OBSESSIVE CHILDREN
A Sociopsychiatric Study

OBSESSIVE CHILDREN

A Sociopsychiatric Study

PAUL L. ADAMS, M.D.

*Professor of Psychiatry and Director
of Psychiatric Education
University of Miami*

BRUNNER/MAZEL • New York
BUTTERWORTHS • London

Library of Congress Catalogue Card No. 73-78725
SBN 87630-071-9

MANUFACTURED IN THE UNITED STATES OF AMERICA

FOR Bingham Dai,
    psychoanalyst and
    teacher

INTRODUCTION

For clinicians this volume is a newfound treasure about a rarely described entity. For behavioral scientists it presents a new and valuable integration of theory about obsessive-compulsive disorders with data from the 49 cases presented and previous clinical data. For all of us Paul Adams has written a human document, moving and poetic as he describes the essential plight of these children and their treatment.

Obsessive-compulsive neurosis in children, a little-described entity, is given the serious consideration many of us in child psychiatry have looked for. Mental health professionals working with children will find it a gold mine of historical and clinical information especially rich in relating conceptual frameworks of the past to known data. I was especially rewarded by the socio-psychological issues described which enhanced my understanding of these serious conditions and forced me to review my own clinical work in the light of the etiologic data presented. Though not specially labeled as such, the preventive implications in the discussion of etiology and early precursors of these disorders are important.

The review of compulsive and obsessive behaviors developmentally and from normality to severe psychopathology is a delightful introduction to the analysis of the dynamics of the full blown conditions according to various schools of psychoanalytic thought.

An analysis of prevalence reveals the rarity of the condition as presently diagnosed and its relation to socio-economic class is reviewed. The genetic relationship of the family to these disorders is scrutinized and synthesized in a new way which has clinical relevance and opens up new vistas in understanding these disorders. The view of Sullivan and others concerned with understanding the dynamics of family systems in psychopathology of obsessive and compulsive conditions is also reviewed. A central concept is introduced in etiology, i.e., how a facade of love which hides actual cruel and sadistic treatment of the child affects the child. The double bind of Jackson and Bateson in schizophrenia is reexamined as pertinent for obsessive-compulsive disorders.

Genetic and biologic evidence in etiology of these conditions are also reviewed.

The most striking synthesis of thinking by Adams comes in his review of the work of Bingham Dai and Leon Salzman and others from their clinical experience which indicates that obsessive-compulsive parents beget obsessive-compulsive children and that basic lack of empathy of the parents for a child and the condition of childhood are important determinants of these disorders.

The analysis of Adams' 49 cases indicates a sociopsychiatric relevance of great interest to child therapists and investigators and ties together the preceding theoretical discussions in a very satisfying and enlightening way. Of particular meaning to me was the elucidation of data to indicate that some basic tenets of psychoanalytic drive theory are not born out by the data. The anal character problems derived from conflicts around toilet training are not special areas of disturbance in the children studied. It would seem that competence in the sense that White uses it and healthy obsessive-compulsive behavior which creates order and meaning out of chaos as described by Sullivan, Silverberg, and

Szurek may be more meaningful than libido theory in understanding development.

The clinical description of these disorders as delineated by Paul Adams is especially moving and poetic. The vivid clinical description of the driven, sad, unloved and unloving child and his need to use the magic of words to perpetuate the "fog" in his own mind and others begins to make sense of a clinical picture so difficult to understand and take hold of.

The 49 case histories bring a wealth of clinical detail as they range from the mildest to the most severe obsessive-compulsive disorders. I would urge the reader not to skip any of the brief case histories for fear of losing the theme and variations which run through them so vividly.

Following the case histories there is a review of pathogenesis and etiology. This chapter integrates the data from clinical material with the previous review of the development of thought about these disorders. Again the nature of the parental relationships to the child emerges powerfully. The authoritarian nature of the parents' attitudes and behaviors is coupled with lack of parental empathy for the small and growing child's nature and needs. Both the necessary and sufficient conditions to produce these disorders are considered.

The discussion of treatment, like the description of the children, carries the Paul Adams stamp of humanness, honesty, and respect for the child with the capacity to look with the child for the unconscious meaning of symptoms especially in the here and now of living and in the process of treatment. A discussion of transference and countertransference emphasizes again the open relationship necessary to lead to increased clarity and honesty of verbal expression rather than fog. It is clear in my mind that Paul Adams provides a new and restitutive relationship in which the direct and honest interpretations are coupled with a concern which permits the child new developmental experiences with a new parent model leading to reduction of symptoms, efforts to behave and live differently, and finally toward character change. The duration of treatment between 1-2 years and a frequency of

3-4 times a week for very sick children indicate that there are no short cuts to treating these serious disorders.

Finally, obsessive-compulsive neurosis as it relates to our society, to socio-economic class and our society's values is described in a chapter. This relates previous discussion of psychiatry, culture, and Marxian ideas about economics and social class in a meaningful closure.

The book ends in an excellent psychiatric historical chronology of obsession and compulsion and there is a valuable Bibliography which I am personally using in a soon to be published *Bibliography for Training in Child Psychiatry.*

Those of us in child psychiatry training programs are especially grateful to Paul Adams for his unique and valuable contributions to our teaching about obsessive-compulsive neurosis.

IRVING N. BERLIN, M.D.
Professor of Psychiatry and Pediatrics
Head, Division of Child Psychiatry
University of Washington School of Medicine

TABLE OF CONTENTS

PREFACE

More properly, what I am reporting here would have been a prede-signed study of obsessive children and their families, studying their interaction patterns and communication styles. But as it is, it is an *ex post facto* study of the clinical records of 49 obsessive children, and their parents, from three southern U.S. states. Instead of being a controlled study it is exploratory. As a result of all these charac-teristics limiting the study, I can attempt to put forth only a few reasonable generalizations. The information on the children and their families is not as complete as would be desired, for ideally one would want complete, systematic data on more than two generations. A carefully taken *and recorded* family history of men-tal illness, especially of schizophrenia and the affective disorders, would have been desirable. Publication time prompts a host of rather perfectionistic regrets and longings.

Under the pressure of trying to help people, we often sacrifice the time-consuming gathering and recording of worthwhile infor-mation. Our ethic of service impedes our scholarship, at times. Most child psychiatrists do not apologize for their being unheedful of scholarly study. They are simply too busy "delivering services." For the committed clinician, research is a luxury, secondary to service and teaching, in most medical colleges. The academic child psychiatrist, however, often has some opportunity for a bit of research. There is some stimulus and encouragement for professors to inquire, investigate, and not merely to transmit child psychia-try's untested clinical lore. So, during my eleventh year there, the University of Florida chose to give me, along with about two per cent of its faculty, a "sabbatical" of three months at full pay. I used those weeks for this project. Also, nights and weekends were helpful.

Circumstances have not afforded me the luxury of doing the

best kind of study, so I can say in justification of this work only that I am trying to get some investigation of childhood obsession started, trying to be as honest and unbiased as I can, and hoping that better studies will protect themselves against the errors that I have committed.

Obsessive children are rather rare in outpatient psychiatric work. But they do provide a fascination and a challenge for students in the mental health disciplines, no matter how infrequently these children are encountered. As we shall see, there is something about obsessive young people which makes them not only emblematic of our times but also rewarding for the therapist who is in the process of learning how to help them best.

My special thanks go to four women who had a big hand in assisting me toward completing this monograph. Evy Adams was the loving wife and companion who always inspired me to do my best. Kirstie Ollendorff was the loving hostess in London while I was writing and using the library at the Maudsley Hospital. Virginia Sasek was the friend and loyal secretary who did at least two complete versions of the typescript, always with good cheer and unstinting industry. Mignonne Groetzinger was the tactful and lenient editorial adviser who made good points well, never seeming to interfere too much.

Also, Steve Nadeau receives my deepest thanks for helping me with the bibliography and the computerization of the data. The time of our working together is now a fond memory for I have moved to the University of Miami. I hope that Steve goes on to success with medical studies as soon as he completes his alternative service as a conscientious objector.

Finally, all the children with whom I worked, and whose identities I have striven to respect by disguising them in this book, deserve my gratitude. They have my thanks and best wishes as they move through life.

PAUL ADAMS

Miami, Florida
March 1973

OBSESSIVE CHILDREN
A Sociopsychiatric Study

1

Childhood Without Spontaneity

CHILDHOOD BLIGHTED BY OBSESSIVE DISORDERS is what this book is all about. It surveys the literature, describes 49 children and their families, and presents some generalizations about the psychiatric treatment of these unhappy people, both the children and the adults.

Childhood itself gives us trouble.

Childhood has been portrayed repeatedly as, ideally, a time of ecstasy. The juvenile era has been declared by both Christians and Jews to be an epoch, in the human life cycle, that is stamped by the reign of happy innocence. This shows at least that there is some belief in extolling childish ignorance as if it represented moral superiority. Heaven is commonly supposed to lie about us in our childhood, if for no other reason than that we do not know any better. Other culture groups, such as the ancient Spartans, viewed childhood as a time for serious enculturation—learning to be a proper citizen—and, therefore, while the Spartans required a somewhat lowered performance and fewer responsibilities from young people, nonetheless, they expected children to get on with the

3

acquisition of the responsibilities, duties, and remunerations of a mature citizen. Still other civilizations bore down harder on children than on adults. Social customs varied across cultures and through time.

In the United States, despite our cultural heterogeneity and rich diversity, adults do seem unified in one thing, namely, a clearcut ambivalence about childhood. A public profession of concern for the welfare of children is hastily inundated by deep unconcern and neglect. Governmental priorities are given to economic and political institutions, to wars and space races, and to the schemes and projects of *a more docile age group who produce, not consume as children do*. The non-producer is disvalued and feared. "Welfare" is a word said with a snarl. Nevertheless, except for several million black and poor children, North American children are supposed to be happy and carefree. Children generally receive smiles and pleasantries from sometimes patronizing adults. Adults expect, and forgive, childhood spontaneity or naturalness, even when they might not wish to encourage it. The young, in some way, are simultaneously taken to threaten the established social order.

Does an obsessive child fit any picture of romanticized childhood? No, the obsessive child is altogether unhappy, unnatural, forced, and lacking in spontaneity. That is the critical issue: how to help the obsessive child to naturalness and spontaneity. It would be easier if we had a happy "premorbid state" into which we could reinstate him, but the obsessive child of ten years, for example, has often been markedly unhappy all of his life—he needs habilitation into happiness, not rehabilitation. The discovery of the child's real self is the goal of therapeutic work. That is, he needs to learn some naturalness even if it *is* for *the first time in his life*. For he is not at all the fantasied happy child of the primitivist. Instead, he is a miserable example of human misery—the misery of over-reflection to diminish his anxiety about himself. That it is a needless misery, because it can be helped, is one of the optimistic messages of this book. That it is a misery in which nearly all of us, children and adults, participate is a sobering consideration.

The obsessive child is *forced*, constrained, in a special way. He feels driven by fate to do things, to think certain thoughts or carry out certain rituals, which may seem trivial and silly even to the child. Yet he cannot stop himself. If he does not do as driven to do, he fears that he will fall into a devastating disintegrating panic. His forced quality is his "anancasm" (from the old Greek *Ananke*, signifying a Fate by which one is tied and by which one's life is invested with a feeling of inevitability, a feeling of not being free, and a feeling that there is no escape possible). The ancient Greeks believed that a "daemon . . . magically controls all the individual's actions from the beginning of his life to the end." (Jaeger, 1943). That is much more crippling than the kind of constraint felt and displayed by an ordinary shy, timid child. It is felt by an obsessive child as a *life and death matter*. He feels as if he were Fate's victim and craves for release. The etymology of our term *obsession* tells us something: the Latin, *obsidere*, means to be sieged. The obsessive child does feel besieged. In his heart he longs for the siege to let up.

After all, what could be more cramped and woeful than the feeling of a child of 12 years that he has committed *an unpardonable sin*? And this they do often feel. To have the phrase "blaspheme against the holy spirit" return again and again to his awareness, and to feel opposed and misunderstood by his relatives, especially the much-valued Mother? And, although sensing, perhaps, death and decay in the air all around him, to be able to look *openly* only to the sweet side, the side his family may not possess but only profess? A childhood in the shadow of death, dirt, sadism, and victimization is not fun. Certainly, it is not healthy. A childhood in which decay and cruelty are hidden behind a hypocritical mask holds no pleasure. And that lack of naturalness is specifically the core deficit of a child who is inordinately obsessive- compulsive.

Not every obsession-compulsion in childhood is of serious import. There is a spectrum of obsession among children that covers a wider array than Leon Salzman (1968) found among adults. Salzman, with the outlook of a neo-Freudian analyst, described three adult groups, i.e., normal obsession, obsessive personality, and obsessive neurosis. That is an apt general categorization for childhood obsession too, but children will often add a string of phenomena to the adult series. They are prone to use obsession "playfully," which adults are not so likely to do, and children more than adults will show obsessive maneuvers as secondary manifestations of other conditions. To demonstrate this, let us take a quick survey of how obsession operates in childhood, proceeding from the most benign to the most pathologic uses of obsession by children.

Ritualized collective play is the form of obsessive play in which peer group norms and group influences are at the forefront. Several children are at it together and "in common." It has a less pathologic orientation than other forms of obsession. The jacks, for instance, counting out by rhymes, the hop-scotch and jump rope that school children play for seemingly interminable hours are illustrative of games that have a compulsive flavor. This aspect of their play suggests that the children seek a substitute for sex play and erotic fantasies. The substitute, in the play itself, is being constructed, and, almost certainly, under a sizeable amount of pressure. Further, play of this type betrays children's efforts at group formation or group rules, and their very "overdoing" of rules leads a sensitive observer to suspect that an assemblage of young lawbreakers (according to their inner longings) is trying to police itself into being straight and law-abiding! Overdoing is always undoing, in a sense, but it makes for childish fun, it would seem.

The elementary school children's game of "cooties" is a good illustration of how sexual seductiveness is the issue in some "natural" collective play. Sexiness breaks through, coexists with, and, at times, comes under the control of relatively harmless ritualization. Cooties is a sexy tag game based upon the notion that girls possess a magically noxious influence which can infect boys and which boys must avoid or pass along at once. Girls give boys cooties, according to the game, and boys dramatize greatly the anxiety they feel about being "infected" by girls. They run, dodge, and scream in fright. Playful diversion, magical thinking, compulsive avoidance, genital excitement, superstitiousness and ritual making are all intermeshed in the school child's game of cooties. But it is not a highly pathologic form of obsessive tactics: it is shared; it is play.

"Phase appropriate" rituals and other obsessive behavior are often reported, as with the two- and three-year old child who must have everything "just so" in eating, toileting, bathing, dressing, and play. The young "anal stage" child becomes transparently compulsive whenever uncertainty looms. By his ritualization he essays to cope, and magically to ward off uncertainty. It is often assumed he is trying to force object constancy, to make his significant people more static, more reliable, through enmeshing them in a transitory obsessional web. Parents of these young children often sense the child's imperative to reach the parents and to control them. And many parents respond good-naturedly to this, even if they have not read Anna Freud's comment (1965, p. 162):

> In the ordinary course of events the compulsive manifestations disappear without trace as soon as the relevant drive and ego positions have been outgrown.

Peter Blos (1970, p. 71) and Edith Buxbaum (1970) wrote that preadolescence, and possibly any other stage of childhood, can temporarily show "normal obsession." Melanie Klein (1932) found obsessive-compulsive features such as "repression of phantasies" and "clinging to reality" (but not rituals) to be characteristic of a normal latency period.

Ritualized solitary play that is not in the second or third year of life, that seems driven, insistent and perseverative, is a bit more pathologic, probably. Hence, this is a third position on the obsessive spectrum. The support of numbers seen in group play is lacking, and the emotional isolation and withdrawal of a child with repetitive activity carried out in solitude comes nearer to being at least a precursor of obsessional disorder. In all these instances I have found Melanie Klein's (1964) avowal—made in 1927—to provide a useful reminder: "a fundamental mechanism in children's play . . . is the discharge of masturbation phantasies." Play with string figures, with marbles shot down inclined planes, and even the compulsive "solitaire" or "Patience" played by school-age children seem only a small removal from substitutes for masturbation. Even in families wishing sexual freedom for their children, I have seen the children contrive elaborate bedtime ceremonials that guard against the "evils of masturbation."

Obsessive collecting is still closer to being pathologic, it would seem. Rock collections are popular. In Florida, petrified shark's teeth are commonly gathered. Leaves, butterflies, nude photos, news clippings (the Viet Nam war was one escalatingly burdensome example), match covers, stamps, telephone pole insulators—some children become avid collectors of these and similar items that have more of a symbolic than a manifest importance. The avidity with which they collect has a *driven* quality, and it would look as if a full-blown symptom of neurosis is present, were it not short-lived, usually. However, Lauretta Bender (1954), for a long time the senior and leading figure in child psychiatry at Bellevue Hospital, remarked that later in life these children may return, in the same or other ways, to obsessive behavior and obsessive style.

Circumscribed interests (Robinson and Vitale, 1954) or impulsions (Bender, 1954) are a still more serious fifth station on the obsessive spectrum in childhood, but even these can be dropped or overcome as the child grows and changes. Children with circumscribed interest patterns are children who "go nuts" or "ape" about very specialized, oddball interests to the exclusion of all other activities. Included are rocketry, shortwave radio, high fidelity sound recordings, and the reading of children's books, if they are engaged in to the exclusion of other activities or areas of thought. Children with circumscribed interests may make reputations as child prodigies. These children are one-sided in development, like *idiots savants*, although they are usually of at least normal intelligence. Leo Kanner (1954), author of the first textbook on child psychiatry, in his discussion of the Robinson and Vitale article on circumscribed interest patterns saw these less sick children's specialized and constricted preoccupations in contrast to the ways of children who are autistic.

Although I have seen the phenomenon in bright, somewhat lonely children, I have not included any of these children among the 49 grouped for report in this book because they either did not use obsessive tactics generally or because they quickly cultivated peer relations shortly after being exposed to, and evaluated by, a psychiatrist. The differentiation of sick children and those with circumscribed interests cannot always be done with an easy dogmatism, however.

Obsessive character, still more pathologic, is included in the obsessive disorders exemplified by 10 of the 49 children described in this book. In the language of the Freudians, the child with an *obsessive character* shows more pregenital arrests than those children listed in the five conditions above, as being less pathologic than obsessive disorders—children with circumscribed interests, collectors, etc. These children make a more pervasive use of an obsessive and compulsive style, although there are fewer stark *symptoms* than in an obsessional neurosis. For example, "obsessive character" or "obsessive personality" would be an apt label to give to that zone of the obsessive spectrum at which were placed children numbered and named as follows (see vignettes in Chapter 4):

1. Bernice	21. Chuck	31. Hank
3. Chloe	22. Crown	32. Harry
14. Billy	29. Eric	33. Henry
17. Burt		

These were not children who utilized rituals, but they were uptight and obsessive almost as second nature.

All of the other 39 children showed definite neurotic formations with definite symptoms. These make, therefore, the seventh group, and they *are* ill: *obsessional neurosis*. These, with the sixth group, are discussed at length in Chapter 3, "The Clinical Picture," and Chapter 4, "The Children."

Still an eighth group is comprised of those children, also ill, who show obsessive-compulsive symptoms *secondary to depression, to schizophrenia or other psychosis, and to brain damage*. No children of this sort were included in this study, unless my appraisal of Miles C (#39) and Chester E (#20) is wrong. However, these sick children are important, and they are returned to in our discussion of differential diagnosis (Chapter 3).

To recap at this point, obsession is everywhere, in all of us. Among children, it characterizes a life style, or a transient and recoverable state, or an unrelenting neurosis, or a severe psychotic illness, or a collective "game." Obsessive behavior appears all along a broad and diverse spectrum of childhood activities.

THE COMPONENTS OF OBSESSIVE ILLNESS

Normal children's everyday speech and play are filled with "obsessive-compulsive maneuvers." Whenever a child broaches the topic of his being weak or afraid, but quickly shifts to his strength and bravery, he is using a compulsive, or obsessive, maneuver. Obsessive maneuvers of this type have a very human face, for all of us. They assist all of us in everyday life to keep polarities in some sort of balance. The obsessive maneuver of the normal child is seen with a much greater frequency in the children studied and described herein. Children who are ill with obsessions make a caricature of "normal obsession," so to speak. Furthermore, children who are pathologically obsessive have a lot of symptoms too. Not all child psychiatrists are agreed as to what an *obsessive illness* rightfully includes. There seems to be room enough for honest dissent and disagreement.

The major expressions of obsessive illness can include a lot or very little in the way of psychopathology. It all depends on one's perspective in using the term "obsessive illness." Pierre Janet (1903) included a great many more forms of psychopathology than Sigmund Freud (1895). Janet saw "psychasthenia" everywhere, certainly in both obsessions and phobias. Freud was exercised to refute Janet's inclusive views and to remove phobias from the obsessive spectrum, so Freud wrote:

> Obsessions and phobias are separate neuroses, with a special mechanism and aetiology which I have succeeded in demonstrating in a certain number of cases, and which, I hope, will prove similar in a large number of new cases.

Let us look a little further at this dispute between Freud and Janet about phobia and obsession. It is a good example of how psychiatry goes about its argumentation and growth. Freud's insistence that phobias are "a part of the anxiety-neurosis" and, consequently, not akin to obsessions meant that he could attribute phobias rather simply to unvarnished Oedipal anxiety. But he would need a complex array of concepts to account for obsessions—he needed fixation and regression theory, anal character-ology, a psychology of libido and aggression, and of ego and super-ego, and more. Janet's contrasting view was that phobias, neuras-thenia, obsessions, compulsions, tics, depersonalization, and "excitements" were all to be combined under the rubric *psychas-thenia.* Janet's blanket concept might have been overly inclusive, as North Americans and/or Freudians have often contended. But, as we shall see, it was Freud's choice of phobias to be strictly distinguished from obsessions which now seems *overly exclusive.* Most European child psychiatrists have elected unhesitatingly to side with Pierre Janet, and not with Sigmund Freud, in this quar-rel. Hence, the psychologist Hans Eysenck (1952) was in a rather large and comfortable company when, being anti-Freudian, he lumped anxiety neurotics, reactive depressives and obsessives all together as "dysthymic." British, French, and other European psychiatrists do not go quite as far as Eysenck. They do lump phobic-ruminative states with obsessions, yet they keep *obsession-al neurosis* separate from anxiety neurosis. When the American Psychiatric Association issued its first *Diagnostic and Statistical Manual, Mental Disorders* (1952) it adopted the Freudian view, separating "phobic reaction" from "obsessive compulsive reac-tion" and "anxiety reaction." The 1952 publication was common-ly called "D.S.M." By 1968 a second edition, "D.S.M.II," ap-peared, showing separate listings for:

anxiety neurosis
phobic neurosis
depersonalization neurosis
obsessive compulsive neurosis
obsessive compulsive personality.

I. M. Ingram (1961) found that *the predominant childhood pre-cursors* of adult obsessive illness were "phobias, phobias and ritu-als, stammer and psychosomatic illness." Those adult obsessives who had suffered from childhood disorders had had more child-hood phobias and rituals than any other clinical signs or symp-toms. The Freudian view contends that phobias and obsessions are discrete, while in fact they are merged and coexistent in reality.

This makes one speculate that a situation in which psychodynamic theory violates evidence needs new psychodynamic theory if—after all—obliging new evidence does not occur. Unless, as another alternative, we want to have it the way Bertolt Brecht ironically put it about East Germany: *when people do not love their government, the ungrateful* people must be dissolved—and a new populace found. Facts (and populations) may prefer to dissolve theories (and governments) instead.

Adopting the Freudian view has arduous consequences, for one must be surprised if phobias and obsessions ever exist simultaneously. Moreover, the meticulous and time-consuming attention given to "Frankie" (a phobic boy analyzed by Berta Bornstein but who became an obsessive man analyzed by Samuel Ritvo) showed to what lengths theoretical commitments can carry an International Congress of highly intelligent, compassionate people. Much concern was devoted, at the 1965 International Psycho-Analytical Congress, to discussing what could have accounted for Frankie's changing from a phobic to an obsessive. Was it the techniques of Frankie's childhood psychotherapy? or some fault in diagnosis? or his subsequent drive regression, or his subsequent ego progression, or what else? Anna Freud (1966) pointed out that the basic trouble might have been that the Congress participants (1) took childhood diagnoses too seriously, and that they (2) presumed too little developmental progression (or too much personality standstill) in growing human beings. Another possibility, to be added to the other two, I believe, would be that psychoanalysts (3) evaluated too dearly their own learnings and teachings concerning the "dynamic incompatibility" of phobias and obsessions. People often transcend theories about people.

Anna Freud (1965) already had singled out some of the problems, and had entered a plea that commonsense empiricism be allowed to take precedence over partisan theory-commitments (p. 151):

> In the early days of analytic practice, when only a small number of preselected children reached the analyst, it was expected that the majority of young patients would belong to

the category of the infantile neuroses ... with Little Hans and the Wolf Man as their prototypes ... But this notion changed with the step from private practice to the opening of consultation centers and clinics for children where a whole mass of unsorted case material arrived. . . .

In children, symptoms occur just as often in isolation, or are coupled with other symptoms and personality traits of a different and unrelated origin. Even well-defined obsessional symptoms ... are found in children with otherwise ... hysterical personalities; or hysterical conversions, phobic trends, psychosomatic symptoms are found in character settings which are obsessional.

And, in furtherance of respect for "the truth as it is," Anna Freud could write (p. 152):

... early delinquent behavior need not turn into a true delinquent state; the child in question may develop into an obsessional character or obsessional neurosis rather than into a delinquent or criminal. Many children who begin with a phobia or anxiety hysteria grow later into true obsessionals.

Her solution to this unexpected confrontation of what is with what was hoped for is to stress that "mental disturbances are more frequent in number and more varied in kind in children than they are in adults." The myth of the uncomplicated child got exploded again. Certainly, in children depersonalization, phobias, dissociation, hysteria and anxiety neurosis can coexist with obsession.

What, now, from a more empirical, phenomenologic standpoint, are obsessive children like, regardless of psychodynamic theory's requirements? One of our best leads up to now stands in the praiseworthy essay by Lewis L. Judd (1965), who undertook to examine the clinical pictures of five obsessive-compulsive children and to give a descriptive account of the children. He enumerated the most frequent items found *in all five of the* obsessive children:

1. sudden, often dramatic, onset of illness
2. higher than normal intelligence
3. obsessions and compulsions always occurred in combination, and never separately
4. the child's symptoms "disrupted" and brought "conflict with" his interpersonal environment
5. guilt feelings about their thoughts and acts persisted and were frequently verbalized by all the children
6. initially the children appeared to have a "rigid, absolute, adult-like moral code"
7. fantasy life was unconstricted and very active
8. no evidence of psychosis.

Then Judd reported the six items that occurred *in four of the five cases:*

1. normal premorbid record except for over-compliance and hyperconcern for rules
2. parents and near relatives gave positive histories of psychopathology, often obsessive compulsive
3. bowel training was normally timed, with no regressions, and was "non-punitive, uneventful."
4. some precipitating event was identifiable
5. transient and shifting phobic responses were frequent
6. one or both parents became object of the child's strong ambivalent and openly aggressive feeling.

And, finally, *in three* of the five cases Judd found:

1. strong emphasis by the family on religion
2. erratic, inconsistent discipline carried out by the parents.

The result of Judd's itemization is to depict, with clinically rich imagery and documentation, a "real, live" group of children actually suffering from obsessive problems, warring with their parents, intellectually bright but very active in fantasies and feeling, preoccupied with compliance, guilty, obsessive, compulsive and hurting. Typical textbook characterizations lack the realistic descriptiveness of Judd's report. It is interesting, too, to see what, although they are reported to occur in other clinical material, *the children studied by Judd did not show:*

1. obstinacy
2. pathologic envy
3. frequent constipation
4. history of sexual trauma
5. depersonalization.

Some of those "missing traits" are virtually required by classical concepts of an *anal character* which predisposes to obsessive illness! The child picture is undoubtedly more fluid than certain psychodynamic formulations may have anticipated. What we need to find out is probably more empirical than logical. A closer look at a larger group of obsessive children may be empirically rewarding.

INCIDENCE AND PREVALENCE

Obsessive illness appears to be a relative rarity among children. We have no certain indications of how many children suffer from "obsessional neurosis," so we are hard put to estimate its frequency among children as a group, or for that matter among the entire population of adults and children. We cannot guess how many treated cases there are in the U.S., for example, because many cases among lower class and working class children cannot afford, and do not receive, treatment and, as a consequence, are difficult for us to identify. This high "selectivity" of cases has given some private practitioners the notion that obsessive children are always of patrician background. The situation is, it would seem, that only the patricians can afford child mental health specialists, and even they for rather brief time periods.

Statistics are dependent upon good recording and reporting of most cases of illnesses. We *can* turn up figures concerning the number of children who are *labelled* as obsessive neurotics, and who are treated in outpatient facilities or inpatient units. In some parts of northern Europe, owing only partially to the geographic dispersion of culturally homogeneous, mono-national populations, a tradition has developed to hospitalize obsessives of all ages. Hence, Einar Kringlen (1965, 1970) selected 91 adult inpatients for a follow-up study—patients who in the U.S.A. might have been kept ambulatory. Likewise, in Denmark and England obsessives have been hospitalized liberally, and studied rather closely as a result. Avoidance of hospitalization has been the vogue for disturbed children for many years. In the U.S. we justify keeping children out of mad-houses on humane grounds. This now appears to be true all over the world. We in child psychiatry generally have the opinion that outpatient clinic care, although superior for the patient, may attend an impoverished record keeping. By contrast, inpatient records are ordinarily more complete. In Florida, for example, a few years ago outpatient clinic records frequently were found to contain little clinical matter, and in some clinics children were "coded out" routinely as "adjustment reaction of childhood." Using this single diagnosis for all cases saved the time of professionals for better things, the clinics' workers felt. Needless to say, this made it impossible to get information about the incidence of obsessive illnesses among those clinics' clientele.

In Table 1 I have shown some of the "incidence" figures extant for obsessive illness. Sources marked with an asterisk drew upon child populations, and might seem to have more direct relevance. Yet it should be pointed out that a majority of obsessive adults report to psychiatrists that they were obsessive and ill during their childhood, so groups of adult obsessives are pertinent to our purposes. From 20 years old onward, certainly, the risk of an obsessive illness declines for all population groups. Obsessions are cripplers of the young, first and foremost.

Some adult obsessives who did not show obsessive traits before their illness are probably in a transiently obsessional group whose deeper-lying illness may be brain damage, depression or schizophrenia. These three illnesses do result in many obsessive-compulsive symptoms and to such a serious extent that the obsessions may come to dominate the clinical picture. Demetrio Barcia and Pilar Fuster (1969-70) make the case strongly that epileptic and brain damaged children show a higher incidence of obsessions. There are, for sure, sub-groupings of young people whose risk of

TABLE 1
INCIDENCE OF OBSESSIONAL NEUROSIS
IN VARIED REPORTS

Source	Place	% of Patients Seen	% of Neurotics Seen
Goodwin et al. (1969)	St. Louis, Missouri	1	4
*Berman (1942)	Providence, R.I.	0.8	—
*Berman (1942)	New York, N.Y.	2.2	—
*Judd (1965)	Los Angeles, California	1.2	—
*Despert (1955)	New York, N.Y.	17.0	—
Lo (1967)	Hong Kong	0.35	—
*Nágera (1965)	London, England	rare, <3	—
Kringlen (1965)	Oslo, Norway	2.5	4.3
Ingram (1961)	Dumfries, Scotland	0.9	—
Pollitt (1960)	London, England	3	—
*Bender (1945)	New York, N.Y.	0.16	—

obsessive illness becomes elevated. The brain damaged youths are one such group. Therefore, the wise clinician, in my experience, tries to look at the underlying mood and cognition status of the patient, and to assess for neural impairment. This assists the doctor to be fairly certain whether a given case actually is a case of obsessions springing up unheralded, or whether it masks a more serious affective or thought disorder. Yet let us keep a sensible perspective, for the entire occurrence of obsessions and compulsions in childhood is pathognomonic of an obsessive illness *and not of some other disorder.* The apparent reasons for this are taken up in Chapter 3.

Robert Woodruff and Ferris Pitts (1964), by reasoning from available incidence figures, and from population statistics, came forth with an estimate of how many people (of all ages) in the U.S. have obsessional neuroses. Their estimate of maximal prevalence is the figure of 5 persons of all ages in every 10,000 of the general population (0.05%). They considered this prevalence rate to be maximal and emphasized that the actual frequency could be only one-tenth of 0.05%—i.e., 0.005% or 5 in every 100,000 people. That makes obsessive neurosis, unquestionably, one of the rarest forms of mental disorder. Consequently, it would seem reasonable to state that fewer than 2% of large groups of emotionally disturbed children are obsessional neurotics. That is the report of many child guidance clinics to the author, and it has been the experience of the University of Florida's Children's Mental Health Unit. It would seem that the incidence of some *compulsive or obsessive traits* is increased in brain damaged and schizophrenic children, but that the incidence of *obsessive illness as a neurotic entity* is increased in the subgroupings of intelligent, lower middle class, male, Anglo-Saxon, Protestant children. Obsessive children largely come from middle America, even though they do not constitute a big group of middle America's children.

Why, if not for the numerical frequency, are the obsessive children so important? Some immediate answers to this can be given: 1) These haunted children suffer more poignantly than most adults can imagine. Although voluntary subscriptions pour in for physically handicapped children, crippled children in groups abound in gaiety and mirth by comparison with a group of obsessive children. What advertising and promotion work can do bears no close correspondence to realities when one tries to relate funding to the suffering of children. The obsessive children cry out for relief. 2) They put a therapist's empathy and flexibility to a severe test and put the most skillful doctor on trial. Working with them can be exciting and is, most certainly, demanding. 3) If a therapist can deal successfully with an obsessive child, he can deal with almost any other. We need better and more telling evaluation devices in academic child psychiatry. Consequently, when adjudging the clinical work of residents in child psychiatry, I have found that the topnotch people are the ones who—perhaps less from a mastery of any specific technique than from a personal wholeness— can treat obsessive children. Because of this, an obsessive child is like a representative test question, in some ways.

Character disorders and antisocial reactions abound in urban North America, probably outnumbering all other disorders. Most disturbed children scarcely need to see a psychiatrist to get themselves unleashed.* There are more children "in need of acquiring

---

*One is reminded of the saying that a poor black, living in a rat-infested ghetto, hardly needs a psychiatrist to find out what "bugs" him (the black one)!

controls" than in letting go and being impulsive or natural. Where the obsessive child stands regarding his inner controls is not a formidable site, but more of that later. The point I want to underline now is that I am not certain that everybody needs to take the lid off. I am certain that, in highly specific ways, the obsessive child must take the lid off. Hence, he "was made for derepression, the goal of early Freudian analytic therapy"—although unfortunately analytic therapy's techniques do not always benefit an obsessive child.

The sex distribution of obsessive illness is generally reported as being identical to that of the more general psychiatric caseload carried by a given hospital or clinic. As a result, where female patients predominate most obsessives are female. This is the case in studies made by Ingram (1961), Kringlen (1965), Pollitt (1957) and Edith Rüdin (1953). In all of their study populations there were about 60% females and in 1903 Pierre Janet found that 71% of the obsessives whom he encountered were females. And, in clinical samples where males predominate, the majority of obsessives are male. Lo (1967) found only 27% female obsessives among adult psychiatric patients in Hong Kong. Sigmund Freud (1926) noted greater frequency *in males.* Certainly, in U.S. groups of obsessive children, reported in psychiatric literature, the sex ratio is largely male-oriented, as shown in Table 2. I include the current group of 49 children in that table. Among children, obsessiveness is not primarily a female but a male disorder. As many psychiatric residents have observed, "adult" psychiatry is work with women, but child psychiatry is mainly work with boys.

TABLE 2
GENDER DISTRIBUTION OF OBSESSIVE CHILDREN

Source	Total	% Female
Berman (1942)	6	50
Despert (1955)	68	23.5
Judd (1965)	5	40
Adams (herein)	49	20

The male child is possibly at greater risk for obsessions than the female child. It is the same with school problems, conduct problems, bedwetting, and so on. Most of the child psychiatry patients at the Children's Mental Health Unit, University of Florida, were boys—aged 9, 10, 11 years in the period 1960 to 1972. Why this is so is probably more culturogenic than biogenic, despite growing evidences of the female's biologic superiority. As the years pass, more and more girls are brought in, to become child psychiatry patients. The times change.

Gerda Willner (1968, p. 201), without citing what her evidence was, wrote:

> The neurotic personality of today seems to develop more obsessive ideas and compulsive trends than ever before. This may have something to do with recent advances in technology and science, and an emphasis on college education and acquisition of academic degrees ... Our culture breeds compulsiveness and probably contributes to the increase of the so-called 'obsessive-compulsive neurosis'.

Some psychiatric authors insist that the overall incidence of obsessive disorder is increasing, but cite mainly their own personal case-logs as evidence. Naturally, people who see increasing numbers of obsessive children in their own clinical work would be expected to say that they are seeing more and more. But those estimates by clinicians are tricky matters, for one or two swallows do not make a summer. If I had not looked at the total number of referrals to our clinic, it would be relatively easy for me to conclude that more and more obsessive children were being produced in northern Florida. Actually, I have no reason to assume that the incidence is increasing any faster than the population of young people is increasing. The word does get around that I am interested in working with obsessive children, and am trying to find ways to serve them better. I, consequently, may, for these reasons, see more than the estimated mean.

2

Familial and Social Roots of Obsession

IN THIS CHAPTER I will undertake to review the literature of obsessive family studies, to outline what seems to be a fruitful sociopsychiatric approach to obsessives' families, and then to examine the principal social characteristics of the 49 families. The social characteristics are studied from both a demographic and an attitudinal standpoint. At the end of the chapter some efforts are made to look at the social roots of children's obsessive illness, a matter to go into more fully in Chapter 7.

Families of Obsessives in Psychiatric Literature. There is a relative dearth of reports on the families of obsessive children. Few articles or books have said very much on the subject, beyond a scanty side line comment. To undertake to construct a literature review is a demoralizing project, for most of the "evidence" on the subject comes from unsupported impressions, assertions by clinicians and, of course, those from-between-the-lines extrapolations that entice the faithful readers and followers of Freud, Adler, Klein and others. Hence, as a way of ordering the review of literature, I will keep drawing contrasts between the various approaches

21

("schools") not for their scientific substance and merit but for their "theoretical positions." These are the approaches that will be reviewed:

a) Freudian, classical
b) Freudian, ego psychology
c) post-Freudian psychoanalytic (Sullivanian, neo-Freudian)
d) communication theory
e) organic determinism
f) behavior modification
g) eclectic.

Are family relations important in accounting for obsessive children? Some clinicians place the obsessive child's style squarely into the middle-class family with its uneasy, almost unbearable, admixture of equalitarianism and patriarchism. Many clinicians see the family configuration as a critical, and perhaps even an explanatory, social datum. Alfred Adler could be characterized as the forerunner of this inclination to give a familial and *social* explanation of the origin of neurosis. To say that Adler sought a social or interpersonal explanation of *neurosis* as a generic category is to say that he sought that way of explaining obsessive neurosis as a particular sub-category, for the greatest volume of Adler's work was concentrated upon what he called *compulsion neurosis*. Adler (1931) contended with an assertiveness bordering on pontification —but with a pioneering assertion:

> We cannot, however, find the explanation of the origin of compulsion neurosis in instincts or drives, for a drive, as we understand it, is without direction. We are equally unable to lay the blame on heredity, since all the factors entering into the neurosis—character, passions, emotions—are shaped within the framework of human society.

Middle-class families do display the aforementioned conflict between equalitarian and patriarchal values. Robert Ollendorff (1966, 1971) depicted the kinds of problems that arise in those middle-class families that only give lip service to female equality while treasuring attitudes and patterns of male priority. When the families profess equality but retain strong components of inequality and constraint, the children suffer inwardly from ambivalence or ambiguity, of social change in-the-making, as their families live out flux and contradiction. Wilhelm Reich in *The Mass Psychology of Fascism* (1933) made some of the first successful efforts at integrating Marxian and Freudian tenets. To that degree Reich, too, was a pioneer in sociocultural analysis of neuroses. Reich related family life, especially sexuality, to economic class positions and economic life chances as well as to political ideologies and political liberties. Reich is not ordinarily credited with his early economic and political views, even by the foremost contemporary Reichians, yet it was Reich who broke the ground worked subsequently by the Max Horkheimer group in their *Studies of Authority and the Family* (1934). I include in this group particularly the writers, Erich Fromm (1941, 1947, 1956, 1962), Theodor Adorno and Else Frenkel-Brunswik (1950), none of whom has championed Reichism. Abram Kardiner and his associates (1939, 1945) dropped the Marxist terminology more fully. But they added important substantive research to existent efforts to combine the societal (or utopic) aspects of the family with the intrapsychic (or ethical) aspects of the individual family member. The Kardiner contributions likewise have been too seldom heralded. When the family is seen as society's microcosmic form, societal interpretations become familial interpretations and family studies become society studies.

Authoritarianism and the Family. Ours has been an age that has washed its mouth out with many beautiful words and phrases. Many times the phraseology has been misleading by design, as with those who speak of Judeo-Christian values while purveying war, greed, racism and sexism, or those who talk of revolutions on behalf of freedom but come to work for authoritarian governments which call themselves dictatorships for the people. It seems plausible that the family is an institution which, along with others, plays an important part in the breeding and rearing of authoritarians. If obsessive children are preoccupied with power relations more profoundly than other children, and I believe they are, they could be expected to have special experiences within the family which implant those values into their lives.

From experiences as German socialists (also influenced by the

politics of the early psychoanalytic movement) there was a group
of "psychologists" who gave a lot of attention to the relationship
between Authority and Family. These scholars were associated
with Max Horkheimer, and included such figures as Else Frenkel-
Brunswik, Theodor Adorno, and Erich Fromm. They were ap-
prised of Marxist as well as Freudian views, and from their many
studies concluded, in general, that it was the German family's
structure and ideology that accounted for its authoritarian personality. Theirs was a credible accounting, by the argument that they
documented carefully, for the nationalist posture taken by German socialists during the first World War, under the Weimar repub-
lic, and finally by the working-class people who flocked together
in support of the Nazis. What made these German working people
fly, in the face of their well-accepted ideology of internationalism
and socialism, into the authoritarian and anti-libertarian camp?

Later, some of these same people, now refugees to the United
States, joined with other scholars to bring out the monumental
study reported in *The Authoritarian Personality* (Adorno *et al.*,
1950). Now they were led to conclude that the appeal of fascism
and of ethnocentrism (anti-Jewish practices in particular) could
"happen here" because of the prevalence of the authoritarian personality in the USA. The Horkheimer group came more and more
to assume the reputation of relics of the earlier European amalgam
of Marx and Freud.

Psychoanalysis found itself early on to be a congenial movement
for socialists (such as August Aichhorn, Paul Federn and Alfred
Adler) and humanitarian liberals, but as the psychoanalytic movement assumed a more conservative orientation, it became more
difficult for the orthodox analysts to maintain fellowship with the
Adlers, Reichs and Fromms. For more and more analysts, to be a
socialist was incompatible with being Freudian. And, since early
analysts began to prize the golden mean—even if it meant non-
commitment socially—the analytic movement began to extrude
religious people, leaving no welcome spot for the later-day Jungs
and Pfisters. None of the early analysts avowed his Jewishness
even when he was a Jew (Fromm, 1959). The psychoanalysts came
to believe that *psychoanalysis* as a vanguard of a somewhat secu-

larist ethical culture movement could "save the world." Melanie Klein's orthodoxy and ardor were so great that she came to recommend psychoanalysis for *all* children, not only for those with emotional difficulties of a more serious kind.

Ultimately, only the neo-Freudians felt secure in harboring Marxist or neo-Marxist notions. The Marxist tradition itself held *not* that character structure reflects early infantile experiences, *but* that *both character and family* are reflections of the economic relations within a given society. For that reason, Marxists placed greatest stress upon the market place, factories, power and party struggles and especially class struggles. The family was diminished by Marxist theory to a degree greater than even Freudian theory diminished the family's influence on character formation. Soon, the phenomenon of leftist authoritarianism made itself brutally apparent in the USSR of Stalin and Trotsky and their ideological descendants around the world. As Albert Camus (1956) stated it, with good effect despite its oversimplification, authoritarianism of the Left saw victims exalt the executioner, hoping thereby to trade off a temporary enslavement for a later liberation. When the intimate lives of Citizens are given no priority, family, or conjugal, life is not a primary focus, and sexual and other repressions become the way of life after the Revolution. Women and children are almost as totally subjugated in socialist and communist countries as in fascist or capitalist ones, according to many reports. As a corollary, family life nearly everywhere in the world today is life pervaded by training in irrational authority.

Jewish-Christian, Roman, Moslem, and Anglo-Saxon traditions all place a premium upon the family as a crusher of children's wills. Under patriarchal doctrines that run as a common thread through all of the major traditions that have shaped our culture, the wives and children, like oxen and sheep, are all chattel. Sober commandments, mostly said to be of divine origin, are invoked to ensure that parents are to be honored, obeyed, yielded to, and deferred to. The fifth of the Ten Words given by Jahweh to Moses ordered: "Honour your father and your mother, that you may live long in the land which the Lord your God is giving you." And to drive home the point more fully, Jews and Christians have held that "Whoever reviles his father or mother shall be put to death" (Exodus: 21:17).

Family life even today is lived against a background of subjugation. Many hold, with Samuel Butler, that family living is odious and enslaving or productive of neurosis. Others contend that family living is an island of intimate relating and sexual opportunity that is unusual in the modern world.

With colleagues at the University of Florida, early in the sixties, I attempted to study the extent to which more "authoritarian parents" had more disturbed children (Adams *et al.*, 1965). Luckily, we recognized at the outset that there are two kinds of authoritarianism which have been discussed in social philosophy and in psychiatric theory. *Authoritarianism A* refers to a fascist-conservative value-orientation. It is the subject of writers such as Camus, Horkheimer and his group, and many others. *Authoritarianism B* refers to lack of empathy, a lack in the parent's capacity to take up the child's role in imagination. The latter type of authoritarianism has been written about by George Herbert Mead, Martin Buber and others.

When we probed for the first type of authoritarianism we had a number of fairly well accepted inventories and tests already worked out and proven by wide use. These included the Traditional Family Ideology, Allport-Vernon Inventory of Values, Religious Conservatism, Political and Economic Conservatism, Parental Attitudinal Research Inventory, and the F-scale (fascism) and E-scale (ethnocentrism) from the original study of the authoritarian personality (Adorno *et al.*, 1950).

To measure the other dimension or form of authoritarian character among the parents, of both disturbed and normal children, focused-psychiatric interviews were designed to elicit information about empathic parenting, effectiveness as a parent, effectiveness as a spouse, self picture, parental evaluation of the reference child, acceptance of the child's peer relations, and view of the child's religion.

Hundreds of hours were spent in obtaining proper matches for the experimental and control families, and then again in studying them by interviews and testing in such a way that bias would be negated. As a crude summary, I like to say that we found *parents of normal children were higher on Authoritarianism A* and *parents of disturbed children were higher on Authoritarianism B*, showing the latter's empathy deficit. Fathers of disturbed children, more than mothers, showed the most conspicuous lack of empathic parenting. In the intervening years, my own clinical work has utilized these findings and they have greater applicability, chances are, in work with obsessive children than with many other types of conflicted children. Non-empathic parents (if not conservative ones) rankle their obsessive children with a special acuity to which we shall return in later discussion.

Authoritarian families do, it appears, breed neurosis, and perhaps they are neurotigenic most notably when the families profess simultaneously to be equalitarian, thereby exposing the children to conflicting ideas and "objects." A nine-year-old boy of my acquaintance forestalled neurosis (I would speculate) by stating openly at breakfast one day that his father, while giving an impassioned speech in favor of women's liberation during the brief meal, twice had remained seated but asked his wife and daughter to perform services for him. The boy sensed the paradox, that a liberated woman ran to get the salt shaker for her libertarian husband! The young daughter must have sensed this too as Dad so naturally and lovingly requested her mealtime services on his patriarchal behalf.

Middle-class families live amidst cultural conflict and contradictions. Conversely, cultural conflicts live amidst the families, and produce a neurotic child. Karen Horney referred to the neurotic as "a stepchild of our culture." When she saw neurosis as deriving from cultural contradictions, Horney (1937) spelled out what she believed these cultural conflicts were, namely, aggressive greed versus yielding altruism, need stimulation versus factual deprivation, and self-regulation versus helplessness. Horney viewed the family as the medium of enculturation. I have found that *lower* middle-class families in the sixties and now the seventies show pervasive conflicts about matters such as materialism, race, religion, war, politics, etc. (Adams, 1971). Herbert Gans (1962) and many other behavioral scientists have emphasized that *upper* middle-class family styles, although prone to equality in ideology, do not *uniformly* practice equalitarianism either within generations or across generation lines. Perhaps, as has been said by certain Marxist scholars, middle classness is especially prey to a position and an ideology of conflict-ambivalence (sociologist Lewis Corey, 1934; social scientist Robert Lynd, 1937). Friedrich Engels of course postulated that the very origins of the family institution lay within conflicts concerning private property.

However, both Marxism and the pre-1926 Freudianism *tend*—it is not total, for either school—to diminish the family by unmasking it as only an epiphenomenon of an economic substructure (Marxism) or of an instinctual destiny programmed into each human being (Freudianism). While the Marxist might look at the family to see enacted within it the vicissitudes of the economic system, the old-line Freudian will study the family to see it as an enactment of the vicissitudes of biologic drives. Both take the family for granted as they go looking into extrafamilial fields. Consequently, in both views, the family is secondary. Real strength and clout are viewed as residing elsewhere.

THE SULLIVANIAN APPROACH TO THE FAMILY

Sullivanians are less radical politically than some of the Freudians (Géza Róheim, Norman O. Brown, Herbert Marcuse and Wilhelm Reich). For when psychiatry is viewed as the study of interpersonal relations, it is possible quietly to "pull its teeth" politically. All that is needed is for one to accept the extrafamilial institutions as they are. Many Sullivanians accept an idealized bourgeois family as being the last word, *non plus ultra.* If Sullivanians are at all concerned with larger sociopolitical issues, it is usually only in the capacity of "reluctant revolutionaries" (John Seeley, 1967).

Harry Stack Sullivan (1956), while omitting any politicized references to class and status, did point his finger to the deceptions in which the (middle class?) mother enfolded her young child and set up a network of interpersonal relations with an obsessive pattern engrained therein. Sullivan (1956, p. 267f.) noted that the obsessive patient typically described a story of childhood brutalization by a parent:

> If this rather brutal recital includes some thin disguise which the parent wore, I think that you may always accept the account as being reasonably close to the truth . . . These people really know that their parents were not happy and that one of the parents, at least, was savagely cruel to them. But what has always been baffling is this constant thin veneer of convention and sweetness and light.

After reading that Sullivanian commentary, there is not much doubt that Sullivan assigned primary importance to the obsessive's infantile intrafamilial experiences.

Sullivan observed that the child is baffled by the deception of his parents, because he comes to doubt that the parent is really cruel, thinking it may only seem so because of the patient's "own cursed perversity." Yet treatment showed Sullivan and his patient that the parental cruelty to the child was real, behind a hypocritical mask.

J. S. Kasanin, although to all appearances a Sullivanian of Freudian extraction, wrote, in 1944, that obsessive children use "fantasy to compensate for the lack of love in their lives." Kasanin, too, gave a place of primary importance to the early Joveless family, but he came back to the Freudian perspective when he viewed the family as important "because Id was there."

Joseph Barnett (1969) notes that early childhood for an adult obsessive is marked by "hostility, rejection, and power struggles." Those ingredients, however, are in the infantile experiences of many children. What is unique about the early family life of the obsessive? Barnett wrote (p. 48) that specific to the obsessional:

> . . . is the hypocrisy typical of his family experience. In such a family, the parents camouflage hostile behavior toward the child with a facade of love and concern. They rationalize their

own needs as being objectively right, and self-assertion by the child as wrong. This private, arbitrary system of morality is mediated through interpersonal operations creating anxiety, shame, and guilt.

Bingham Dai (1941, 1944, 1952, 1957, 1965), Joseph Barnett (1966, 1968, 1969), David Shapiro (1965), Mary White (1952), and Leon Salzman (1968) have continued to apply and reformulate these basic Sullivanian views with respect to obsessive people. These are the views that Salzman called "post-Freudian psychoanalysis," that Bingham Dai called "sociopsychiatric" and that Gardner Murphy—although differing from Sullivanians—labelled "biosocial." The components of this generally Sullivanian orientation are described more fully in a later section of this chapter ("Sociopsychiatric Approach").

Sullivanians, like Freudians, have been content with studying a few clinical cases and forming some generalizations based upon a small sample of cases. Both "schools" have stuck to clinical exploration of one to six cases. Their methodologic approach to population size would *never* allow us to tell them apart! The methods and approaches are very different.

FREUDIAN CLASSICAL APPROACH

Among the Freudians, classical Freudians such as Róheim (1943), Kasanin (1944), Serge Lebovici and R. Diatkine (1957), perhaps Berman (1942), Brown (1959), and Karl Abraham (1921) appeared eager to view the family only as a "playing out" in reality of the intra-individual instincts. Love and hate were importantly there, in the family. To the family are attributed none of the neo-Freudian's views about Family primacy in instigating or teaching life styles (Adler) or interpersonal patterns (Sullivan) or self-concepts (Dai). The classical Freudians see the family as merely the stage upon which libidinal and aggressive instincts are brought out into the open. Melanie Klein (1964), Betty Joseph (1966) and J. O. Wisdom (1966) all appear to be closest to the original Freudian school in their strict emphasis upon the intrapsychic, and de-emphasis of the intrafamilial, when dealing with obsessive children. Indeed, when one reads a Kleinian it looks as if the family is only a necessary sustaining ground for the intraindividual Psyche and at times, perhaps, merely a necessary evil.

FREUDIAN EGO-PSYCHOLOGY APPROACH

The "ego-psychology" Freudians are another group who have contributed voluminously to the current literature. Indeed, in my estimation, their contributions seem to outweigh—in both volume and depth—the writings of all other groups of clinicians. They have been more productive of literature than the Sullivanians, certainly. I cannot do them justice in this brief survey. Anna Freud, along with her many followers and supporters, insisted upon giving more attention to the family as an autonomous system in which human lessons, with anality among them, *are learned from people*, especially mothers or nurturing surrogates, and are not merely unfolded out of instincts or drives. They have to be taught; they do not bubble up of their own accord. In this group we might choose to include Bornstein, Bonnard, Chethik, Erikson, Kalmanson, Nágera, Weissman, and, despite the early date of her writing, Sokolnicka.

The ego-psychology Freudians are capable of deriving some very tight mechanistic formulations concerning the family life of an obsessive child. For example, Anna Freud (1966, p. 119) discussed "the matrix of obsessional neurosis." She summarized the specific ways in which a damaging mother-child relationship can induce *obsessional neurosis*, not neurosis generically, and her inclusions were sparse:

> If we want to restrict ourselves to those factors in the mother-child relationship which are truly specific for obsessional neurosis, then we are left with a few only, such as damage done to the synthetic function, to the capacity for fusion of love and hate, to the ability to maintain object love as contrasted with self-love. Also, where early object loss is concerned, we have to think in less global terms ... What is significant for

obsessional neurosis is not the event (of losing a loved person early in life) as such but the child's belief that it is the result of his own death wishes and the feeling of guilt attached to this interpretation.

In the same 1965 Congress summary Anna Freud (1966) rather fatalistically reminded the assembled group that even a most salutary early relationship to one's mother "may promote rapid ego growth and instead of safeguarding the individual this may be instrumental in creating the very precocity of superego functions which we have met as one of the preconditions of obsessional neurosis." Although the mother-child relationship is what is important for Anna Freud, she is scarcely to be found believing that love is enough always to guarantee a salutary outcome. She believed that Fate governs the mother-child dyad in such a manner that good intentions and good experiences will not always protect against a hellish outcome. Fate shows some determinism and uniformity as it works through the child's id and ego in interaction with the mother. Fate has some patterns, she has said, but who ever said our instincts will make us happy?

ECLECTIC APPROACHES

Eclectic psychiatrists, while not eschewing psychodynamic theory, have given more importance to the family as a recognizable social unit, and have described the family as a social unit in which biologic and cultural features are intricately woven together. David Henderson and R. D. Gillespie (1956), Judd (1965), Despert (1955), Stella Chess and Alexander Thomas (1960), and John Clancy and Albert Norris (1961) have questioned varied facets of Freudian views. That seems to be where eclecticism begins—in debunking Freudian comments. When it comes to Freud, one's mind is either filled with agreement or disagreement, it appears. In any event, for other than Freudian ideas there is no voluminous literature concerning obsession in childhood.

Sandor Rado (1930's, published 1969) appeared to rate his disagreement with Freud as very severe, but the views of "adaptational dynamics" are not highly divergent from classical psychoanalysis, as I see it. The Freudian ego-psychologists are almost as "deviant" or unorthodox as the Rado group. The Sullivanians and the entire group of neo-Freudians are probably the ones who disagree most with classical Freudianism, for they have either dispensed with or ignored libido theory almost fully.

Let me take the illustration of harsh toilet training as an intrafamilial pattern occupying a crucial place in the genesis of obsessive disorder in children. By looking at eclectic psychiatrists' views on toilet training we can see how various writers take sides for or against Freud with respect to maternally imposed disciplines on the child's bowel activities.

Norman Brown (1959) could be exemplary of the view that, no matter what the toilet disciplines might be, a programmed anality of the child will come to the fore and carry the day. Brown sneered at the view that anality is seriously modified by life-experiences—that anality could be taught, or needs to be taught or learned.

Sandor Rado (1959) could illustrate the view that it is not only toilet training but *toilet disciplines along with other features of a battle for autonomy between mother and child* which predispose toward obsessional behavior. This is very akin to Fromm's 1944 views. Rado paved the way for estimating causes other than anality to be important in the formation of obsessive behavior. He gave a slightly more humanistic interpretation of the Freudian metaphors and asserted that it is the general onrush of social learning which the child defies, not solely the toilet discipline.

Let me presume, finally, that Clancy and Norris (1961) could epitomize the eclectic approach, coming at the question of harsh toilet disciplines, as they did, in a pre-designed comparative study of a group of obsessives and a group of patients with anorexia nervosa. They found no evidence that harsh toilet disciplines characterized either obsessives or anorexics. Toilet training certainly did not distinguish the obsessives from the anorexics. It just does not seem to be a big issue, one way or the other, as far as Clancy and Norris are concerned.

Likewise, in the paper of Joseph C. Finney (1963) where the results more or less supported "Freudian" views, Finney tried to set down exactly what would be included in such personality traits as rigidity, anality, stubbornness and submissiveness. Finney studied 31 boys and their mothers—the boys for "anal character, stubbornness and submissiveness," and the mothers for "rigidity." He found that a high correspondence indeed did exist between the maternal and filial personality traits. Until we have more evidence of this kind—that children are like their parents—we have no good basis for concluding either (1) that obsessive children learn obsessiveness from their exposure to their parents, or (2) that obsessive children inherit the illness or the predisposition from their progenitors. The eclectic spirit, tied to research know-how, is what is called for.

A number of authors (F. Bernard and H. Flavigny, 1965; G. Heuyer et al., 1958; Michel Dugas, 1961; P. Fedor-Freiberg and G. Dobrotka, 1964; Muriel Hall, 1935; W. H. Lo, 1967; Salzman, 1968; Finney, 1963; and Kringlen, 1965) have all suggested with varying degrees of certitude that children are like their parents in being obsessive. It would have been welcomed to find adequate documentation of assertions that parents and their children behave alike when the child is obsessive, but no such luck. Often, the best we could glean was a statement such as "some of the obsessive traits and symptoms seemed to be acquired from the mother."

Dai and Weston LaBarre (1945) engaged in a notable debate on the topic of toilet training in the Orient. But Mildred Sikkema (1947) appeared to settle the dispute—at least as far as the Japanese were concerned. She went to Japanese people and got to know their customs. LaBarre as a Freudian found the Chinese to have no obsessive disorder and related this directly to the leniency of Chinese toilet training. At the same time LaBarre depicted the Japanese as rigid in bowel discipline and with a resulting high incidence of obsessive illness. Dai, as a neo-Freudian on both theoretical and practical grounds, asserted that the Chinese assuredly did not practice harsh toilet training, but that other features of Chinese culture and values must be found to account for the occurrence of obsessive neurosis among the Chinese. Dai then adduced evidence from the Japanese psychiatrist, Tsuneo Muramatsu (1951), to show that the Japanese were obsessive but also that they were lenient about the bowel training of their children. Dai was by that time finding fault with LaBarre on two counts, for LaBarre was saying:

1. The easygoing-toilet Chinese are not obsessive, when they often *are*, and

2. The strict-toilet Japanese are more frequently obsessive, for the Japanese *are* obsessive even though they *do not* have rigid toilet training.

So, Sikkema settled the fuss by finding that Japanese people simply did not, contrary to LaBarre's statements, have harsh toilet training of children.

Erik Homburger Erikson (1950, 1959) attributed as much importance to walking and talking as to bowel control for the child's second year of life—the so-called anal stage. Other Freudians of the ego-psychology stripe have in general declined to be as outspoken about the strictly metaphoric significance of toilet training. Anna Freud (1955, pp. 73-74) wrote about the toilet training era that feces are "doubly cathected"—with libido and therefore regarded by the child as love gifts to mother, but also with aggression and therefore regarded as weapons to discharge rage, anger, and disappointment toward the mother:

> While the trends shown by children in this phase are fairly uniform, the actual events vary with the differences in the mother's attitude. If she succeeds in remaining sensitive to the child's needs . . . toilet training will proceed gradually, uneventfully, and without upheavals. On the other hand, such empathy with the child in the anal stage may be impossible for the mother due to her own training, her own reaction formations of disgust, orderliness, and punctiliousness, or other obsessive elements in her personality.

From that quotation it would appear that little has changed as Freudianism underwent its updating. However, merely for placing the critical issues about toileting into the realm of object relations, Anna Freud has been attacked as a deviationist by some arch-orthodox Freudians (for example, Norman Brown, 1959).

LIKE PARENT, LIKE CHILD

The neo-Freudians or post-Freudians do not take up systematically a definite stand on the theoretical dispute between libido theory and interpersonal theory, but they seem to have obtained consensus that it is the mother's tyranny (real or imagined) that determines obsessive illness in a child.

Erich Fromm (1944) in his classic article, "Individual and Social Origins of Neurosis," attributed all neurosis, and all "sick conformity" to an intrafamilial battle of wills. Fromm's case for the social origin of neurosis is especially apt in considering obsessive neurosis. The untamed child is forcibly bent into submission. If "rational" authority is employed in the childrearing, the child is not crippled emotionally, Fromm wrote, but if irrational authority is enforced upon the child, his will is broken and the kernel of neurosis is implanted and nurtured. This mechanism seems apposite to our obsessive children as a group, a matter to which we will return later.

A theme of *battle with mother* for autonomy runs through many case studies (Augusta Bonnard, 1950; Berta Bornstein, 1954; Morton Chethik, 1969; Harvey Greenberg, 1969). The struggle between mother and child formed two interdigitated themes throughout this literature.

COMMUNICATION THEORY AND OBSESSIVE FAMILIES

It was recognized by philosophers such as George Herbert Mead and other North American pragmatists, by Martin Buber and other religious existentialists, and by Edward Sapir and other experts in culture, linguistics and psycholinguistics that the gift of communication through speech and gesture is a distinctive, even elegant, attribute of the human being. Human communication furnishes a medium for the sustenance and change of human relationships. Messages are important, and according to Jurgen Ruesch (1951) communication provides the social matrix of psychiatry. Applying communication theory to obsessions, Ruesch stated (pp. 88-89):

> By and large he [the neurotic] tends to flood others with messages, in an attempt to coerce them into accepting roles

they are not willing to assume . . . The compulsive intellectual and the fanatic broadcast their message uninterruptedly and attempt to influence others without being concerned with the actual effects of their actions upon people . . .

Again Ruesch (1957) wrote of how obsessives are *trained* in childhood (pp. 129-130):

> The events that force children at an early age to make logical statements are related to premature demands on the part of the parents. Activities that cannot be mastered and things which are not meaningful to the child cannot be integrated, are isolated, and escape future modification. Under such circumstances, the child cannot cope with the situation in any other way but by memorizing some external criteria, by forsaking opportunities for experimentation, by avoiding failure at all cost, and by doing things 'just so' and in no other way . . . The parents did not underline the pleasure of the activity or the pleasure of mastery; they rewarded the effort made rather than the effect achieved, and the inherent frustration that the child sensed in his premature attempts was rewarded with (a show of) affection . . . the logical person learned early in life to ape the verbal statements of adults; the memorizing of words and sentences rather than the inquiry into what these words stood for on the part of the youngster satisfied the parents of precocious children. The time needed for developing analogic understanding was not granted them, nor were they shown how to react to other people in non-verbal terms. Pleasure thus was taken out of the process of communication, save for the critical, biting, and sadistic performances which usually took place in the family.

It seems readily apparent that what may be transmitted, received, interpreted, and fed back in the mother-obsessive child dyad is worthy of investigation from the communications approach. But the communication patterns of intrafamilial dyads and larger groups have received psychiatrists' attention mostly when the family contains a *schizophrenic* patient. Those who would emphasize the psychogenesis and sociogenesis of schizophrenia (see Don D. Jackson, 1968) have latched onto a modified communication theory with the greatest zeal. Jackson himself had a background in psychoanalysis although he was prone to repudiate it at times. Gregory Bateson, an anthropologist associated with Jackson from 1954 onward for several years, helped Jackson to bring forth the "double bind hypothesis" which may in the long run apply to families with an obsessive better than to families with a schizophrenic as a member. Bateson *et al.* wrote (1956, pp. 35-36):

> The necessary ingredients for a double bind situation, as we see it, are:
> 1. *Two or more persons.* . . .
> 2. *Repeated experience.* . . . the double bind structure comes to be an habitual expectation.
> 3. *A primary negative injunction.* This may have either of two forms: (a) 'Do not do so and so, or I will punish you,' or (b) 'If you do not do so and so, I will punish you'. . . .
> 4. *A secondary injunction conflicting with the first at a more abstract level, and like the first enforced by punishments or signals which threaten survival* . . . the secondary injunction is commonly communicated to the child by non-verbal means . . . Second, the secondary injunction may impinge upon any element of the primary prohibition . . . for example, 'Do not see this as punishment,' [or] 'Do not see me as the punishing agent,' [or] 'Do not submit to my prohibitions,' [or] 'Do not think of what you must not do'. . . .
> 5. *A tertiary negative injunction prohibiting the victim from escaping the field* . . . if the double binds are imposed in infancy, escape is naturally impossible . . .
> 6. Finally, the complete set of ingredients is no longer necessary when the victim has learned to perceive his universe in double bind patterns. Almost any part of a double bind sequence may then be sufficient to precipitate panic or rage . . .

Bateson and others (1956) stated that the victim of the double bind confuses literal speech with metaphoric speech. They viewed his shifting from literalness to metaphoric speech and vice versa as a protective device. As a consequence, he could not tag or "label" his communication as metaphoric. He would not even recognize what he is doing. Similarly:

> To recognize that he was speaking metaphorically he would need to be aware that he was defending himself and therefore was afraid of the other person. To him such an awareness would be an indictment of the other person and therefore provoke disaster. (p. 39)

The gist of the double bind situation is a restatement of the Sullivanian description of the predicament of the obsessive child, caught up in the "hypocritical mask" behavior of a mother who is afraid to be either angry or loving.

Jay Haley, with a theater background, was an associate of Jackson who published treatises on "Marriage Therapy" (1963) and *Strategies of Psychotherapy* (1963)—always with a focus upon communication processes and overall interaction styles within marriage pairs, and also within family groups but tending to emphasize the parental roles. Jackson described Haley as a "Communication Analyst." Haley, along with other family group therapists, has written more of work with "schizophrenic" families than of any other.

Although I have not seen anything in the family therapy literature that I could call brilliantly illuminating of families with obsessive children, I believe that much will be forthcoming in this field. I like especially the quasi-anthropologic notions and assertions of Howard Mitchell (in Freedman *et al.*, 1965) that the entire family system must first change, and then dyadic and triadic relations within the family and, only at the end, changes within the individuals in the family. This has been very different from my own approach to family problems, but I find it challenging and interesting.

Virginia Satir, with grounding in psychiatric social work, became a popular lecturer and writer during her association with Jackson. Her book *Conjoint Family Therapy* (1967) makes few explicit references to families with an obsessive child, but much of what she says is highly applicable to these families. For example, (p. 92):

> We call an individual dysfunctional when he has not learned to communicate properly. Since he does not manifest a means of perceiving and interpreting himself accurately, or interpreting accurately messages from the outside, the assumptions on which he bases his actions will be faulty and his efforts to adapt to reality will be confused and inappropriate.

And, (p. 94):

> If the parents' own attitudes are uncertain, or if they disagree with each other, the messages the child takes will be equally confused. The child will try to integrate what cannot be integrated, on the basis of inconsistent and insufficient data. Failing, he will end up with an incomplete picture of himself and low self-esteem . . .

> In addition, the child's parents may deprecate his self-esteem more directly. He looks to them to validate his steps in growth; if these are not acknowledged at the time they occur, or if they are acknowledged with concomitant messages of disgust, disapproval, embarrassment, indifference or pain, the child's self-esteem will naturally suffer.

Satir has not been the only family therapist who has conceptualized the family as a systematized set of small group relations designed explicitly for the hatching out of individuals. Their idea is that family therapy helps the group to change and the person to hatch. None of the family therapists insists upon giving Otto Rank (1932) credit for his initial concepts about the family's *collective spirit* which opposes the *individual spirit* of the differentiating person who is a family member. This is the track that Ivan Boszormenyi-Nagy was on, however, when he wrote in Freedman *et al.* (1965, p. 316):

> The main guideline in evaluating the degree of healthy contribution of any family change issues from the members' joint capacity for replacing gratification systems of stagnant posses-

siveness with those of fresh, new involvements and with pride in everyone's gain toward individuation.

Harold Searles, in Boszormenyi-Nagy and James Framo (1965), said it more concisely: "as viewed over the years of the family's evolution, a family is a *process of individuation out of symbiosis.*"

Family group therapy, then, has become the most popular application of communications theory to child psychiatry. Some writers espouse family group therapy without explicit acceptance of the communication-theory background to which it has been linked in this brief review. Nathan W. Ackerman (1958), a founder of this "school," wrote almost nothing of obsessive neurosis in his *Psychodynamics of Family Life*, but concerning other pathologic problems he did not employ a communication model.

One wishes that the effort at quantification of intrafamilial interactions made by Jules Henry and Samuel Warson (1951) and by Henry (1951) had "got off the ground." In their joint paper they described narcissism's pervasion of intrafamilial transactions in a way that comes close to depicting the non-empathic mother, at least, of many an obsessive child. In the paper authored by Henry alone (1951), a family—again reminiscent of some of the preoccupations of the parents of obsessive children—was described as showing:

> The existence of dominance-subordination relationships as a way of life and as a crucial issue between parent and child. . .

By categorizing and counting interactions these authors made a very important step forward in psychodynamic research. That it did not catch on widely (a fate shared regrettably by much magnificent work of Abram Kardiner) does not detract from its richness and, perhaps, some day, its greater utilization. The presence of an improved audio-visual technology ought to enhance their kind of work.

William Westley and Nathan Epstein (1969) in *Silent Majority* depicted *affective* as distinguished from *instrumental* communication within families. They followed the sociologist Talcott Parsons (1955) who had made a distinction between *expressive* and *instrumental* functions of families, when they (1969) wrote:

Two groups of reasonably similar, interrelated variables appeared. They were problem solution and communication, and autonomy ... Problem solution and communication describe the degree of communication in the family, the capacity of the family to see and solve emotional problems, the amount of free interaction among the members, the degree of reciprocal warmth between husband and wife, and the presence or absence of psychopathological problems in handling rage.

We are not referring here to the amount of talking or physical activity in the family, for some of the families of disturbed children had plenty of both ...

The journal literature is exceedingly sparse concerning family therapy when a child-member of the family is obsessive. As Carl Whitaker (1972) wrote me: family therapists do not organize their writing in that way! One article is by M. E. Scott (1966) in the *Southern Medical Journal*, giving a case report of a bright ten-year-old boy with chronic worries (obsessions) about school failure, dirtiness, and associated compulsions to ask questions, change clothes, and count his money. Ostensible precipitants included his maternal grandmother's death, an eight-year-old brother's ill health and the mother's leaving home to work, to work off her nerves and depression. The decision was made to give the mother anti-depressant medication, encourage the boy to become friendly with the psychiatric clinic's gardener, and see the entire family as a group. Within one year the boy had become more physically active, had lost some of his obsessions and had improved relations with his father and his two brothers. But his mother was still caught in his questioning and "somewhat ritualistic behavior." In describing the family group therapy, the author reported only that the mother "became quite open" as to her depressed feelings. Other topics and processes were not reported.

Often, family group therapists proceed to report *changes* that accompany or follow "this magic of meeting with the whole family group," but they do not specify how the family group process emerged as a curative force (instead of a destructive one) during the elapsed time. The family therapy literature is imaginative and speculative, and it also has the advantages of an adequate methodology and technology at hand for doing research into the communication networks in families with obsessive children. Heretofore, however, this research capability or advantage is a promise more than an achieved reality.

"Political" advantages of the family therapy-communications approach have been more conspicuously materialized. The approach is more or less congruent with, and acceptable by,

(1) post-Freudian psychoanalysis: after all, this itself is an effort to use some of the individual-based concepts of psychoanalysis in a small group (interpersonal) setting,

(2) "radical therapists" with a commitment to social change and to any and all modes of psychiatric treatment which do not impede movement toward "socialism," at most, or "restructured society" at least,

(3) proponents of group therapy who believe that modality is intrinsically superior and/or most efficient in "delivering care to a greater number of consumers," and

(4) eclectic psychiatrists who'll try anything "not patently immoral."

Perhaps it would be feasible to add a fifth group who might be congenial to family group therapy—the behavior modification advocates—but I cannot find in literature, or in my personal experience, much indication that the behavior modification school actually does find family group therapy congenial. Indeed, it may be that one bandwagon cannot tolerate another.

OBSESSION VIEWED AS BIOLOGICALLY DETERMINED

Our families influence us by our genes as well as by our nurture in humanness. Hence, "family studies" of obsessives have been both "interpersonal" and "organic" in their subject matter. Erwin Straus (1948) wrote as an existentialist but he had a persisting German bias in favor of heredity and constitution. This bias meant that Straus sought to get back of the family system, and into a biologic-constitutional substrate that could account for the emergence of an individual's obsessiveness. An experientialist who grew up in the organicist twenties, Straus elegantly contrasted the deadly rigidity of the obsessive with the opposing style of free-swinging openness shown by the hashish user. Paradoxically, though, Straus ended by stating that some chemotoxin probably causes both "states of the soul," of hashish taker and obsessive.

Ivan Pavlov (1934) bypassed family and environment entirely. For the obsessive-compulsive, he posited areas of "pathological inertness" in the brain and also pathological areas in the brain caused by an "ultra-paradoxical phase." Do we need further reminders that a commitment to the mystique of biology can produce errors as preposterous as those for which we can blame the adherents of an environmentalist monism? There are numerous other examples of "biologism" standing in the literature.

Constitution. The Danish authors, Theodor Balslev-Olesen and Einar Geert-Jørgensen (1959), illustrated the viewpoint that obsessives are born, not made. They wrote that in a series of 62 adult obsessives the 48 who showed onset in childhood or puberty "belong in the constitutional group." Early onset is equated, naively enough, by these writers with constitutional determinism. In German, E. Kahn had referred to what I would translate as "anancastic constitution." Many appear to want to leave the door open to a hereditary determinism where obsessive children are concerned. Heredity and constitution have allure for the modern mind.

M. Matousek and R. Nesnidalova (1964) found that electroencephalograph (EEG) abnormalities were uncommonly frequent in obsessives and their parents, and from this inferred that obsessional neurosis likely is biologically determined. It would all be part and parcel of a deranged nervous system. Many writers, oftentimes clutching at straws, come to the conclusion that anything so intractable, so fascinating, perplexing, difficult, etc., must be biologically determined! Daniel Hack Tuke (1894) had similar views. Before EEG, it was a matter of "heredofamilial predisposition." After EEG, Pacella *et al.* (1944) found 22 out of 31 people with obsessive symptoms, with varied nosologic conditions, to give abnormal EEG tracings. In 1947, however, Rockwell and Simons contrasted the high rate of abnormal EEG in psychopaths (10/10) with *the low rate* in obsessives (2/11). Several years later, when more was known of the incidence or prevalence of abnormal EEG tracings in the general public, Ingram and McAdam (1960) could report that obsessives had abnormal EEG records no more frequently than the general population.

Nevertheless, in the days after the first World War, with the discovery of obsessive features of many post-encephalitic patients, a growing number of quite highly respected writers speculated that *all obsessives* might have "subclinical" or "soft" indications of brain damage, and so the whistle blew and they were off! Neurologism was in the saddle. Kurt Goldstein, whose works began publication in the US in the late thirties, was a leader in the new blending of psychodynamics with "hard neurological science" and speculative philosophy. That integration was difficult, at best, but some of the best Germanic minds set themselves to the enterprise. Their efforts after forty or more years seem a bit puerile in their scientism. Paul Schilder once declared that two-thirds of his obsessive patients were brain damaged. Yet, being psychoanalytic, Schilder also contended that the organic condition served to set free motor impulses which reinforced sadistic attitudes, as the latter were expressed in compulsions and obsessions. Pollitt (1957) entered a worthwhile detracting note into the discussion when he made the observation that was both so sensible and available to the everyday clinician—obsessives simply do not act the way that brain injured, antisocial children act!

The situation is similar with epilepsy, as Linton Grimshaw (1964) reviewed it. Tuke (1894, p. 191) had commented that: "Indeed, we cannot fail to be struck with the frequent occurrence of epilepsy in the families of persons labouring under imperative ideas." In some cases the interaction of seizures and obsessions *is* startling, but the incidence of obsessions in epileptics is *no higher than in the general population*. Tests of significance are very useful in these matters. Nevertheless, Grimshaw examined clinical records of medical histories for 103 obsessive adults and 105 controls (with anxiety state and hysteria) to see what had been the occurrence within each group of chorea, convulsions, encephalitis, meningitis, epilepsy, heat stroke, von Recklinghausen's, anterior poliomyelitis, subacute combined degeneration of the cord, eclampsia with fits, etc. Having set up some of the formal conditions of experimental control, he could, then, use statistical tests to determine *if one group had more of all kinds of neurologic disorder* to a significant degree. It is interesting that, although it forces nobody to any precise conclusion about "the vulnerable central nervous system and obsessive behavior," the obsessives as a group showed more neurologic disorders on their histories than non-obsessives, significant at the 5% level of confidence with one degree of freedom.

In the final analysis, such studies probably do little more than prompt us to hedge when we write about obsessive children—as did Dugas (1961) who suggested that a familial tendency exists *on both hereditary and environmental grounds* and that the prognosis is better in "environmental" cases where salutary changes might be made to occur. Or, as in the report of P. Fedor-Freiberg and G. Dobrotka (1964), childhood obsession is described as "the result of coinciding dispositional, constitutional and environmental factors," but those writers were consistently eclectic and employed combined treatment with psychotherapy and ataractics. Lucie Jessner (1963), a Freudian, acknowledged congenital influences when she reported one boy in whom the obsessional development "seemed determined by (1) a congenital characteristic (hyperactivity), (2) traumatic experiences in the first two years, and (3) the interaction with the neurotic trends of his parents." Louise Despert (1955) noted that 12 of the 68 children whom she studied were derived from six sib-pairs, a high familial occurrence although in a group of families that were by no means randomly selected.

Aubrey Lewis (1936) tackled the problem of familial incidence when he studied the parents of 50 adult and late adolescent obsessives. He found almost none of the parents to be normal and 37 of the 100 parents to be markedly obsessive. Obsessions, furthermore, occurred in 20 percent of the sibs. Lewis, however, was not as quick as some to draw the conclusion that obsessions are heredofamilial. Lüxenburger (1930) and Rüdin (1953), lacking the caution of an Aubrey Lewis, did jump to that conclusion, based on the same kind of survey data which Lewis compiled. However, of his survey method, Lewis himself acknowledged that ". . . one cannot distinguish satisfactorily by this method between hereditary influences and the environment that is constituted by the parents."

Genetic studies of twins promise to be considerably more enlightening about the hereditary passage of obsessional neurosis. Lewis warned almost 40 years ago that "a striking concordance in one or two pairs of monozygotic twins proves nothing: one needs a series and a control group of fraternal twins. Specially valuable also is the monozygotic pair in whom the conditions of the environment have been very different." Hence, the concordance in a large number of proven monozygotic pairs must be significantly higher than chance, and they must display a significantly higher concordance than that seen in a sizeable group of dizygotic, fraternal twins. Moreover, monozygous twins reared differently do provide telling data about the genetic transmission of obsessiveness. Let us look at the genetics literature in the light of these simple criteria.

Lewis (1936) cited three cases of monozygotic twin pairs, and in one case they had been reared separately. He did not compare this small number of cases to the general population nor to a series of fraternal twins. His commentary is very apt: "But two or three pairs tell very little; it is a pity that twins are so rare."

Rüdin (1953) unearthed from the literature nine cases of monozygotic twins of whom at least one in each pair showed obsessional illness and, adding one case of her own, the tally came to: concordance, six; discordance, four. The diagnostic criteria were not described by Rüdin, she used no comparison groups, and the twins' monozygosity was not assured. These were all rather grave inadequacies.

Woodruff and Pitts (1964) gave an excellent survey of the psychiatric and genetic literature, adding a report on one male-twin pair, aged 17 years, who showed concordance for obsessive illness. This concordance obtained in a general caucasoid population for which the maximal prevalence was computed to be five persons in every 10,000 (or 0.05%). The odds for a monozygotic twin to be obsessive were said to be 1 in every 300,000 (or 0.00033%) and the odds for concordance by chance alone were one for every 600 million of the general population (or 0.00000016%). I think anyone would have to concede that the two twins described by Woodruff and Pitts were concordant for obsessional illness. It is interesting to note that also their father and paternal grandmother were obsessive. But concordance is *not* proof of transmission in the genes, and such a telling genealogy is instructive only if heredity has been proven (Kringlen, 1965) for obsessive disorder.

Eiji Inouye (1965) tried to advance an explanation of the concordance of obsessions in eight of ten monozygotic twin pairs, whereas only two of four fraternal pairs showed concordance in obsessional illness. He postulated these three causes of concordance:

(1) an environmental influence incidentally shared by two members of a twin pair
(2) susceptibility to neurosis in both twin members resulting from a particular situation to twins
(3) heredity.

Inouye (p. 1174) concluded with a two-cause hypothesis in a terminology that was reminiscent—for content—of Paul Schilder.

The deviation in the core of personality in the patients of typical obsessive-compulsive neurosis with chronic course is controlled by a gene or genes, and the development of ego or superego in these individuals is strongly influenced by psychological environment or physiological function of the central nervous system. The ego or superego suppresses or represses the internal impulse coming from the personality core, and this disharmony or conflict in personality is a possible cause of the neurosis.

Neville Parker (1964) adduced some impressive argument to the contrary, i.e., Parker showed that very strong identification does not give concordance. Parker studied two pairs of monozygotic twins with a high degree of identification who were nonetheless *discordant* for obsessions. Parker noted that only the more assertive member of the twin pair became obsessive. His conclusion was that the "purely environmental theory," of identification producing concordance, had to be discarded. Also, since Twin A and Twin B had had identical toileting traumata, he concluded, ". . . disturbance in this area is not sufficient in itself to produce an obsessional illness." In a way, this twin study had been an acid test. However, it is still subject to varied inferences and "explanations."

If, as it appears, all was in order, the kind of twin study reported by L. Braconi (1970), is what is required to answer the question of whether obsessional neurosis can be an inheritable illness. Braconi, working in Rome, collected four monozygotic twin pairs (all female), all of whom were concordant in obsessional neurosis. They had been observed for a period lasting from two to 11 years. Two pairs with family histories of nervousness and depression improved, but the two pairs with family histories of schizophrenia evolved into being schizophrenic.

Braconi did more. He collected five pairs of dizygotic twins of matched sex in which one twin was obsessive, and also two dizygous pairs of disparate gender (one male twin and one female). *In only one pair of dizygotic twins*, both male, was there concordance in obsessive symptoms. That pair had a maternal great-aunt who was psychotic and a paternal grandmother described as anxious. Both of these twins became schizophrenic, suggesting that the hereditary transmission of schizophrenia would be hard to parcel out from the inheritance of obsessive symptoms in that particular twin pair. What Braconi showed, at most, is that concordance in four pairs of female monozygotic twins, but not in three pairs of dizygotic female twins, moves us into the direction of seeing certain obsessive pictures as distinctly hereditary. Now all that is required is replication and critique, and this may be forthcoming from a variety of "gold mines" where twin studies are being carried out currently. This is an area in which anyone interested in the heredity of obsessive children should read the literature month by month.

People working in psychiatric genetics seem to oscillate between environmentalism and hereditarianism. In the matter of obsessive neurosis, there is strong evidence in favor of environmental determination *and* in favor of hereditary determination! Counterevidence to both views is also on record. As more twin studies are done with pairs (monozygotic and dizygotic) concordant and discordant for obsessive illness, we will know more, but twins are indeed rare specimens for study. Brown (1942, pp. 785-90) summed up the potentialities of inheritance of neurosis:

> Assuming then that there is a hereditary factor, what is its nature? It is easier to answer this negatively than positively. It is not a recessive, only one case of consanguinity was found. Simple dominance is also excluded . . . There is a great probability that the inheritance of many commonplace human characters is on the lines of variable dominance, where the environment also plays a large part . . . I would suggest, however, that the development of, say, an obsessional state rather than an anxiety state depends more on the commonplace personality factors, which are probably themselves variable dominants, than on the specific psychoneurotic factor, if it exists. It may perhaps be that there are one or more pathological variable dominant factors, of the order of constitutional emotional sensitivity, determining whether or not a psychoneurosis can develop in a suitable environment.

Jan Ehrenwald (1960, 1963), a dynamic psychiatrist, switched metaphors in hopes of solving some of the problems of spreading neurosis. He picked up the metaphoric terminology of a classical epidemiologist and used this in a report on 14 family members, drawn from four generations, whom he had studied for a total of 859 hours. He concluded that, although some of the 14 "subjects" were obsessive, it is not the nosologic entity but the "maladjusted attitudes" which are transmitted through the process of "contagion." Since Ehrenwald believed that neither the entity, obsessive illness, nor the attitude is genetically programmed into the person, he labeled as "neurotic pseudoheredity" the lineage patterning of neurotic attitudes. This makes "contagion" the basic process, as he saw it. Ehrenwald asserted that *contagion varies:*

(1)   directly with duration of exposure,

(2)   inversely with age of host at initial exposure,

(3)   inversely with host susceptibility (including predispositions) to the attitudes, and

(4)   directly with the virulence and penetrance of the attitudes.

Ehrenwald seems on the right track and to top it off was
equipped with an admirable irony. By borrowing the language of
quantitative biology he could state some basic postulates about
how people make people well or ill, "infecting" one another with
attitudes and values, in such a way that some worthwhile sociopsychiatric research could be taken up within the framework he
offered. He stated *testable hypotheses* about what facilitates, for
example, children's acquisition from their parents of those
"maladjusted attitudes" which lead to obsession. It was a statement of some learning-theory principles in the terminology of a
"medical model" which, although many non-medical people nowa-
days are finding it objectionable, appears to be a model that serves
well for solving the problems of illness, maladjustment or pathology—that is, it serves for clinical purposes. For neutral, descriptive
work it has some shortcomings, it must be granted.

Using Ehrenwald's model to study a group of families with obsessive attitudes (defined later herein), we could test whether:

(1) the child in these families is more at risk—or more vulnerable—with prolonged exposure [Ehrenwald's postulate 1].
Kringlen (1965) found no support for this.

(2) the child is more at risk the younger he contacted the
attitudes [postulate 2]. Kringlen (1965) found *no* evidence of
this in his follow-up study, however.

(3) the child is more at risk with certain attidues than with
others (e.g., toilet training or anality might not be highly
contagious but orderliness might be. See Finney, 1963). [pos-
tulate 4]

I do not know whether we have adequate ways of assessing

Ehrenwald's *host susceptibility* to attitudes [postulate 3] at this point, but social psychologists have explored considerably what makes certain groups and persons susceptible to particular attitudes and behavior. When we know that, with certainty, we will really have some of our deepest therapy problems solved earlier, and perhaps prevented. One "political" advantage in the Ehrenwald approach to these problems is that—being "biological"—it is compatible with a wide range of views, for example, with Freudian, post-Freudian, communications theory, and learning theory approaches.

BEHAVIOR MODIFICATION APPROACH

Of all the schools reviewed, save perhaps for Melanie Klein and the classical Freudians, the behavior modification authors seem to be the most uninterested in other members of the obsessive child's family. Behavior modification literature is fascinating and the "believers' " devotion to their arts shows a deep, loyal commitment that is rare in contemporary life, whether it be in politics or in science. But their literature should be read as the *non plus ultra* in taking the family as given. Behavior therapy, or operant conditioning, or behavior modification, is all-out for parents. Behavior therapists see to it that children are shaped as parents want them to be. The child is told to shape up or ship out, in effect. Hence, parents are not regarded as a "problem," *but as a datum*, for behavior modification workers (Carrera and Adams, 1970). Parents and their power are so accepted, so taken for granted, that parents and family members—when they are not set up as ancillary "shapers" and reinforcers—and family styles, and family history, can be "ignored," more or less. One does not delve into what he takes as axiomatic. Witness the *entirety* of Irving Weiner's (1967, pp. 27-29) reference to an obsessive adolescent's family:

> Almost every moment of his waking life was governed by one or another of these rituals, and he was terrorized by thoughts that if he failed in any way to execute them, either 'something terrible' would happen to his parents or 'I'll be drafted into the army and sent to Viet Nam and killed.'

The boy was the only child of middle class, apparently emotionally stable parents, and he had no history of serious psychological [sic] disturbance.

He had been seen for psychological consultation four years earlier when his parents had been concerned about his then mediocre school performance and overdependence on them to the exclusion of peer relationships . . . The next four years had passed without significant psychological [sic] incident, and it was only the recent onset of the patient's compulsive rituals and attendant acute distress that had led his parents to arrange the current psychotherapeutic contact.

Any less attention than this to a child's family would surely constitute an airy disregard of family relations!

All told, operant conditioning shows the parents' wishes being imposed upon obsessive children, with the help of a "science," itself plausible but very poor in conceptualization. Whatever the operant conditioners think of family life, their work at the present time does not tell us about families.

SOCIOPSYCHIATRIC APPROACH

Bingham Dai (1957) selected four features of the approach which he called *sociopsychiatric* and *biosocial*.

(1) Uses, in a modified form, of Freud's epochal discoveries of the 'unconscious' and 'infantile sexuality.'

(2) Views of childhood sexuality "as essentially a biosocial form of relationship between the child and his elders and as only one aspect of the role the child occupies in the total family constellation."

(3) Cognizance of how "the forces of culture" shape and pattern the roles and self-images of persons at various chronologic ages in their development.

(4) Emphasis of "the importance of the immediate situation" as a totality, including both self-concept and individual perceptions of the culture, against which behavior can be understood.

More recently, Dai (1972) expanded his earlier statement about the situation by saying:

> This view is a field-theoretical conception of the total situation which consists of the interaction between the individual as he conceives of himself and the situation as he perceives it. Behavior is considered as a function of this total situation.

In short, then, the *sociopsychiatric* focus is upon *an individual's* early life, his carryover into the present of his early family-circle patterns, his cultural milieu and especially his own definition of his culture, and finally his all-important self concept as a human being of human merit. Dai (1965), although usually empirical and clinical, and not highly abstract, carried his explanation further when he stated:

> Through the pioneering work of Freud, the role certain biological drives play in human behaviour has become abundantly clear. But it is still not sufficiently recognized in certain quarters that man is more than an animal. What seems most characteristic of man is his consciousness of self as an object. This momentous emergence of the self in experience takes place somewhere in the second year of an individual's life and ever since then his entire existence may be thought of as a ᵖrolonged struggle to achieve a picture of self that will be acceptable to himself as well as to other humans and to arrive at a style of life that will do justice to his own nature as well as to the requirements of his culture. This may be called the task of being human, and, as a rule, it takes precedence over the gratification of any isolated impulse.

All of Dai's written work (1941, 1944, 1952, 1957, 1959 [with Braganza], 1965) concerning adult and adolescent obsessives has been carried out within that "sociopsychiatric framework" wherein the most telling psychiatric datum is the self concept in relation to the intimate familial "culture." In doing this, Dai elaborated upon the viewpoints of Harry Stack Sullivan and Karen Horney concerning the self-regarding attitudes of the obsessive. He gave renewed emphasis to the interaction between the individual and the sociocultural environment. In conversation, in 1972, Dai told me rather insistently that the self picture of the obsessive child—the self picture being an intrapsychic phenomenon of interpersonal genesis—is always in conflict with some "cultural emphasis" that is communicated to the child as it is embodied in the parental attitudinal system. Dai (1972) asserted, based on his cross-cultural study of young obsessives, "Any cultural emphasis which goes against the child's inner nature is what leads to an obsessive disorder. In China this has occurred as a result of the emphasis on filial piety or on maternal indulgence of the child. In North America it is a consequence of such emphases as sexual purity, self-help, romance and so forth."

Dai's views suggest a philosophical commitment to a Rousseau-like humanistic ethic. There seems to be postulated a "good" Human Nature within the child waiting to be let out in a finite range of interpersonal milieux. If the cultural emphases of the parents do not allow the child's nature to unfold, or if their values distort the child's essence, or negate what the child *is* "in his heart of hearts," then, according to Dai's viewpoint, we will see the genesis of childhood obsessional neurosis, an overuse of obsessive maneuvers to the point that obsessive symptoms occur to the child.

The Dai point of view was a sophisticated one, taking into consideration the cultural base of behavior, but at the same time it was filled with hope that the obsessive child's nature only needed liberation.

Leon Salzman (1968) propounded a similar theoretical approach to adult obsessives. Salzman called the generic theoretical approach not *sociopsychiatric* but "post-Freudian psychoanalysis." Salzman went against the Freudian grain which emphasizes the intra-individual (Wisdom, 1966; Nágera, 1965; Anna Freud, 1966; Melanie Klein, 1964; Norman Brown, 1959; Géza Róheim, 1943) to such a radical extent that he could state (Salzman, 1968, p. 88):

The role of early patterning of obsessional behavior is undoubted, as is the influence of the parental figures and their own obsessional difficulties. It is conceivable that there could not be a severe obsessional problem in the child unless it were already present in the parents.

In that way Salzman (1968) propounded the view that the obsessive attitudes of parents beget obsessive attitudes in children. The diffusion "from generation to generation" could occur by what Ehrenwald (1960) called "homonymic contagion." Surely, the social scientist and the epidemiologist ought to be able to enlighten us on this problem . . . some day.

FAMILY CHARACTERISTICS

In line with the sociopsychiatric approach we have elected to take, let us now see what kind of sociocultural phenomena play through the families of the 49 obsessive children gathered here. First, certain demographic features of the parents and sibs, and of the entire household, will be given. Second, to close the chapter there will be presented some of the ideological and attitudinal aspects of these households—especially of the parents.

Size and Composition of Households. Taken all together these 49 households included 230 white people, 129 males and 101 females. No obsessive child was black. Subtracting the obsessive child from his family, we find our 39 obsessive boys surrounded by 71 other males and 71 females, and our ten obsessive girls living in households with 20 other females and 19 males. That is a very even distribution for gender of others in household. Adding them back into the lot, we can see, because of the small average family size, that the obsessive boys lived in predominantly male households and the girls in predominantly female households.

These families contained 132 children, total. The mean number of children in the families was 2.7, approaching a zero population growth level! There were 83 sibs. Only three families had five children and one family had six. Each obsessive child had, therefore, an average of 1.7 sibs, and these were older than the obsessive child, but 60 sibs were younger. And in five of these households the only child was obsessive.

Grandparent(s) lived in only three of these households. Other than these only the conjugal family was present in each of 46 households.

Two boys lived in homes rent by the death of the father and two boys lived in homes broken by divorce, giving four families that were fatherless. All the girls and 35 of the boys lived in intact homes.

Age of Parents. The mean age of the group of living parents was 40 years (SD=7.76). Parental age co-varied positively (r=0.30, p=.033) with pathology in the family members. Age of parents also co-varied positively with *neurosis* as opposed to *personality* diagnosis in the 49 obsessive children (r=0.38, p=.007) suggesting that older parents produced the sicker, symptomatic children.

Place of Residence. Three of the 49 families were rural dwellers, seven lived in towns with fewer than 25,000 population, 28 lived in towns with populations between 25,000 and 100,000, and 11 lived in metropolitan areas (over 100,000). Hence, they were highly urbanized.

Religious Affiliation. Eighty-five of the parents of these children were Protestants. Eight were Catholics, four were Jews, one parent had "no religion;" and of the 98 parents, eight were involved in mixed religious marriage. That is to say, four of these families showed mixed marriages on religious criteria. The overall view was of white Anglo-Saxon Protestants being endogamous.

A few of these families (10, or 20%) took religion seriously and made it "significant in the home," but in 39 families (80%) religion was not given an explicit, outspoken part in daily family life. Mostly Protestants, they carried their religion lightly.

Occupations of Fathers. Table 3 depicts the fathers as having a preponderance of professional vocations (30 out of 49). Eleven of them were medical doctors. Big business managerial and ownership occupations brought the total to 39 out of the 49 fathers. These were an elite group occupationally, undoubtedly. Only five fathers were as "lowly placed" as to be in the clerical and sales fields, and there were no lower socioeconomic status (SES) jobs than these.

TABLE 3
FREQUENCY OF FATHER'S OCCUPATION

Work Title	Number
Professional	30
(Physicians	11)
(Educators	4)
(Lawyers	2)
(Clergy	2)
[Professors, also included under other titles	8]
(Assorted titles	11)
Managerial	6
Clerical and sales	5
Big business proprietors	3
Inadequate information (father out of home, etc.)	3
Draftsman or foreman	2
Total	49

Occupations of Mothers. The mothers, as a group, were mostly housewives (34 of them). However, eight practiced a profession (mostly teachers). Three mothers were full-time students. Three held clerical jobs and one was a domestic service worker. All together, seven held jobs that could be described as "students and workers." The mothers too were very upper middle class in life style, as a group.

Family Income. The average annual household income for the U.S. is around $10,250. The mean income of $19,400 for the households which contained the 49 obsessive children was almost twice the U.S. average. The median family income for the families of obsessive children was $17,000, however, since the three millionaires "skewed the curve" and elevated the average income for the study group.

If we used not reported income but the SES score which Green (1970) advocated, taking occupation, income and education as the chief criteria, we would have found an average SES score of 68.86, which goes with an approximate income of $25,000 per year. This shows us that even Southern professionals are not as highly paid as those in other regions. If we derived an SES score by using The Duncan Decile ascription (Reiss, Duncan *et al.*, 1961), the mean score would be in the 8.18 decile, also a high score.

Parental Education. The educational attainment of these parents is presented in Table 4, where it is readily obvious that they were an advantaged group, especially the fathers.

TABLE 4
EDUCATION OF FATHERS AND MOTHERS

Education Level	Fathers	Mothers
Graduate/Professional	23	2
College graduate	9	17
Partial College/Business School	10	17
High School graduate	4	10
Partial High School	2	1
Elementary only	1	2
Total	49	49

Psychopathology in the Family. Records were scrutinized, for family history of mental illness, in both mother's and father's respective families of origin as well as in their current family of procreation. We did not search further than the parental families of origin and, regrettably, the records were not as complete on sibs, grandparents, aunts and uncles as would have been desired. *No mention of psychopathology* is not a disclaimer; it is equivocal. What we had to settle for was a count of mentioned psychopathology in our available case records. The results, summarized in Table 5, suggest that these families were at high risk for mental illness and that family members other than the study group of obsessive children were obsessionals. A positive history in 71.4% of the families suggests some interpersonal transmission, either through genes or learned attitudes, or both!

Some Family Disciplines and Practices. In 33 families (67%) there was a report of inconsistent or erratic discipline. For most of

TABLE 5

FREQUENCY OF OBSESSIVE AND OTHER PSYCHOPATHOLOGY IN FAMILIES OF OBSESSIVE CHILDREN

	No. of Children	%
Positive Record of Obsession in Family		
Yes	35	71.4
No	14	28.6
Positive Record of Other Psychopathology in Family		
Yes	27	55
No	22	45
Both Rows Total	49	100

the children this was bound to developmental stages—for example, permissiveness in pre-school era and strictness in school era with abdication of any pressures when symptoms flared up, etc. The other third of these families showed very strict consistency in their disciplinary strategies. Among child psychiatry populations, this third who were consistent disciplinarians probably make up the unusual, large group, and not the mere two-thirds who were "erratic or inconsistent" disciplinarians.

Bowel training was rigid, punitive or prolonged in at least 41% of the cases (N=20). This will be considered more fully in Chapter 4 where the 49 children are described.

To summarize the demographic findings all too briefly, these 49 families were people who epitomized urbanizing, affluent, middle-class, middle-aged, white, Anglo-saxon, Protestant "middle America" in that period of U.S. history, from Eisenhower through Nixon, which saw cold war prosperity give over to a real-war economy geared toward an unpopular war in Southeast Asia. These families lived out their lives, with considerable personal and interpersonal unhappiness, in that unhappy epoch, being made by History more than making it.

ATTITUDINAL CLIMATE IN OBSESSIVE CHILDREN'S FAMILIES*

During the time of collecting most of the cases considered here the clinic procedures typically were *not* to do family-group evaluations and treatment but to concentrate upon working with the child patient and his parents, with other members of the family being encountered primarily during home visits or as a more or less accidental accompaniment of the mother, father and obsessive child. As a result of this way of working, and of my heavy reliance upon clinical records, I have had to formulate some general statements about the attitudinal climate within the families of obsessive children on the basis of information derived from closest study of parents and obsessive child(ren), not of sibs—nor of the entire familial group. Hence, what follows is more impressionistic, and more subject to some of my own biases, than some other items reported. In any event, one does form general impressions about these families from a survey of the clinical records, and it is with a statement of the general "flavor" of these households, of their values, roles and relationships, that we now proceed. In what follows I make general remarks. The specifics are reported in the vignettes reported in Chapter 3.

First of all, it was not surprising to discover that the parents set the tone of a household that was *highly verbal*. No silent majority could keep its name if it contained these parents. Indeed, on behalf of the obsessive child, one might wish to prescribe the reduced talking that is said to occur in culturally deprived households. These parents were motorically underactive but verbally hyperactive, and as Harry Stack Sullivan (1956, p. 247) stated of the talk of an obsessive adult, so we can say of the talk of the parent of an obsessive child:

> (while it) sounds pretty good, it actually does not communicate—or rather, it miscommunicates, misinforms, and misdirects attention.

*Some of the material in this section, although based on an earlier group of 30 children and some older adolescents, appeared in Adams (1972).

They acted as if talk, as long as it is involved, sadistic, hypocritical, or pointless, has a magic that dispels all sinister forces. Physical activity on the other hand was disvalued by the parents studied. This was reflected in their reluctance to encourage their children to play games, swim, hike, ride bikes, etc., during psychotherapy.

A second feature of the life style of these parents of obsessive children was their high *positive evaluation of etiquette* and of conventional correctness. "Rectitude" was revered by them, and they advertised it strongly as they perceived it in themselves. The mother in particular was convention-bound and prone to proclaim her personal nobility of character as well as the exalted status of her family of origin. She derived pride from her discernment that her son or daughter morally was better or "deeper" than others, was scrupulous even to a fault. She felt gratified that the child was so deliberative, so "thoughtful"—not in the sense of being considerate of others but in the sense of doing nothing rashly.

A third characteristic of these parents' values was *the premium they placed upon a form of social isolation or withdrawal.* Warm interpersonal dealings were not prized; nor were numerous club-memberships. These parents were not joiners. They had few friends for exchanging family visits. They were more snobbish and, calling themselves highly selective, often they were hard-put to name anybody whom they genuinely liked. They spoke in disapproving, barbed and caustic tones of those few chums whom their children might seek out. Small wonder that their obsessive children frequently opined that the human world is steeped in malevolence and Death Instincts. The children's symptoms paralleled the parents' strengths as proponents of "privatism" and rugged independence.

A fourth psychosocial attribute of these parents was their *emphasis on cleanliness,* approaching in several instances a sphincter morality which equates cleanliness with godliness. Only cruel fate would send such parents a hippie son or daughter! The mothers as a group had been insistent about bowel and bladder disciplines; and "anal-stage problems" while not universal were more numerous, especially in the histories of the children of elementary school age, than might have been foreseen out of this author's sociopsychiatric perspective. Rarely did a child patient recall toilet training difficulties, even in the later phases of psychotherapy, but almost half of the mothers (N=20) supplied positive information on toilet training pressures. Yet, even the mothers supplied such information late rather than early in the period of psychiatric work.

A fifth attribute of the parental ethos lay in the parents' *adherence to an instrumental morality*, to goodness not as a goal but as a means of reaching heaven, or of achieving conquest, or of asserting moral superiority. This was the case with Bible Belt and other Protestants, with Jews and Catholics. Family life was replete with admonitions to be good, to think good thoughts, and to uphold the counsels of perfection. Over-goodness as a way of control was very much in evidence in these households. Likewise, there were strongly articulated examples of what might be called the parents' "narcissistic morality"—meaning the equation of what gratifies the parent with what is right and sacred, and conversely "what bugs Mother is plain wicked." Saul C. (Chapter 4, Child #46) perceived this when he said, "Adults enjoy life themselves but they won't let kids have any of it." Parents who take all the gratification for themselves, and who dub any complaints from the child as wickedness, stir up vicious little cycles of defiant rage and guilty fear. Such adults were often hated by their offspring, the young patients studied.

Another attribute that stood out in many of these families was the *derogation of maleness*—particularly exhibited in the derogation of the fathers who as a matter of fact did appear to be persons with few id-strengths, and with little zest or vigor, as compared to their more energetic wives. The wives (mothers) studied were often described as "castrating females," "more aggressive than the father," etc. The mothers were more "workable" than the fathers and mobilized more discontent with their life patterns.

In religion, as in politics and social views, the parents were far from being zealots. As middle class parents *they practiced a form of limited commitment*, emphasizing relativism, restraint, and moderation that often prevented their taking a definite stand on civic affairs. They typically denounced the views of the child's grandparents, however, especially if the grandparents held traditional religious attitudes. The parents viewed themselves as being better than their own parents in matters religious, and often stated they were seeking to avoid the "mistakes" made by *their* forebears.

As regards money, the attitudes of these parents are those of what Erich Fromm (1947) called "the hoarding orientation" and what Sigmund Freud with an earlier and earthier metaphor called "the anal character." They devoted much time and effort to saving, spending and accounting—as if they lived amidst scarcity instead of in their actual abundance. Money was employed as a favorite reward or reinforcer for these parents in their relations with spouse and children. Nothing is freely provided; all must be earned by effort; and love itself is doled out as merited. These are all ostensibly remnants of a patriarchal ideology; however, the vestiges persist in families with *weak* fathers!

What of the social perspective of these parents regarding childhood sexuality, spontaneity and maskless behavior? Lip service was given frequently to childish impulsiveness, but these parents weren't really convinced. They viewed children as miniature adults, who are frigid and impotent—and devoid of sexiness if they are being reared properly. The family creed denied aggression and libido but vaunted precocity of the constraining ego. Stated more truthfully, these parents vaunted not the ego but that *deficiently socialized pseudo-self* which is the outcome of living in the family of an obsessive child. And again, what is often called an overdeveloped superego appears on close appraisal to be a conscience decrement in both obsessive children and their parents. Perfectionistic virtue is far afield from genuine moral sensitivity.

Camilla Anderson (1950) believed that the self-image of a child, resulting from his many experiences with "significant others," became structuralized in early life, and (p. 192):

> Once the image has been formed, behavior loses its free or experimental nature and becomes compulsive. . .

Anderson stressed the universal neurotic need to be virtuous and to maintain a moralistic worthiness, features of both obsessive children and their parents. In an exhortation to parents to ease up, she wrote (1950, p. 101):

> If they [parents] could give up their sense of righteousness it would help a great deal. Let them pursue the courses they must, in order to be comfortable, but with at least a flicker of awareness that they are selfish and obsessive and fearful and lacking in wisdom and that they are often hampering the healthy development of their children, instead of with the fictitious assumption that whatever they do they have only the best interests of the children in mind. To become really honest as a parent is equivalent to becoming truly humble.

3

The Clinical Picture

CLASSICAL OBSESSIONAL ILLNESS in children has, as a pervasive and striking part of its picture, these three ingredients:

1. intrusive ideas or images or impulses;
2. a subjective sense of these being forced, of compulsion; and
3. a concomitant feeling the compulsion must be resisted.

All of these experiences can be internal. The obsessive child might also have to do certain compulsive acts, or rituals. But his symptoms can be strictly mental and not involve any conspicuously pathological overt behavior at all.

The obsessive child, ordinarily, is said to exhibit a prizeworthy ego and superego, to show highly developed cognitive functions, and to be hypercorrect socially. These time-honored views will be questioned herein; and the familiar obsessive syndrome of obstinacy, orderliness, and frugality will be elaborated. The following presentation will adhere somewhat to the conceptual framework of Sigmund Freud who remains highly instructive after eight decades because of his organized presentation of overt actions, followed by consideration of thoughts and affects. The concluding section of this chapter covers differential diagnosis.

SOCIAL BEHAVIOR

The countenance and bearing of the obsessive child is characteristically unhappy. Always humorless and serious-looking, the child often appears tormented and anguished. His anguish lies in a rigid guardedness. His every action looks, as Federn said, like forced labor. He displays lack of zest, and distaste or disgust for life, in every action. His ubiquitous deliberateness and unameliorated stiffness—"unnaturalness" or "uptightness"—is readily obvious. Such a boy or girl might also exhibit ritualistic behavior, but even without the rituals the gross lack of spontaneity, the complete absence of gracefulness and fluid coordination, is striking to see. Indeed, the child is often awkward and ungainly, though without the postural bizarreness that might characterize the psychotic child. The lack of joy and exuberance is more akin to whatever makes the child have the appearance of a bookworm, or a sad little professor, rather than the melancholy mien of a withdrawn, depressed child. Sad the obsessive is but deep melancholy is not present. He looks, often, very similar to a cautiously phobic child, to whom he is, after all, a not-too-distant relative in regard to life style and psychodynamics. The child who told me he felt robbed of a happy childhood showed his rage, disgust, and unhappiness on many occasions before he put his feelings into such commonplace but eloquent words. His strained gracelessness and pseudo-maturity gave abundant prior notice.

Similar traits are observed in obsessive children by family friends and neighbors. They find it difficult, if not impossible, to compliment the child except for his proficiency in some circumscribed interest or skill, or because he is so "pensive" or so well behaved. They never say that he is a swinger, with admirable social skills. He is more often a respected "nut" about his hobbies or narrow interest-areas than good company. His virtuosity is in fact unnatural and driven, and variably executed. Nobody loves an obsessive, it can be said, and the obsessive child himself does not radiate any convincing self-regard or self-love.

The *verbal communications* of the obsessional are often thought to be his forte. That is what both adult and child obsessives and many psychiatrists think, but there is ample ground to wonder whether the obsessive child is not simply a precocious and expert talker who is, at the same time, an extremely feeble communicator, who, indeed, says little or nothing in his outpouring of polysyllabic words. Moreover, obsessive children are quarrelsome and rebuking toward therapists on the grounds the therapist "misuses" words, states things imprecisely or emotionally, and so on. Skeptical and pedantic, the child judges the adult, and with a harshness both pathetic and, eventually, annoying. The obsessive child is certainly successful in putting the therapist on his mettle as a conversationalist. It is sometimes painful for a therapist to speak at all with such a sharp-tongued little critic all set to hang him for making one slip. Talk for the obsessive child is always the *last word*, a kind of verdict on any subject. The therapist is obliged to tell the child over and over in simple terms that what the therapist says is aimed at eliciting talk, dialogue; getting a conversation *started;* embarking on a verbal adventure in mutual understanding.

Although the child is boringly literal and demands precision of word definition, he is *always* a sender of garbled messages. Content analysis shows he says little that makes much clear sense, that his speech while cautious and often grammatically impeccable carries little or no meaning, and that he is faking it when he appears to be scientific and logicoempirical. Beneath the surface, his "science" reveals itself as voodoo and superstition, and his true intention and longing are most assuredly for murkiness and unreality, not clarity of exposition.

The obsessive and perfectionistic child's marked overevaluation of his linguistic fluidity brings to mind a deprivation analogy. It has been noted that the child who is prone to overvalue material possessions may have gone hungry earlier. Nobody is as greedy as a deprived child, one who has suffered from poverty and neglect, one who adores what he is lacking. Likewise, the child who overvalues talk may be a severe stutterer. Coming to place less value on talk can be the stutterer's cure. Obsessive and perfectionistic children sometimes stammer severely and block in their speech. Indeed, I have not seen a clinically noticeable stutterer who was not also profoundly obsessive, and I have seen stuttering disappear when the obsessional neurotic core is extirpated. However, the experts in communication disorders, people working in speech and hearing clinics, are often of another persuasion. As such, they aver that in some cases stuttering is psychogenic and obsession-related, but that most cases are not associated with obsessions or emotional disorders. It would not be news to announce that child psychiatrists see a restricted and selected clientele of children who have speech problems. Good judgment dictates that the psychiatrist respect and defer on such issues to the language expert.

More ordinarily, however, obsessive children do exhibit a remarkable and continuous verbal fluency, a linguistic competency, as stated earlier, often employed to muddy and mystify and not to "level" and communicate meaningfully. These children use wordiness to evade communication. Their pattern of utterances is diphasic and contradictory. Beginning hot, they wind up a single sentence lukewarm and often freezing cold. Beginning strong, they end a sentence weak. If they begin with a genuine expression of love or tenderness, they undo this before drawing a second breath.

The phenomenon of going compulsively from one topic to its diametric opposite is also omnipresent with an obsessive child. When angry and about to say so, the child talks instead of his freedom from wrath; when feeling some love toward the therapist, he suddenly becomes uncomfortable and often exhibits a "fantasy" (obsession) that he sees in his mind's eye of himself killing the therapist. Indeed, a close look at the sound or video recording of a session with an obsessive child is useful to dramatize this feature of switching from a topic to its counterpoint. It is in fact the obsessive's conversational maneuver *par excellence*. Jumping from weakness to omnipotence, from "good" to "bad," etc., demonstrates compulsive behavior within the therapy hour itself. The compulsive maneuver is always present in the "free field" verbal behavior of the obsessive child. Its presence is not fully pathognomic of obsessional neurosis (for all of us use it, and so do most school children) but I have come to rely upon it as a useful index of the severity of the obsessive character, of the extent to which the child is living in the energy-draining obsessive mode. The more he uses this device in his speech, the more severely obsessional he is and the more he may be approaching a "breakdown," as the older terminology referred to that paralysis of doubt and indecision which can sometimes grip the obsessional neurotic.

There are other pertinent elements of obsessional speech-content. One important substantive feature is that the speech is quite often inclined toward uncertainty and the unknowable. Uncertainties and unknowables are for most children simply parts of the human scene and human condition. Indeed, for most children, they add a mysterious dimension to life and may provide the background for ghost stories, amusing horoscopes, science fiction, and even a kind of theological disputation. Yet with the obsessive child there is an unabating insistence upon unravelling the great human riddles and knowing that which only mystics have stumbled upon. The true mystic, however, is willing to let these questions be, and to accept namelessness, indescribability, etc. The obsessional child, however, sets himself up *to know*, and scientifically at that, what is unknowable. Could I have committed the unpardonable sin? Why does God let children die? Is there a life after death? Are all human beings born with a death instinct? Can you prove there is no reincarnation? Can you be certain the coat is in the closet when the door is shut? Can you be sure that lightning will not strike my mother? These are matters preoccupying and terrifying obsessive children. Let it again be stressed that these arcane matters may engage many children for brief periods of time, and certain familial and subcultural mores literally place a premium on certain of these topics, but in the obsessive child the preoccupation is suffering. There is no lightheartedness or emotional release or satisfaction whatsoever in these ruminations—far from it, there is only woe. Furthermore, the ruminations are not scientific, or even prescientific: they are in the realm of that which cannot be proved *or disproved*, far afield from the logical-empirical statements of science. As idle thoughts or idle chatter, some momentary entertainment or other benefit might be derived, but these are far from harmless musings. They are time killing, life negating and anhedonic thoughts to which the child feels driven, frequently worn out by his experience of them, he is hungry for respite.

It seems to be the craving for certitude that is beneath the obsessive overconcern with whatever is unknowable. The obsessive child is thrown into a dither by the laws of chance. He becomes panicky about risking an earthquake or a hurricane, or the sudden appearance and eruption of a volcano. Feeling so unprotected, he returns over and over to his desire to foretell, foresee, and *exert control before the fact.* Perhaps the encounter group movement with its emphasis upon "risk taking" should be made available for more obsessive children and their families. Experience in taking risks, in being human, in living within the limits of man's fate— these are what the obsessive child needs. This craving is not for deep answers but for comradeship in life.

Let me amplify a bit upon the remark that certain familial and subcultural values can encourage obsessive behavior of children. This is described in Chapter 2, but some general commentary is in order here. Parents who produce an obsessive child are parents who without exception manifest acts such as the following:

> Encouraging a wakeful, frightened child to say his prayers again.
> Telling a child with a nightmare to think good thoughts instead.
> Showing fascination with a child's religiosity.
> Talking away feelings instead of accepting them.
> Advising half-heartedness, and feigning neutrality in matters of race, religion, politics, sexuality, economic inequality, etc.
> Covering brutality with sweet, undoing talk.

Unsatisfying *interactions with peers* provide yet another ingredient of the pathological social behavior of the obsessive child. He is not a good mixer, and will prefer solitary play even when he is in a comfortable group setting. He does not seek fun for himself or for

others; quite the opposite. He is often so openly belittling or
antagonistic to his peers that they reject him before a relationship
can get started. The obsessive is often both giver and receiver of
cruel ridicule and contempt. "Punishment," in particular, is meted
out to the obsessive child by children who are not themselves
obsessive. The child who is obsessive is unaccustomed to being in
the company of his age-mates and as a result behaves "like a
weird-o," does things awkwardly, idiosyncratically, inappropriately for his age and gender. He is thus likely to be called a sissy or
a queer or a fag or baby. Juvenile wit and humor, not notable for
its subtlety in any event, is often "inflicted" upon him. One boy
whom I saw was so slow in his walking and speaking that his
classmates were given to tell him, "Do it or get off the pot" . . . or
"Spit it out for Pete's sake." Or, most poignant of all, he came to
be called "Tiger"—a deliberate emphasis on his fearful, deliberate,
and tentative manner of existence. Peer relationships are unsatisfying, indeed, but the obsessive child is oriented toward a very special adult person.

The focal point of the obsessive child's life *is usually the
mother.* Sometimes, the child lives unhappily as his mother's constant companion. Often, whether male or female, the obsessive
sleeps in the mother's bed, and in general is as strongly attached as
ambivalence allows him to be. Any efforts by the mother to get
away, even to a movie or for a short weekend, are countered by
vigorous protest and fear. The child displays separation problems
marring school attendance, engendering morbid fears of maternal
death or illness, and producing continuous detailed reporting to
the mother of the numerous ritualistic acts to which he feels
driven. The latter maneuver is explicitly attention-getting, and a
way of enslaving the mother in a sadomasochistic bond. Often the
mother feels appropriate anger, but pretends she is not angered by
her child's hostile dependency. Because the relation with the
mother is so pervasive it becomes axiomatic to the child, as if it
were "the order of nature." Indeed, *only* obsessional patients will
say "I dreamed that she and I were on a trip," and look irritated
by the doctor's stupidity when he asks, "Who was with you on the
trip in the dream?" To the obsessive child, mother is the center of

the universe and he cannot understand that others do not know his mind or share his viewpoint. The crux of the neurotic struggle for the obsessive child is with his mother (or with her mother). For the male adult it will be the wife or girlfriend who triggers off some of the obsessional behavior that only a mother can elicit in a child. The therapist of obsessionals must look for that female with whom is being waged the patient's battles for control, autonomy, and independence. *Cherchez la femme.* The male obsessive child is more unduly sensitive to what women and girls think about him and his behavior than his female counterpart. He bends over backward to please female teachers, neighbors, and age mates.

Other behavior of the obsessive stands out, making the obsessive child both a pitiable creature and a museum piece of odd and perplexing psychopathology. Obsessive doctors in particular find themselves eager to disaffiliate from the obsessive child and to claim, reassuringly, that they have never seen such things as those which are presented in his behavior repertoire.

Obsession is madness, and madness is not health, but obsessive behavior is possessed of a "very human face" which makes it not so totally foreign or alien to any of us. The physician, who has had to undergo long years of mechanistic training, to deprive himself of certain feelings and to learn a variety of masked roles still *usually* seems to be bending backwards in self-congratulation when he sees the obsessive child as bizarre, alien, and unbefitting as an object of a physician's empathy. The same is, likewise, true of a psychologist. Hence, the symptoms to be listed now must be viewed as reflections of a very human style, even though it is a style that leaves much to be desired. In truth, that doctor who feels that the obsessive child is bizarre had better find out if he is not dissociating from a part of himself.

Obstinacy (mulishness and pigheadedness are the common apellations) is a characteristic that has been associated since the third century B. C. days of Theophrastus (1946) with both *orderliness* and *parsimoniousness.* Even those obsessive children who have not suffered physical want and deprivation tend to hoard, to be ungenerous, and to emphasize any shortage of supplies. They are cautious about wasting the therapist's play materials, at first, and, in fact, an index that psychotherapy is working appears whenever the child becomes freer within a milieu that obviously has come to be fuller and more abundant for him He shows this change as he moves about more expansively and easily in the psychiatrist's play-room or consultation room. Both grownups and children who live with obsessives are pleased when the obsessive child's life grows easier and more abundant—when the child becomes less orderly, rigid, thrifty, and stubborn. Therapy has assuredly taken hold when these children can begin to let go. "Easing up" or "letting go" is indispensable.

One further word needs to be added concerning the magical acts, the rituals, of the obsessive child. Rituals are the secondary symptoms of obsessive behavior much as the hallucinations are secondary in schizophrenia. The pubertal young man, Alfred (Child #12), showed many rituals in his daily life as a schoolboy in a small Southern town. He washed his hands compulsively. He ritualized both urination and defecation and returned long dis-tances to mop up drops of urine that might have fallen on the floor or the toilet. Getting dressed in the morning was an ordeal of stylized, ceremonial behavior. His "routines" went far beyond the "habits" of expressive movement that characterize most men as they—usually automatically and easily, that is, not obsessive-ly—put on undershirt before undershorts, left sock before right one, etc. The young obsessive's *every movement* was studied, planned, tense, in contrast with typical modes of dressing proce-dure. This had the interpersonal consequence of baiting and irritat-ing his mother who somehow detected his wish to delay and drag his feet as well as the ritualized compulsion to forestall panic. His mother certainly knew the "logic" of his rituals. She understood the rationale of fending off sinister forces by magical movements and incantations; but she was accustomed to doing such acts in connection with church related, more socially accepted beliefs and practices. It all added up to her having some empathy with his ritualistic activities but feeling that he drove a good thing to an absurd excess.

The boy in fact did *many* queer things to ward off his obses-sions, His body movements had dwindled as part of his magical ritualization. I thought he was catatonic, or hovering upon psychosis, when I first saw him—sitting almost frozen. When he did move, he took great pains to hold his palms and fingers rigid and pointing downward. All that was required was for me to comment upon his unnatural stiffness. Then he told me he was preventing himself from raising his middle finger to God in an obscene salute defiant to every value his Christian upbringing had implanted. He shuddered at the thought. He was not catatonic, I realized, but in the throes of an obsessional breakdown ... brought on by some events, affects, and relationships still to be determined and eased.

Ritualism is indeed the forced behavior of children who have lost heart and become profoundly alienated. Robert K. Merton (1957) characterized ritualist social response as that which evinces surface conformity while rejecting the values and goals customarily associated with the overt ritualistic behavior. The *obsessive* ritualist, however, has nothing with which to replace conventional values. The obsessive ritualistic child partially rejects the motor impelling him into his rituals but feels that maintaining the pretense put forth in the rituals is the only safe course which, however weird it looks, provides him with some protection against panic, forestalls his having to face the notion that reality is not cut and dried, and, moreover, gives him a magical guarantee that little or nothing is risked.

A child with this disposition toward life will readily adopt the "rituals and etiquette" of psychotherapy, playing every safety game a therapist can invent for himself and his patients. The therapy hour will become stylized, with a written agenda brought in and rigidly adhered to; and even the riches of a child's dreaming and reporting of dreams will be converted into a sterile obsessive avoidance unless the therapist is wary of all these impending developments. Ritual avoidances, "manias" of counting and touching, are all evidences of how the child, estranged from his natural feelings and honest opinions, strives to keep up a front to ward off the dreaded, but ill-defined, danger threatening his very existence.

Almost pathognomonic of the obsessional child is his asking, "Have you ever before had a patient with my kind of problems?" Many determinants can be at work when the child asks this—for example, he feels pride in his possible uniqueness, superiority, and claim to fame; he is competitive and seeks reassurance that he compares well with others by not being crazier than they are; he shows his convention-ridden existence by wanting to look like others; he reveals his doubt that the therapist is competent to help him; he implicitly emphasizes the fact that he suffers greatly; or he may simply be trying to sidetrack the interview by changing the subject.

Summarizing the obsessive child's social behavior, we would remark that the cardinal signs and symptoms have to do with his uptightness in his bodily movements as well as thoughts and feelings, with his plodding unhappiness, with his overvaluation of words, with his penchant for magic, with his peer isolation, and with his close sadomasochistic tie to the mother.

COGNITION

A thread of recurrent importance in obsessional disorders in both adults and children is the question of whether the illness consists mainly in thought distortion or affective distortion. Is the trouble cognitive or conative? Aubrey Lewis wrote in 1936 (p. 255):

> Those who have occupied themselves with this question [of what an obsessive is], from St. Ignatius Loyola onward, are divided by their emphasis on the formal disorder of thought on the one hand, and on the disorder of affect on the other.

This section is a description of cognition, both the child's disordered *process* of thinking and his disordered *content* of thought, that is, his attitudes and values.

The mention of thought disorder makes many people think at once of schizophrenia, but as mental illnesses are studied more and more from a cognitive standpoint it is being learned that more of them are cognitive as well as emotional. Writing in 1896, Freud in rather characteristic fashion paved the way for a lot of later argumentation. He acknowledged the cognitive, affective, and behavioral distortions in obsessional neurosis. But at the same time that he gave a kind of parity among them he sided very definitely with the notion of supersession of the affective lesion. While ego deals in cognition and behavior, id in libido theory supplies the basic resources for obsessional neurosis, namely, the affects. In "Notes upon a Case of Obsessional Neurosis," Freud (1909) illustrated his stand that the affects have primacy and play an initiatory role:

> Our patient was compelled to overestimate the effects of hostile feelings upon the external world . . . His love—or rather his hatred—was in truth overpowering; it was precisely they [his hostile feelings] that created the obsessional thoughts, of which he could not understand the origin and against which he strove in vain to defend himself.

One fundamental aspect of the cognitive styles and patterns of the group of 49 obsessive children comprising our study consists in *the obsessions themselves*, the necessary ingredient of their emotional disorder. An obsession is hardly the finest flower of human thinking. Some people actually take pride in their own obsessions and compliment the thinking of other obsessives. I recall an adult obsessive, a psychiatrist, who was a teacher and supervisor of mine some years ago. That gentleman seriously believed being obsessive indicated he possessed a form of moral and intellectual superiority above the common run of humanity. He stated often, and not without a note of vanity, that obsessive neurosis was "a patrician illness." Contrarily, simply on the face of it, obsessions represent outright pathologic cognition. It requires little that is gifted or creative to be obsessive. Obsessive children are both different and defective in their cognitive patterns, regardless of their overblown reputation among some intellectuals.

The obsessive's very knowledge of the obsession is distorted. Freud (1909) acknowledged that the obsession itself is not easily reported by the patient. Although the obsessive has had the forced idea, or done the act, many times an hour for many months, he is unable to "spell it out" and sometimes he appears confused as to what the obsession is really all about. Clarification and exposition of the symptom is, of course, part of therapy for obsessive children. We strive to make them more productive thinkers than they were when locked into their obsessions.

The non-obsessive or comparatively healthy child learns, masters, and grows intellectually by adoption of the thought-forms conventional among the people who nurture him; occasionally, he may even use creatively deviant thinking processes. There is, however, something radically amiss in the thinking of the obsessive child. His thought processes reveal an irrational, absurd logic—and a private logic. His thoughts do not arise naturally in the daily process of adapting and growing, of living a pragmatic and functional existence. No, his thoughts are alien to him; although perceived as originating compulsively and forcibly, they are from "out of the blue."

The *deliria* are secondary elaborations of obsessions and admirably exemplify cognitive distortion. Freud's classical example was of the man who believed his niece would die every time he felt any erotic attraction to an adult female. Among the children surveyed here, the older ones demonstrated deliria most fully. Fourteen-year-old Daniel, who obsessed about his father's death, spread his spiralling cycle of fear and doubt and magical, compulsive thinking so that there came to be included in it any adult male as a part of—and as a trigger to—his illogical thinking. His father had proved himself vulnerable by dying. The son, therefore, saw himself in a constantly precarious position because of the possibility of his own extermination. Even the therapist was in a risky position because he, being a man, was "definitely" mortal and, indeed, a poorer risk than any woman. For Daniel, males had come to be feared, feared for, belittled, revered, and the objects of a great diversity of complicated private meanings. It is exactly these ever extending, interrelated ripples of increasing murkiness which constitute the so-called deliria, the obsessions upon obsessions. The capacity to engage in such networks of symbolism is not a very fortunate thing for a child, in my opinion, but many writers take such elaborate symptoms, and clusters of symptoms, as being indicators of the highly developed wits or intellect, or ego functions, of obsessives.

The obsessive child becomes deeply bound to his elaborate

obsessive symptoms, as if the obsessions and deliria are real things which he can love and cling to. Solomon (1962), a libido theorist, said it graphically:

> ... fixed ideas can be invested with libido and can be treated as though they were substitute objects in themselves.

This falling in love with obsessions, said Solomon, can be at oral or anal or phallic levels, but the most immutable ideas are the ones which serve as "oral transitional objects." In the latter type, the patients "suck on their ideas as they did their thumbs when they were little." They are like addicts, he stated, and:

> A statement such as, 'you hang on to your ideas like a scared infant hangs on to its mother,' may prove highly significant in focusing upon the structure of the patient's defensive framework.

Alfred North Whitehead (1925) described the logical fallacy of this operation as *the fallacy of misplaced concreteness*. At the hands of obsessive children we can see this fallacy writ large! Can we go along—after all—with the classical view which sees obsessive children as advanced thinkers with precocious egos?

Ego Precocity. Freud and the Freudians became concerned early in the development of psychoanalysis with the ego's developmental phase as well as the id's or libido's. Freud (1913) was already trying to bring an updated ego psychology into the body of libido theory when he wrote in "The Predisposition to Obsessional Neurosis":

> ... developmental disposition to a neurosis is only complete if the phase of the development of the ego at which fixation occurs is taken into account as well as that of the libido.

It would matter greatly in this theoretical system if the ego developed faster and earlier than the id. Freud used this speculation as an entry into some typically Freudian dicta concerning ego precocity:

> ... I suggest the possibility that a chronological outstripping of libidinal development by ego development should be in-

cluded in the disposition to obsessional neurosis. A precocity of this kind would necessitate the choice of an object under the influence of the ego-instincts, at a time at which the sexual instincts had not yet assumed their final shape, and a fixation at the stage of the pregenital sexual organization would thus be left. If we consider that obsessional neurotics have to develop a super-morality in order to protect their object-love from the hostility lurking behind it, we shall be inclined to regard some degree of this precocity of ego development as typical of human nature and to derive the capacity for the origin of morality from the fact that in the order of development hate is the precursor of love.

In other words, Freud's price for admitting the precocious ego into libido theory was the unmasking of human morality as a "love system" derived from hate! By 1923 Freud had settled into a more mechanistic id-dominated psychology that diminished the ego in obsessional neurosis, for he wrote in *The Ego and the Id:*

The defusion of love into aggressiveness has not been effected by the work of the ego, but is the result of a regression which has come about in the id. But this process has extended beyond the id to the super-ego, which now increased its severity towards the innocent ego.

Anna Freud, however, has continued the Freudian school of *ego psychology* and has persisted in emphasizing that both "ego and drive" development require assessment in obsessive patients. Heinz Hartmann (1950) stressed ego as much as id and stated a cautionary word about the much heralded "precocious ego" of obsessional children:

. . . actually only the intellectual or the defensive functions of the ego have prematurely developed, while, for instance, the tolerance for unpleasure is retarded.

It could be said that psychoanalysts, whether emphasizing id or ego, have almost universally regarded the cognitive (intellectual) aspects of the ego to have flowered in obsessional neurotics; and for that reason assertions such as Hartmann's need to be made.

Fixation and/or Regression. The same psychodynamic theorists who belabor the precociousness of the obsessive's ego have, of course, looked long and hard at another aspect of libido theory, namely, fixation and regression in obsessive adults and children. (See Chapter 5.) The most judicious summary to be made at this point is probably to take Freud's earliest views as quite generally applicable. Those views are:

1. a phallic Oedipal stage must be achieved before a "true" obsessional neurosis (or indeed any "infantile neurosis") can exist.

2. regression from the phallic Oedipal phase to the anal stage (anal sadistic phase, explicitly) occurs in obsessional neurosis.

3. specific fixations in the anal sadistic phase "stack the cards" in favor of the "choice of *obsessive* symptoms" (as opposed to paranoid, psychopathic, etc.).

4. modicum of (pre-anal phase) oral gratification occurs so that oral fixations are less weighty (as "fixatives") than anal ones.

Utilizing these four "principles," the followers of Sigmund Freud and id theory, of Anna Freud and ego theory, and of Melanie Klein with a "super-id" and "super-ego" theory have created a considerable body of literature. On specifics there has been much disagreement—hence the literature—but on generalities there is considerable consensus among the varied psychoanalytic-libido schools. If one accepts as working postulates the four principles previously listed he can choose to emphasize:

1. id or ego or superego—or sub-parts of each or all.

2. oral phase or anal phase or Oedipal phase-or sub-stages.

3. fixation or regression—or both in diverse admixtures.

4. conscious or preconscious or subconscious.

5. innate or acquired factors (instincts or familial values).

6. libidinal drives or aggressive drives.

7. gratification of, or defense against, certain drives.

In short, then, fixation and regression theory can send one off in many conceivable directions of investigation and speculation.

Returning to an appraisal of the obsessive child's cognitive process, we are left with one primary consideration. Is it a superior thing? Maladaptive and dysfunctional, his thoughts take over and, instead of thinking in the service of coping (with self and others), his thinking is largely in the service of obscurantism, neurosis, deception, and fake reassurances. Alfred Adler (Ansbacher and Ansbacher, 1956) was "on" to how the obsessive uses thinking for the winning of fake battles, and stated in admirably succinct Adlerian phraseology:

> The patient who feels a compulsion to jump out of windows has built up this compulsion into a safeguard. He acquires a sense of superiority by successfully overcoming the urge, and employs the whole situation as an excuse for his lack of success in life . . . The compulsion neurotic retires, so to speak, to a secondary field of action where he expends all his energies instead of devoting them to solving his primary problem. Like a veritable Don Quixote he fights windmills, concerning himself with matters which have no proper place in our social world, and only serve to dally away time (pp. 305-6).

Adler insisted that obsessive-compulsive symptoms have their genesis in social, interpersonal relations however much the obsessional might want to negate or deny the interpersonal context.

Obsessive children show *a longing to be unaware of the meaning of their obsessions,* and are inclined to refuse ("resist") consideration of when and with whom and in what meaningful context the obsession made its appearance. The obsessive child has had long training in paying more attention to grammar than to syntax. Context, meaning, and significance are the forest he cannot see for the trees. He is a bit like the researcher who devises an elegant design for studying an inconsequential issue. The virtue of cognition for the obsessive child lies in the formal and manifest characteristics of a thought, not in its significance, its relevance, its relation to living and meaning—and obsessive children value only the superficial and formal. They are "precocious" in the superficial and discrete, but they have a strong aversion to reading between the lines and truly reaching out to living and phatic communication with others. Joseph Barnett (1966) restated Sullivan's view of one possible genesis of this obsessive attitude toward language, namely, that what has nearly always been said outwardly to the obsessive child is "all sweetness and light." The outward and formal message is one which gives security and comfort to the child. Unfortunately, however, the message is not true. The parents say, "Mother and father love you more than they love life itself," and the child receives some consolation for his hideous discernment that one or both of his parents hate him, or wish him dead. If he plays along and clings with obsessive tenacity to *what* is stated, without heeding any of the undercurrents of parental hatred, he can stay fairly "safe" from his fear of being "wiped out," punished, and subjected to parental sadism. He becomes adept at working within a form of "double bind." A fake security, an ersatz comfort, is thus derived for the child, and he is trained over and over in the modality of what has been said literally—ignoring what people really feel and really mean for one another. He learns to pretend there is no iceberg under the water, and that all that matters is what is above the waterline. The superficial and blood-less thought is his only protection from parental wrath. That the thought is irrelevant only intensifies its usage. The child comes to belittle himself, because he sees he is not loved, and from low self-esteem he can only leap, compulsively, to some form of gran-diosity. Many writers have stressed this compulsive leap as *per-vasion of thought by magic.*

Fantasies enrich the thinking and the speaking of people who are fairly open and direct in relatedness to the people around them, but for the obsessive child omnipotence and omniscience become the goal of thinking. The obsessional is rarely able to proceed beyond his mastery of reality *in thought* to a mastery in fact. The grandiose thought, in and of itself, is the obsessional child's dead-end street, leading nowhere from a cognitive stand-point.

Now, we can turn to a related characteristic of the obsessive child's thinking, namely, to his *urge to think ahistorically.* He wants, it appears, to conceptualize his life out of context. He wills to forget the past; even the recent past is often beyond his recall. He forgets the occasions on which certain of his most gruesome symptoms occurred, even if they happen on the same day as his appointment with the psychiatrist. He cannot remember, with cer-tainty, he stipulates, whether it was his mother or father who said something that sent him into orbit. It could have been a visitor, etc. What comes through in all this is the conclusion that the child must feel trapped by contexts, he who indulges in so much nit-picking about concrete facts when others are talking to *him*! He has an urge to globalize—to undertake a superficial expansion of ideas. This is what many would call his intellectualization. It makes him feel safer to refuse to "get down to cases." His prefer-ence is for inattention to what is happening to him. It aids his self-deception, his living only amidst stereotypes and sterile gener-alizations. His categories of thought are sometimes as "primitive" as the psychotic child's, and as highly personal and unshared. He needs "training" in a more conventional cognition, if only because the more conventional way is infinitely more useful.

Contending with the child's inattention to contexts is not an easy task. The therapist needs to be active enough, for example, to stop the child outright in his narration of a dream whenever he cannot recall the night on which the dream occurred. This need not be put forth as therapeutical obstinacy, although it might be just that. What I have done is to tell the child, "Well, let's leave it if you can't place it. We can learn so much more from a dream that occurred on a day that you know more about. So, when you can, tell me a dream that happened on a particular, definite night. Then I can show you how important a part of life your dreaming can be." I hope that such directions are not too intrusive or authoritarian; I believe that in the long run they are warranted interferences. They certainly promote clear thought and focused therapeutic work, and in this way are helpful to the obsessive child.

The therapist needs to let the child know that help comes when his unhappy behavior can be understood and that understanding requires a knowledge of situations, fields, and contexts.

Existentialists would probably disagree with our contention that children learn something worthwhile from the specification of contexts. Existentialist therapists themselves might do without the excess baggage of contextual understanding in order that they might be free to live in the immediate moment, but obsessive children could be said *to require* skills in contextual assessment in order to set straight their pervasive cognitive shortcomings. An event can be understood and discussed only when it is made concrete and unique by stripping it of the obsessive child's generalities and abstractions which serve only to becloud the matter. On that point everyone might agree.

Isolation, or severance, of affect from thoughts and speech is a highly distinctive feature of the obsessive child's cognition. When Daniel D (Child #24) talked, he spoke either in a low pitched monotone with a deadpan face or in a high pitched "mad robot" voice lacking intonation, inflection, any variation in voice quality, and all the other paralinguistic factors that help most children to speak from the heart and to enjoy the riches of genuine symbolic sharing. Daniel could only feel a modicum of safety when he both talked around the point and said everything in an affectless way. His psychotherapist dropped all vestiges of orthodoxy and asked Daniel in effect to be *more histrionic*, to attempt to say his angry thing *angrily*, his sad obsessions about the death of his father *sadly*, and so on. Sometimes these children cannot speak in anger until a grownup not only has condoned it but also has encouraged such speaking.

When the obsessive child speaks unfeelingly he is *not necessarily being affect-poor*. He may, in fact, have overwhelming feelings flooding him with their breadth and depth. He has to control so strongly because what he feels appears to him to be so strong. As with his diligence, where his hard work betrays a very sizable "lazy streak," so it is with his pruning of affect. He is hiding and trying to subdue a formidable affect, deep and strong. His affect-free thoughts, then, are only *defensive* constructs. The substructure may be enough, or too much, affect.

Sandor Rado (1959) depicted the obsessive as having lowered "id strengths" and as constitutionally lacking in the zest, vitality, libido, etc., which provide non-obsessives with batteries to keep their motors running strong. Some adult obsessives with whom I have worked do seem short of warmth, lust, anger, *joie de vivre*, and even of stamina. I could well say these adults look "constitutionally" lacking in spiritedness. On the other hand, obsessive children do not impress me with any possibly inborn deprivation of affect. Oddly enough, those who work with adults may yet turn out to be the *mavens* who concern themselves with constitution and heredity. To look at anyone with a chronic lack of spontaneity spanning over many years is to look at a final product depleted and leached out. These same adult obsessives also convince one of the propriety of leucotomy for relief of severe, intractable obsessional disorder. Obsessive children do not elicit that. The adult picutre, looking very barren, makes one think more regularly of a constitutional lowering of affect. Those who work with obsessive children, however, do seem, in general, to be more impressed with what is learned and taught to these children than by what is constitutional.

Not one of the 49 children in our group was mentally retarded. Not included in this study because of his age was an older adolescent with an IQ below 65 who suffered from the most severe handwashing compulsion that I have ever seen, as well as from severe obsessions. The precocious, highly developed intellect is not a prerequisite for obsession.

Indeed, as I have suggested in this chapter, the cognition of the obsessive child is not the sterling product it is so often claimed to be. The obsessive child has a cognitive defect along with a behavioral deviation and an affective disorder. His cognitive pathology lies in: the illogical obsessions themselves, the compulsive split between affect and thought, the secondarily elaborated deliria, the pervasion of thought by magic, and the longing to "think" but inability to attend context in any kind of "honest" or meaningful way.

Attitudes and Values. Obsessive thought processes are both deviant and deficient, I have said. Next, I want to extend the field to include the *thought content* of obsessive children. What do they think about? What values do they harbor? What do they hold dear?

1. *Respect for internalization.* Whatever happens inside—that is, covertly—is what the obsessive child prizes. He literally spends every hour of the day on internal affairs such as brooding, doubting, obsessing, and so on. He respects these solitary actions. Although they are disadvantageous in some ways, they have their

compensations for his pride and self-glorification. He wants to remain riveted to "thinking," to inner as opposed to extrovert activities, to solitary as distinguished from gregarious acts. He wants to cling to mental maneuvers. The internal is his preferred arena. He is, at times, so patently afraid to be "outer" that I have been inclined to see his respect for internalization as purely defensive and "secondary." However, even after becoming symptom free, these children persist in respecting what goes on in one's head more highly than what goes on in outer reality. They, like psychoanalysts, emphasize the ethical individual more than the utopian society (Nunberg, 1955, p. 284). Seemingly, this is all a matter of life style that reaches above and beyond pathology. Some people prefer to look inward—in the manner of yogis, not commissars.

2. *Respect for fog.* The obsessive child is in love with paradoxes, as long as they are his own, and not the always-inferior property of someone else. He dislikes a therapist who "calls a spade a spade." He sees it as a sign of his moral hegemony that he thinks cleaner thoughts than others and has religious worries that seldom give a moment's pause to ordinary mortals. He derives some odd glory from his preoccupation with heinous crimes he doesn't commit. Adler was right: he does thank God aloud that he has been so good that he does not throw himself out of windows or burn down buildings. He praises himself inordinately because he does not blaspheme against the Holy Ghost, or because he does not kill his parents—all a part of his excessive goodness.

This entails both a penchant and a necessity for fog, for murkiness, and for absurdity, along with some self-proffered praise. Clarity itself seems to make the child more anxious, and indeed, when one refuses his mad premises and comes across directly, the child does become more anxious. When I told Chester E (Child #20) rather early in therapy that I could understand how he both loved and hated his mother, he turned white with fear, became angry, and told me that I could never say anything right. I put my foot in it; he preferred to go at it diphasically, indecisively and indirectly. He was proud of the neurotic fog he emitted. At first, he was made very uncomfortable by anything direct and natural.

Solomon (1962) stressed the obsessive's love of turbulence, his wish to keep himself and his interpersonal world in a continual stir. Certainly, the proclivity for sadomasochistic bonding has the effect of making life more complex than it needs to be. I believe this is closely related to what I am describing as the obsessive child's "respect for fog."

3. *Respect for intellect.* Obsessive children are, by and large, little "eggheads." U.S. populism would be dead if the country were made up strictly of these youngsters, for they idolize being *unequal.* They take equality literally, only in order to denounce it and declare their affinity for the thinker, the philosopher king. "Equality" does not mean that no one has unusual social or economic advantages, but it is made to mean, for them, absurdly enough, *that everyone is exactly the same.* They fight equalitarianism by making it absurd. They "go for" intellectual inequality. They love their intelligence quotients. They denounce children who are action-oriented (coincidentally, usually, lower class) as being stupid clods and clunks. They are the only children whom I have seen who aspire to grow up and become professors! And indeed one of the 49 surveyed has now grown up and done that. They become medievalists, archeologists, psychologists and anthropologists after they lose enough of their obsessive symptoms to free them for a modicum of work and love.

They value intellection before, during, and after their obsessive illness. After their illness they are less likely to abuse intellection and less prone to misuse thinking in the form of unproductive and ambiguous intellectualizing. As one young adult, a scholar, told me, "I fell driven to *reduce the variables* both in my research and in my personal life." At his sickest, the obsessive child does caricature intellect—but at his healthiest he is a child eager to learn, to abstract, to verbalize, to conceptualize; and he reads and studies with diligence and enthusiasm. In the final analysis, I respect these children's respect for their own heads, and for the heads of others.

4. *Viewing life as a power struggle.* Nobody, unless it be an anarchist, can see political significance in everything to the extent of the obsessive child. The obsessive is, however, predominantly concerned with intrafamilial power relations, and his preoccupation is with dominant-submissive, passive-aggressive, ruler-ruled. The obsessive child goes to great lengths to be one-up.

Psychiatrists, who themselves often like to dominate and control without acknowledging what they are doing, are "called" very frequently by obsessive children. This makes the children seem obnoxious to the psychiatrist and "obnoxious" becomes "unworkable" and then "borderline psychotic." Eventually, residential treatment is suggested—and so on. Thomas Szasz (1970) has a small point, at least, in saying that mental illness functions for the benefit of certain specific socioeconomic classes.

Other children spot the obsessive's ruthless competitiveness. He competes more in classroom activities than in sports or gymnastics, and indeed may seek medical excuses from "physical education." In general, he prefers to compete and to excel in classes taught by women teachers, and, hence, receives an added incentive to avoid physical activities at school. He competes to win. He does not display a notable sense of fair play, nor competition for the sake of the fun "our team" derives. Fun loses its fun for this child.

5. *Preoccupation with death and death-fear.* Obsessive children seem to have had more frequent encounters with death than normal children. In the group of 49 there were many who had witnessed the agonal crises of their siblings, parents and grandparents, and those who had seen playmates decapitated by speeding automobiles. Death in the family seems uncommonly frequent among this group. Yet this is only an appearance, not a real distinction. What is the explanation? I feel the crux of the matter is in the obsessive child's greater lingering over death in all the brooding and ambivalence that are so characteristic for him. They have actually seen no more death than other children, but they are more "hung up" on death, decay and disgust. Their fears of death are truly devastating to their daily lives.

Non-obsessive children have more abundant lives and, therefore, a better preparation to take death in stride. Norman O. Brown (1959) described an ego that was strong enough to accept the inevitability of one's own dying, and Brown's metaphor is most appropriate for non-obsessive children. They grieve but do not brood about death, even when it occurs abruptly to someone near and dear. Erwin W. Straus (1966) called this the acceptance of "the provisional," the willingness to conceive, or to concede, that behavior begins and ends—and that life itself ends:

> We live 'for the time being', and we know—more or less
> clearly—that we live in the *provisional.* However much we
> strive for conscientiousness, we still put an end to our deliber-
> ations. In all action, we give up certain things and entrust
> ourselves to the future, relying on ourselves, on the circum-
> stances, and on others. (p. 315)

Entrusting himself to life is not the manner of an obsessive child.

6. *Strives to guarantee his self-preservation and safety.* The
obsessive child has a Hobbesian view of human nature, as brutish
and violent in an ecologic setting of scarce supplies. Nobody is to
be trusted and no risks are warranted. It is as if the child, who, as
we have seen, comes in actuality from a rather affluent background, is afraid that he will starve and freeze. He is healthy but
fearful of death. Nobody is out to do him in but he is untrusting,
at least until he has worked through some of the intrafamilial
conflict and, in particular, his ambivalent relation with the
mother.

Adults, sitting in their armchairs, perhaps are entitled to a
gloomy view of themselves and of human nature. Many psychoanalysts and ethologists, and political theorists, too, expect the
worst from themselves and other human beings. But young children need remediation when they have that dreary *Weltschmerz*
point of view. As they utter their phrases of despair, obsessive
children look sick, not wise. They *are* sick. They need help.

All children strive to build and maintain a concept of self as
fully and acceptably human, and that seems to be what at base
also fires the obsessive child. The obsessive child, however, is more
hounded and his fears border on delusional thinking. He looks as if
his very existence as a worthwhile human being is threatened. He
lives in an imaginary jungle where he is always ready to annihilate
and to be annihilated. That scarcely makes for a happy childhood.
The quandary of the obsessive child lies either in a hatred which
he overestimates and against which he overdefends or in a hatred
which indeed is of grandiose proportions—a matter we will have to
return to in the next section of this chapter. Yet we cannot completely separate his cognitive ruminations about hatred from his

actual hatred, although this is an isolation and alienation to which the obsessive child is as devoted as to a holy crusade. The cognitive aspect worth underlining is that in self-concept he judges himself to be a no-good hater. He hates but rejects hatred. The mother was the primordial object of this ambivalence, that selfsame loved and hated mother who can hate her child whilst advertising all of her love and sweetness. She suggests that only a defect in the young child could make him "discern" such hateful feelings.

The child's *self-concept as an obsessive* does indeed seem to be laid down between ages one and two, that is, the second year of life. It *is* a concept of self that is not loving or accepting or trusting.

The self-regarding attitudes of the year-old infant are largely borrowed (or appropriated) from the mothering person. If the mother were depressed during the child's second year, the child would suffer from this deadness and social withdrawal—there is no escaping it. The child's self-picture, acquired from the mother's picture of the child, easily takes on a negative stamp. Needs unmet are needs unwarranted, in the child's eye. He wants but does not receive, so he concludes somehow that he is undeserving. In this way, a depressed and in-turned mother implants a negative self-picture.

Similarly, if the mother "talks a good line" of loving care but in her heart of hearts wishes the child were dead, the setup for construction of an obsessional negative self-concept is crystal clear. This appeared to be the situation with almost every one of the 49 obsessional children studied. Alfred's mother actually deserted him and his father during his infancy. Daniel's mother was overwhelmed by the disarray a messy infant brought into her life. Milton's and Chloe's mothers were depressed when the children were learning to walk and to talk. Sam's mother had back trouble and could not hold him or pick him up. Interestingly enough, *negligere* (the root of our word neglect) means *not to pick up*. Douglas's mother, resentful of giving up a profession, chronically complained of life's shoddy treatment of her but (with no obvious awareness of contradiction) saw herself as the most giving of mothers. Small wonder that Douglas was perplexed and had to cope with deep ambivalence as to his own worth. To oversimplify, the situation is for the child: *If I were really worthwhile my mother would love me without my receiving, and so strongly fearing, an undercurrent of hatred and rejection.* I do not believe that these mothers as a group, as I showed in Chapter 2, are malignant by design and intention. Their problem may simply be a difficulty in accepting natural-enough anger, but their problem is perceived by the child in magnified distortion as murderously punitive. Such a child can hardly think well of himself and of *his* "natural enough" affects.

The obsessive child, therefore, lives as if extermination were impending. He fears for his existence, for his autonomy, and he doubts his worth. His adaptive devices are sick ones: compulsions to act out rituals lest panic wipe him out; doubting; and the impossible combination of halfhearted commitment and striving for superhuman performance. His compulsive grandiosity is in the service of a deep alienation from a loved, positively valued self.

AFFECTS AND DEFENSES

The Freudian libido theory would hold that the affective disturbance is primary. The earliest Freudian view was that the incipient obsessive was actively lustful in infancy and committed "active seduction." It was, then, this "childhood immorality" of a phallic Oedipal variety which put the obsessional's guilt, shame and doubt, conscientiousness and fear of punishment into working overtime. Castration fears by this same token would be prominent.

Without relying too strongly on libido theory, I have come to believe the "basic anxiety" of the obsessive child is typically a fear of annihilative punishment. This inculcated set of "jungle ethics" is often called a precocious superego, a rather flattering statement for what must probably take place. Less rosy is the idea of an archaic, strict, and punitive superego. The phrase most apt must somehow refer to the child's fear of debasement because of his "sins"; that fear was present in each of our 49 children. Moreover, the accusation is self-initiated, not ostensibly from others. A scrutiny of the mother-child relationship, however, provides ample evidence of the mother giving the message, "Whatever you do that displeases me or diminishes my pleasure is sinful on your part." This cannot fail to produce a guilt-ridden fear, and, for example, caused Daniel, Alfred, and Miles to phrase ritual prayers to their mothers: quite literally a *deification* of the parent.

The mother does not threaten the child directly and primarily with loss of her love. That is the second line of attack, and also the secondary affect against which the child's secondary defenses must be deployed. His basic anxiety, therefore, is in his fear of being punished unmercifully. His anxiety's secondary wellspring is in his fear of losing the love and esteem of his mother.

Consequently, the foremost affects in the obsessive child's clinical picture are fear of punishment, fear of loss of love, a strong hate and a profound loneliness. His capacity for love and lust is impaired, but this seems rather an augmentation of his hatred. Freud (1913) wrote, ". . . in the order of development hate is the precursor of love," whereas in 1909 he had asserted:

> The doubt corresponds to the (adult) patient's internal perception of his own indecision, which, in consequence of the inhibition of his love by his hatred, takes possession of him in the face of every intended action. The doubt is in reality a doubt of his own love. . .

What are the basic defensive maneuvers that obsessive children set up against these affects? They are of one piece with the cognitive and behavioral maneuvers already described, but taken in sequence they are isolation of affect, repression, ceremonialism, displacement, undoing, and reaction formation.

1. *Isolation outweighs repression.* The obsessive child's capability for saying ordinarily upsetting things with a deadpan, "unemotional" expression has led a long line of observers to contend that he separates ("isolates") affect from the content of what he says. As stated earlier, I see this separation as *in no wise* resembling the control which is so vital a part of scientific communication. The obsessive child says things that are nonlogicoempirical: that is, the statements are not conventionally logical, and they cannot with-

stand empirical testing. He may even emit sounds that are "affective"—snarls and purrs—if you or I utter them, but from him they are sounds both monotonous and unfeeling. A little robot talks mechanically even when he speaks of love, hate, fear, and loneliness. Perhaps what the obsessive child overuses as an ego defense is *the selective repression of affect*, not facts about past events.

What he does, in any event, when he isolates and conceals feeling is merely a reenactment of the way people communicate within his family: literal-minded, more concerned with grammar than with the message's meaning, striving to be neutral and objective in delivery if not in original intention, and so on. In short, his mother and father "before him" set the tone of speaking as if everything a family member says "may be taken down and used in evidence" against him! The child comes by these communication patterns "honestly"; as they say in the South, he "did not suck them off his thumb." The course of relative security demands that one be as cautious and "pseudo-factual" as possible. This pretense at rationality is like an inefficient bureaucrat who feels ultrarational when he merely keeps to the letter of rules and regulations, disregarding that the rules may be highly dysfunctional to begin with.

When the obsessive child does recall infantile traumata, of either a sexual or a violent form, he recalls them as being divorced from emotion, both then and now. Freud (1909) stated this as:

> The trauma, instead of being forgotten, is deprived of its affective cathexis; so that what remains in consciousness is nothing but its ideational content, which is perfectly colourless and is judged to be unimportant . . .

Freud contended in the same paper that the earliest infantile "preconditions" of the obsessive neurosis were more shrouded in amnesia, though only a partial amnesia, than were the "immediate occasions of the illness." With the 49 children presented here, that seems accurate as a generalization only in the first half of the statement. These children not only evidenced considerable amnesia for their infancy (even for infantile events such as harsh toilet training and the like), but also had difficulty recalling the "immediate occasions of the illness," the precipitants of the rash of obsessions and compulsions which led to their becoming patients. In other words, their memory disturbance is for both remote *and* recent events. Moreover, the parents, too, have considerable amnesia, and it is only after a long warm-up period, of trying to make changes in the present and becoming freer to recall the nearer past, that parents and child can recover the precipitants and the infantile background data.

One very practical impact of the obsessive child "using isolation more than repression" is to be seen in therapy. The goal is not to undo infantile amnesia as much as to restore naturalness *here and now*, so that the child can come to accept the wholeness of a vital experience, the entirety of an event—all of it with idea and feeling in continuity. He can come to accept the experience as a past happening which is stored, for human beings, with its factual components wedded to its emotional components. Treatment strives, as a top priority, to help with direct experiencing—including affects—in the here and now, thus taking cognizance of the child's neurotic craving to use isolation more than repression in the defense bulwark. Concentrating on the here and now is a technique that unseats isolation most effectively. What does it gain the child to repress affects and recall "facts?" The only gain is in neurosis, not resolution.

2. *Ceremonialism* itself, purely and simply, is defense against anxiety. The 49 subjects often understood the defensive nature of their ceremonies better than all their other defenses. They would state that a ritual act "protects me against a horrible thing" or "I don't know why I do it, but I just know I have to do it or nothing would be safe" or "it gives me insurance, the way people take out insurance before they fly on an airplane . . . they do it to make them feel better." Again, "I feel like if I do it, things may go all right, but if I dare *not* to do it, it could be terrible, like even D-E-A-T-H." Or, "If I don't, then everything is thrown out of whack and I couldn't predict the bad things that could result."

Protection, defense, guarantees against the possibility of panic—these are the meaning of obsessive ritual, the compulsive motor activities.

3. *Displacement* is another defensive maneuver which, as Freud (1907) recognized, is a main part of the obsessive's repertoire. The obsessive child is a veritable expert in substitutive behavior, He may, for instance, let the German language stand for his father and, safely unaware of anger for his father, come to feel enraged or frightened whenever he hears a word of German. His therapist had better not say "Gesundheit" when that child sneezes. Obsessive children go from important complexes to associated words which, barring the displacement operation, seem totally nonsensical and trivial.

Displacement operates too when the obsessive "deliria" are being formed. By displacement, one idea—halfway sensible but with obsessive, illogical premises still a part of the picture—slips to the forefront as a less bizarre expression than the original obsession itself. Chester E (Child #20) stopped retaining his feces when he began collecting his urine in bottles and jars. Finally, as an unconscious equivalent, he began wearing the same socks and bathing trunks, night and day, and kept this up for several weeks. His substitution of dirty clothes for bottles of urine and for masses of feces was salutary because he was choosing less bizarre substitution. Similarly, if the ceiling of one's bedroom displaces erotic or hateful obsessions about his mother, the defense of displacement reduces some of the sting of the child's anxiety. Sometimes, however, the displacing act or thought is more, not less, "bizarre," and then the only gain is that the weirder symptom is more baffling and mystifying. Then there is a third variation. The child who obsessively fretted about the "unforgivable sin" emitted a smokescreen that was neither more nor less socially acceptable, but which was only a good way of hiding his worship of, and his hatred for, his mother.

4. *Undoing* is a defense that aims to deal with ambivalence by separating the two goals into diphasic temporal sequence. As exemplified in a walking ritual, taking five steps forward and one step backward, for example, is a characteristic defensive procedure of obsessive children. It is the defense behind much of the child's ritual-making. Talking ritual is the same. When Daniel D (Child #24) punctuated his compulsive prayer with the phrase "so be it,"

he was attempting to cancel out his approaching awareness that it was actually his mother to whom he was praying. "So be it" was a magical diversion that reassured him and allowed suppression.

A patient, an adult, referred to his behavior of undoing as "like a pendulum. When I have a thought on the hate side, I must swing over to the favorable side, and vice versa." By his doing and undoing, the obsessive child plays a game of pretending that neither feeling exists, when in reality both are in evidence. The game is difficult to win, for the undoing cannot fully neutralize the original deed. The hymn of praise is not loud enough to drown out the vicious curse. The loving thoughts cannot kiss away the mother's cut throat. The angry thoughts cannot wipe away loving, incestuous longings. The obsessive pyrotechnics do not give the security which is sought.

5. *Reaction formation* is often held to be the prime defense of obsessives who are, in general, exceedingly eager to ward off fear and who go to great lengths to "deny" their ambivalent feelings. Freud (1909) wrote:

> ... the neurotic phenomena we have observed arise on the one hand from conscious feelings of affection which have become exaggerated as a reaction, and on the other hand from sadism persisting in the unconscious in the form of hatred.

I think we must call it *reaction formation* when, deeply unawares, hatred is "negated" by contrived love. But when that negation is more deliberate, more conscious, we might tend to call it *compulsive*. Reaction formation, hence, is more enfolded in the generic blanket of amnesia than is compulsive thinking, feeling, or doing. If the child is less aware of what it is all about, we think of it as more akin to reaction formation, and less like a conscious compulsion.

Psychodynamic literature is steeped in the observation that hysterical patients use more amnesia than obsessives. In my view, obsessive children do not seem to show any more useful (or healthy) awareness than the hysterical child. The obsessive's awareness is more of the nature of what the Marxist might call "false consciousness"—that is, it is an ideological fabrication that runs counter to observable data. Furthermore, some writers such as Nunberg (1955) assert that reaction formation is an even more "primitive" defense than repression. Freudians have conducted a voluminous discussion of who is the more regressed and what maneuvers are more primitive. Probably the most weight has fallen on the side of the more "advanced" ego functioning and the defending of the obsessive as compared to the hysteric.

As a summary statement about the obsessive child's affective experiences, I would say that defiance, anger, hatred, loneliness, and fear of punishment are his predominant feelings, while the fear of losing the parents' love is of secondary import. Among his security operations for the guarding of self-esteem, the outstanding mechanisms are repression, isolation, ceremonialism, displacement, undoing and reaction formation. The blight is in the child's inability to feel comfortable in his humanness, to feel truly in touch with his real self.

DIFFERENTIAL DIAGNOSIS

The major mental illnesses need to be ruled out before a child is considered to be suffering from an obsessive neurosis. The neurosis itself is not the benign "transference neurosis," as claimed by some writers. It can be rather intractable, malignant and difficult. It might herald very serious illness such as childhood psychosis or schizophrenia. It might, on the other hand, be a transient way station denoting recovery from encephalitis or psychosis. It is a "good sign" when it makes an appearance in the antisocial or delinquent child because it makes for a better prognosis, given treatment, than a "pure culture" antisocial reaction in a child.

Diagnosis has its place, decidedly, although my wish is not to commit work with obsessive children to an ordeal of hairsplitting diagnosis. Still, one of the virtues of the medical approach is its emphasis upon diagnosis as a prerequisite to rational problem-solving. The medical model teaches us how to come to know what problem it is that we are trying to help to solve. As such, diagnosis in the medical tradition is a set of serviceable operations that we had better not discard.

Schizophrenia, according to Despert (1955), is best differentiated by its lack of ego functions such as "reality testing and reality defining." She wrote that, "However bizarre the obsessive thought or compulsive act, if the patient experiences them as alien to his personality, the break with reality has not taken place." Despert also believed that the preservation of abstracting ability and the onset age at five or six years for the obsessional illness assisted in distinguishing schizophrenia from obsessional illness. But the magnitude and pervasiveness of the symptoms in severe obsessive illness make it rather difficult, at times, to distinguish from schizophrenia or from borderline psychosis. Ten of the 49 children were considered to be possibly psychotic, at first. We probably do well to err in the direction of giving a tentatively serious diagnosis at the outset and later softening that to a diagnosis of neurosis. As Aubrey Lewis (1936) wrote, "The surprising thing here is not that some obsessionals become obviously schizophrenic, but that only a few do so." Lewis viewed obsessions as presaging *adolescent* schizophrenia, at times, but not adult schizophrenia.

In my experience, psychological testing can be of great help in the first appraisal of the child who is obsessive. The Rorschach test, as interpreted by an accomplished clinician, specifying the sequence of the child's defenses, can be most instructive. The child's attention to detail, to minutiae, his compulsive swinging from one extreme of affect and ideation to its polar opposite— these are all observable by a competent psychologist and can enrich and illuminate the assessment that is so useful as a precondition of treatment. Especially with older children, the preadolescents and early adolescents, psychological testing often gives a more serious picture than will be borne out later; but that is only a small but pertinent example of how the big picture is all that counts in clinical psychiatry with children.

Depression in childhood is not easy to spot, nor easy to differentiate from obsessive neurosis in some instances. The depressed child often "misbehaves" or "acts out" antisocially instead of appearing to be saddened and detached. The obsessive child may also have periods of antisocial behavior. The *antisocial* child suddenly may develop a flurry of obsessions at times. A good rule of thumb for differentiating obsession from depression is this: When in a child there are *obsessions and an affect of sadness*, the odds are greatest that the child is an obsessional neurotic, but when there is more antisocial behavior than either of the foregoing, the scales should be tipped in the direction of a real depressive illness. Sullivan (1956) observed the grief that accompanies the obsessive's gaining of insight.

More and more, the prospects of early detected manic-depressive disorder appear on the psychiatric scene, especially for some of the British "organic" child psychiatrists. It is conceivable that some of the obsessive children in our sample of 49 will, in adulthood, turn out to suffer from endogenous depression or other forms of severe affective disorder. If this proves to be the case, then, in retrospect, we may learn that certain types of clinical pictures of obsessive children were, in truth, childhood affective disorders. Just to bow to the manifold complexity of reality, the mentally-retarded obsessive adolescent of whom I spoke earlier in this chapter was in the midst of a hypomanic episode when I first saw him. Hence, he was obsessive, hypomanic and mentally retarded. His affective disorder responded to chlorpromazine and his obsessions diminished apace. Abraham (1921) pointed up the similarities and congruences, not the differentiating features, of obsessive and affective disorders. Manic-depressives in adulthood are often said to adjust as "obsessional characters." Maudsley (1879) regarded obsessive illness as a "latent affective psychosis"—and certainly adults often do present severe obsessions and compulsions in a setting of depressive illness.

Impulsions, as described by Bender and Schilder (1954), are more "ego syntonic" than are compulsions, and they are probably identical with the "circumscribed interest patterns" described by Robinson and Vitale (1954). Such children are "nuts" about geology or stamp collecting or high fidelity or shortwave radio, and they have one-track minds to such an extent that all normal interests and relations are sacrificed. They do not, however, undergo the anguish of the obsessive child. The lack of suffering is probably the most important differentiating point.

Paranoid reactions are not common in children, unless the Kleinian view (1932) be accepted:

... in the early anal-sadistic stage the individual, if his early anxiety-situations are strongly operative, actually passes through rudimentary paranoid states which he normally overcomes in the next stage (the second anal-sadistic one), and that the severity of his obsessional illness depends on the severity of the paranoid disturbances that have immediately preceded it. If his obsessional mechanisms cannot adequately overcome those disturbances his underlying paranoid traits will come to the surface, or he may even succumb to a regular paranoia.

A child with obsessions does not have such fixed notions about the malevolence of others as would a paranoid patient. Yet, Kleinian or not, we do have to acknowledge that there is a kinship between the obsessive and the paranoid maneuvers. In both, there are dissociation, self-deception and unhealthy goals.

Tics, phobic reactions and psychophysiologic disorders are less easily differentiated from obsessive neurosis, and each or all of them might occur as accessory symptoms in an obsessive child's clinical syndrome. Janet (1903) contended phobias are but one of the four types of obsessional symptoms, as are ideas or images, thinking or rumination, and impulses to motor acts. From a pragmatic standpoint, the phobic child, and the child with separation problems generally, might use obsessive maneuvers to such a degree that he is clinically obsessive, and could quite properly be diagnosed as suffering from an obsessive-compulsive neurotic reaction.

Otto Rank (1945) addressed himself predominantly to the needs of obsessives when he formulated his views on will therapy and separation-individuation, implicitly taking cognizance of the similarity between the obsessional and the person afraid to individuate and "be himself." Freudians have stressed a very different genesis and clinical course for phobic reactions, by and large, but that there can be an overlap with obsessive reactions Freudians also have accepted. The effort of Humberto Nágera (1965) to clear this up is admirable:

Several of the cases studied at the Hampstead Clinic showed a completely developed obsessional neurosis sometime between the ages of 9 to 12 years. This was usually preceded by one form or another of anxiety hysteria with typical phobic symptoms. In some cases the picture of anxiety hysteria had lasted for several years (six or more) until it had been finally replaced by the obsessional neurosis and symptoms. All the cases showed quite clearly at some point in their development the phallic-oedipal conflicts from which a final and massive regression had taken place.

Nágera's view saved intact the fixation-regression theory whereby no infantile neurosis can be formed until the phallic-oedipal stage has been achieved. Nágera did this by explaining obsessive neurosis as a massive regression from the psychosexually advanced phase required by a phobic reaction. The viewpoint of Janet, however, is less involved than the Freudian one, to be sure, and gets to the point more simply. Phobias are not discrete from obsessions.

The *tics* of Gilles de la Tourette's syndrome have frequently been seen as blending into obsessions and especially into the compulsion to voice obscenities. Named *la maladie des tics compulsifs avec coprolalie* in 1885, the disorder involved enough coprolalia and compulsion to fire the imagination of the psychodynamicists for many years. Within the past two decades, more and more psychotropic drugs have been found to remove those symptoms most akin to obsessional neurosis. Consensus grows that it is not predominantly a psychogenic disorder (Lucas, 1964, Polites *et al.*, 1965, Fernando, 1967 and Corbett *et al.*, 1969). Haloperidol seems to have cleared up a lot of the copious speculation about the psychodynamics of the symptoms of Gilles de la Tourette's syndrome.

Other tics, especially facial tics, are much more common among children in the age group we studied. In fact, 11 of the children either were tiqueurs at the time they were seen for their obsessive problems, or were recorded as tiqueurs on their histories. The psychogenic tics described by Paula Elkisch (1948) and by Mahler (1949) were found in children whose case reports were not dissimilar to some of the obsessive children depicted in this study.

The most cogent generalization seems to be that the psychogenic tic is closely and directly related to the obsession or the compulsion. And, although classical psychoanalytic theory prescribes that the tiqueur and the obsessive have both reached the phallic-oedipal stage, the actual clinical picture is not a clear one—at least for children. Indeed, phobias, tics and obsessions may all coexist very cozily.

This same coexistence—despite often made formulations—is in evidence when we turn to the psychophysiologic disorders. The obsessive is not spared his physical signs and symptoms. In our group of children the physical difficulties ranged from gastrointestinal complaints as the primary organ system to be worried about, to asthma as a close second among the psychophysiologic disorders, to testicular torsion and other rarer difficulties.

All in all, obsessive children will be relatively easily diagnosed as unlike other suffering children. But obsessive children may also suffer from mixtures of neuroses, and from mental retardation, and from general medical problems. The words of Harry Stack Sullivan (1956) are fitting: "An obsessional neurotic does not have a good time, but he could have a much worse time."

4

The Children

FORTY-NINE OBSESSIVE CHILDREN seen over a period of 15 years make up the study group described in this chapter. This is a population aged 15 years or less, excluding a group of older adolescents who were included in an earlier report (Adams, 1972). These children were cared for by child psychiatrists, either by the author (17 cases), his colleagues or psychiatric residents or medical students at the University of Florida. Sixteen cases were seen by psychiatry faculty members or students under their supervision. The remaining 16 were seen by residents whose work was supervised by the author at least at *some* point in the therapy. These "subject children" lived in North Carolina (3), Florida (44), or Georgia (2), but their places of residence are not identified in order to further anonymity. Some of the demographic characteristics of these young people are presented in Table 6, along with a general description of the group. Case vignettes make up the remainder of this chapter, supplying some of the clinical materials from which the generalizations are made. Unfortunately, neither demography nor abbreviated case reports do justice to the vivid, real-life misery—or the assets—of these youngsters. The case vignettes, nonetheless, come nearer than the demographic group-characteristics in giving some of the flavor of how it is to be an obsessive child living in the world today.

Incidence. The 49 children were drawn from a clinical pool of some four thousand. Hence, about 1.2 percent of the children were obsessive.

Race. All 49 children were white. Although black children are increasingly referred to child psychiatry at the University of Florida, no black obsessive child was referred in the 12 years during which the Florida cases were gathered.

Gender. Table 6 shows that there were ten girls and 39 boys in this assortment of cases. At the University of Florida child psychiatry outpatient clinic between 1960 and 1972, the proportion of males to females shifted from at least five to one to a ratio nearer three males to one female. Girls, generally, in other words, came into psychiatric treatment more frequently with the passage of time in our general clinical work; but obsessive girls, by contrast, *did not* appear any more frequently with the passage of those 12 years in time. Males among adult obsessives outnumber females, and, indeed, Freud (1895), Adler (1931), Sullivan (1956), and Rado (1959) wrote as if females might be exempt from obsessive illness.

One in every four of the Florida group was female. At the same time, though, it must be noted that there was nothing distinctive about the girls—meaning that there were *no significant differences* between the boys and the girls on any of the variables studied. The girls were neither more sick nor more healthy, more briefly or easily treated, or the obverse, and so on. Age, IQ, onset age, ordinal position, socioeconomic status, bowel training harshness, phobias, evidence of psychosis—none of these was associated, at a significant level, with gender. Because of this, and despite the pleasures of speculation on the subject, not much attention to gender will be given in this description of the obsessive children.

Boys lived in households as follows:

Predominantly male	14
Predominantly female	13
Neither gender predominant	12

Girls showed no sexual preponderance in their households, either:

Predominantly male	2
Predominantly female	2
Neither gender predominant	6

Age. The average age of the children studied was 10.06 years (SD=2.44). The girls as a group were younger, but not significantly so.

The average age of onset was 5.84 years (SD=3.5) but the mean period that elapsed between onset and appearance for our treatment was 4.42 years (SD=3.06). When onset is abrupt and dramatic, the likelihood of early treatment is generally enhanced. Yet only 17 of the children (34 percent) showed sudden onset. The remainder (66 percent), 32 children, were said, by parents, to have shown a gradual onset of their symptoms.

"Age when seen" co-varied positively with the age of onset of illness (r=0.516, p=.001). Too, when the onset age moved upward, toward puberty and young adulthood, the lapse from onset until the child was referred was considerably shorter (r=0.7324, p=.001). It could be said, on the basis of this finding, that older children are more precious. At least, they get more attention.

Among the children showing gradual onset there was a significant positive correlation with higher socioeconomic status (r=0.4313, p=.002). However, 22 (45 percent only) of the children showed a precipitating event.

Intelligence. With eight children (16 percent) showing average intelligence (actual range of IQ, 93-110), 41 (or 84 percent) of these young people were above average (actual range of IQ from 111 to 160). This IQ picture certainly does make this an intellectually advantaged group which appeared at an outpatient clinic in which every fourth child of the total populace was retarded or

TABLE 6
FREQUENCY OF SEVERAL POPULATION TRAITS

Incidence	—	1.2% of clinical populace	
Gender	—	10 girls, 39 boys	
Age	—	Mean, 10.06 years	
Intelligence	—	Below average 0, average 8, above average 41	
Ordinal position	—	32 firstborn, 9 lastborn, 8 in-between	
Adoption	—	Affected 6 families	
Diagnoses	—	Obsessive-compulsive neurosis	33
		Mixed neurosis	6
		Obsessive character	10

brain damaged. By any norms these were a collection of very bright children.

Ordinal Position. Thirty-two of the 49 children were either solitary (five of these were the only child) or firstborn (27). This agrees with the findings of Kayton and Borge (1967). Nine were lastborn and eight were "in-between" firstborn and youngest. These 49 children lived in families averaging 2.7 children.

Adoption and Family Composition. Adoption played a role in the families of six children. Two of the obsessive children themselves were adopted. One of these adopted obsessive children remained the only member of his generation in the household. The other adopted child later acquired younger sibs by adoption; three biological children gained their *older* sibs by adoption outright while one acquired older sibs by parental re-marriage and subsequent adoption.

Diagnoses. Thirty-three of the children (67 percent) were diagnosed as suffering from obsessive-compulsive neurosis, six or 13 percent from "mixed neurosis," "adjustment reaction with obsessional neurotic features" and so forth, making 39 of 49 (80 percent) carry a diagnosis of some type of neurotic reaction. Ten children (20 percent) were diagnosed as "obsessive character, compulsive character, obsessive personality, compulsive personality."

Obsessions and Compulsions. These data are depicted in Table 7 where it is shown that 92 percent of the children complained of obsessions and/or compulsions, with 78 percent complaining of both. Four children (8 percent) complained of neither obsessions nor compulsions but were recorded as having "a compulsive style" that influenced the entire clinical picture even if some other aspect of that picture received major emphasis in the diagnostic labelling operations. In all events, simultaneity of obsessions and compulsions co-varied significantly (P<.01) with neurosis, but not with obsessive character or mixed neurosis.

TABLE 7
SYMPTOMS BY DIAGNOSIS

Symptoms Complained of	DX Neurosis	DX Character	Total
Both obsessions & compulsions	34	4	38 (78%)
Obsessions only & compulsive style	2	3	5 (10%)
Obsessions without compulsive style	1	0	1 (2%)
Compulsions only & compulsive style	1	0	1 (2%)
Compulsive style only	1	3	4 (8%)
TOTAL	39	10	49

Disruptive Symptoms. Substantiating a longstanding maxim of child psychiatrists, these children upset their parents. Otherwise, they might never have been brought to a child psychiatrist. Sullivanians would call this the "interpersonal significance" of the symptoms and Freudians might call it "affect on the environment." In 42 families the child's symptoms were considered *disruptive to the family.* In seven cases (14%) the parents were able to accommodate to the child's symptoms without feeling disrupted by them. However, in 48 of the 49 cases the children were reputed to show "ambivalence or aggression to one or both parents." Perhaps the parents were extra-stoical, or should have been!

Evidence of Psychosis. In 43 (88%) of the children there was no suggestion of psychosis, and even where there was explicit commentary sometimes, it was questionable in my opinion. Young psychiatrists between 1957 and 1972 in the USA were, if anything, overly bent toward "rule out schizophrenia" as a remark to be made about obsessive children.

Presence of Phobias. Since so much attention has been given by psychoanalysts to the question of the discrete difference between phobias and obsessions, I decided to scrutinize the medical records closely on this issue. It is noteworthy that 26 of the 49 children did complain of phobias along with their obsessions and compulsions. In nature there are more paradoxical coexistences than would ever be allowed in certain forms of psychodynamic theory. (See Rosenberg, 1968, p. 36.)

Also, the age of onset showed a positive association with the presence of phobias (r=0.297, p=.038)—i.e., the older the age at which these children became obsessive, the more likely they were to have phobias along with obsessions and compulsions. This finding jibes with that of Gunnar Skoog (1965).

Bowel Training. Data about bowel training are shaky, even if the child psychiatrist or social worker is questioning the parents of three-year-olds, in my experience. Parents know that it is *outré* to be harsh about toileting, even if they actually are punitive. Try as hard as we could, we found only 41 percent (20) of the children (as reported by parents mainly) with a history of "bowel training rigid, punitive, or prolonged." In 18 cases (37 percent) there was a history of *no difficulty with toilet training* and in 11 children there was *no report of difficulty.* Some psychiatrists and social workers did prolonged work with obsessive children and their parents but either did not know about the details of toilet training or did not refute the sometimes nonchalant claim that "everything was normal on that score." As a result on 11 children we can only say "no difficulty by report."

Testing for significance, I found that punitive or eventful bowel training was *significantly associated with obsessional neurosis* but not with obsessive character or mixed neurosis (p⟨.02).

Active Fantasy Life. Were these 49 obsessive children vapid, unimaginative and unemotional? Indeed, no, for 45 (92 percent) gave definite information in favor of having an active fantasy life. Only four children (or 8 percent) seemed to be so up-tight that they were rather washed out and had no fantasy life, no inner life of richness, that they would admit to other persons. Alas, neither fantasy nor reality is always able to give happiness to children.

Guilt Feelings. Forty-three (88 percent) of the children had prominent guilt feelings while six (12 percent) did not. This is not to say that their guilt was "neurotic guilt" exclusively. Many times, the children "had a lot to feel guilty about" and reassurance and explanation practically never helped in subsidence of their guilt.

Helen M. Lynd (1961) made the case eloquently that children opt for guilt *instead of shame* in our society. Obsessive children especially show a great preference for guilt, not shame. Shame is too illuminating, too soul-searching; hence, the obsessive child prefers to construct his moral superiority out of incessant professions of guilt, banking on easy expiation if backed against a wall. But shame, and life along the shame axis, with exposure of oneself, gives too much "emphasis on quality of experience, not only on content," for the literal-minded obsessive ever to choose shame. Doubt and shame, in fact, may haunt him so that he strives to convert syntactic shame, compulsively, into grammatic guilt. As Lynd (1961, p. 209) stated: "Surmounting of guilt leads to righteousness. Transcending of shame may lead to [a] sense of identity, freedom."

Moral Code. We looked closely to see if the records displayed that each obsessive child had a "rigid moral code." We found that 26 children did not, but 23 (47 percent) did give pictures of a super-strict moral code, manifested in obsessive moralizing, preoccupation with goodness and badness, and the like. In other words, the yea-nay split was nearly even on considering rigidity of the child's moral code.

Table 8 presents a comparison of these results with the report of Judd (1965) on his five cases. The Judd sample, one-tenth the size of the one currently reported, showed more homogeneity. This may well be a consequence of smallness and nothing else, but cultural differences between southern California and southeastern USA might also enter the picture.

Case Vignettes. In the rest of this Chapter each of the children

TABLE 8
CHARACTERISTICS OF CHILDREN,
COMPARING JUDD AND ADAMS FINDINGS

Characteristic	Adams	Judd
Size of Population Studied	49	5
Age Range	15 and under	12 and under
Mean Age of Onset	5.84 years	7½ years
Range of Onset Age	1 to 13 years	6 yrs. 4 mos. to 10 yrs. 2 mos.
Gender	39 boys, 10 girls	3 boys, 2 girls
Onset	Sudden 34%, gradual 66%	Sudden 100%
Intelligence	Normal 16%, above normal 84%	Above normal 100%
Obsessions & Compulsions	78% had both; 22% did not	Both in 100% of cases
Symptom Disruptive	86% yes, 14% no	100% yes
Guilt Prominent	88% yes, 12% no	100% yes
Moral Code Rigid	47% yes, 53% no	100% yes
Fantasy Life Active	92% yes, 8% no	100% yes
Psychosis Possible	88% no, 12% yes	100% no
Bowel Training Punitive	41% yes, 37% no, 22% not by history	20% yes, 80% no
Precipitating Event	45% yes, 55% no	80% yes, 20% no
Phobias Present	53% yes, 47% no	80% yes, 20% no
Aggression to Parents	98% yes, 2% no	80% yes, 20% no
Premorbid Normality	73% yes, 27% no	80% yes, 20% no

studied will be described in capsule form. My goal is to show certain basic information about each of the children studied—age, gender, family relations, clinical picture, etc.—but mainly to give a quick picture of the child as a case, and also as a growing person. All of the children were seen as outpatients. The first ten vignettes describe the girls, the last 39 the boys. If the reader wishes to identify those children who were given diagnoses not of neurosis but of "obsessive character," they are those with these names and numbers: 1. Bernice, 3. Chloe, 14. Billy, 17. Burt, 21. Chuck, 22. Crown, 29. Eric, 31. Hank, 32. Harry, and 33. Henry.

Child #1
BERNICE J

Bernice was eight years old when her parents, the father a physician and the mother an artist, first asked for a psychiatric consultation. They were especially concerned about Bernice's immaturity (baby talk and thumb sucking), her apparent "insecurity about herself as a person" and her "hysterical episodes" when she cried in anger, lost control and threw a tantrum four or five times daily. Particularly when challenged or outdone by her sister two years older or her brother three and a half years younger, she seemed to "break up" but would also go to pieces at school when she was not performing according to her or her teacher's high expectations.

Bernice, though "overly affectionate" to her father, was a friendless little girl whose parents were rather untrusting of the non-Jewish neighbors who surrounded them in their new home in the South. Bernice's father had health problems that unsettled the entire family, and at age five Bernice became obsessively concerned that her father might die leaving the family helpless. The father adored Bernice's older sister who performed well academically and socially, showing none of the self-doubt Bernice possessed. For the little brother, father was both a loving mentor and an indulgent patriarch. But, for Bernice, he had a lot of criticism and impatience. Yet he showed her his troubled side, complaining to her of his health worries, his daily exposure to all sorts of infectious diseases, the competitiveness of his professional colleagues, and the multiple annoyances he experienced at work. These recitations were designed to keep Bernice from "bugging" him when he was at home where he expected everyone, certainly females, to cater to his wants. Besides, he felt socially superior to his wife. By rights, she should serve him. However, any of his talk of his troubles only fed the Oedipal longings of little Bernice and increased her testing of her father's love. It appeared, though, that father had time for everyone except Bernice.

After four play sessions the psychiatric consultant met with the parents to discuss his findings and to plan for no further psychiatric intervention at that time. The psychiatrist wrote, "At this time I do not find her to be overly fearful or overly obsessive. She is an inhibited child with mild obsessive tendencies that are congruent with the rest of the family. It is a family with very high aspirations for social, cultural, and intellectual achievement. [Bernice] sees herself as being put upon, uncomfortable, unhappy, and overworked."

Twenty-one months later Bernice returned to the clinic. In the interim she had become more socially isolated and withdrawn and had openly stated that she wished to kill herself. By this time, she was ten years old. She had dropped most of the infantile manners displayed during the earlier sessions. She talked of her longing to be loved by her father without always having to perform, to prove herself to him. She also revealed much more of her attitude to her mother, of the battle between her and her mother, of the explicit "obsessional" instructions that her mother gave her when she felt angry (think about something pleasant), and of the marital unhappiness of her parents. When speaking of herself Bernice showed a conspicuous "up and down tendency," as her new therapist called her practice of stating an idea and then negating it or taking it back by stating its opposite. Loneliness plagued her, but she felt unable to earn human companionship, hence her fantasy world had to do with animals, dolls and toys. She felt that her prospective girl friends were too gauche, too tomboyish or too energetic. She felt too small, too weak and too clumsy compared with other ten-year-old girls. And she felt that in order to win her father's love she needed to be strong and "super." Bernice played, did drawings and squiggles, initiated psychodrama and role playing, and came to report dreams with genuine interested involvement. She built a strong relationship with the resident who was her therapist. She began to feel less misunderstood and friendless. Her dealings with peers, sibs, and parents all improved.

Since Bernice's obsessive character defenses rarely broke down to the degree that she "needed" to have overt symptoms, she was adjudged to be troubled by an "obsessive personality" and not neurosis.

Child #2
CHERI S

Cheri was a very bright 10-year-old brought in mainly because of her complaints of headaches, fainting spells accompanied by nausea and vomiting and followed by long periods of sleep, trouble at school and strong rivalry with her six-year-old brother. These problems had been recurring on and off for five years—since her brother had begun to walk. Her parents very much liked Cheri's personality and desired only to alleviate the distressing somatic symptoms. She had been hospitalized for a complete neurological workup. Although she had had two convulsions, no abnormalities were found on EEG. All three of the consulting physicians (none a psychiatrist) who had seen Cheri before she came to us tended to the opinion that her problems were psychogenic.

Cheri proved to be a rigid, compulsive, unfeeling little girl who definitely feared showing any emotion. She had a morbid fear of criticism and a magnified desire to achieve in academic pursuits. It quickly became apparent that she had adopted this value system *in toto* from her father, who was a successful businessman but similarly compulsive and perfectionistic, a man who valued academic achievement, fame, and financial gains above all else. While her father had "infected" her with an overbearing need to achieve, Cheri enjoyed her reasonably close relationship with him and she warmed up noticeably when she talked of him. This stood in marked contrast to her rigidity whenever she discussed her mother. Unfortunately, her father's compulsive nature made it unlikely that he would ever be of any help to Cheri in working out her problems. And his obvious love for Cheri's younger brother had impressed her with the value of being tomboyish. It was clear to her that the tomboyishness was going to become more and more difficult as puberty advanced, despite its being the only way she felt she could keep her father's love.

Cheri's mother appeared to be cold, unfeeling, and somewhat compulsive. Mother was on good terms with her husband, although the two of them did not appear to be close. She over-protected but covertly criticized and rejected Cheri. Her MMPI profile suggested a tendency to somaticize anger and frustration. Both Cheri's mother and the maternal grandparents had a history of migraine.

Cheri, in adopting her parents' value system, had placed great pressure upon herself to achieve. When she began to feel overwhelmed by the school situation, her mother helped her to project the blame onto the school itself. At the same time, her mother gave Cheri very little support, and from Cheri's point of view, gave most of her love and attention to her younger brother who reportedly was "just the opposite of Cheri." More difficult to keep compliant and subdued, little brother got more attention. Cheri clearly resented her mother's overprotectiveness and her father's implicit demands that she act like a boy—with all the resultant guilt and anxiety. Cheri's mother seemed to sense in the mother-daughter relationship many of the characteristics of her own childhood, and her own resentment of the lack of freedom she had as a child apparently colored her behavior and attitude toward Cheri. All this, combined with the family style of noncommunicativeness concerning intimate feelings or problems, actually overwhelmed Cheri. Her somatic and obsessive defenses and her obsessive-compulsive style had not proved sufficient to deal with her anxiety, and she had not even been able to let down enought to "blow" in a tantrum. The result was her somatic problem, which definitely became worse during, or was precipitated by, stressful situations. The interwoven parental and child pathology, mainly characterologic on both sides, made treatment an arduous matter. Nevertheless, it was undertaken, and, although of relatively short duration, resulted in some final improvement.

Child #3
CHLOE C

This enuretic girl, nine and one-half years old, was second in a sib group of five and had been unenthusiastic about her mother's recent pregnancy when psychiatric care commenced. Chloe was the darling of the family: perfect, gifted, very special. Her mother, aged 39, was in psychotherapy for obsession and depression. Her father, aged 40, and in a mental health profession, also knew well the values of reflection and pondering. In fact, neither parent saw Chloe's fears and obsessions as the major problem, for they had identified her bedwetting—itself deeply enmeshed in her more pervasive obsessional state—as the chief problem requiring remediation. In the first hour before Chloe came to the psychiatrist the parents described her as "bright, talkative and communicative." Asked for an illustration the father replied, "A week ago, in the living room, she told me she wanted to let me in on a secret worry. It was a worry of her, at age 18 months, taking a doll out of her doll carriage when she was not supposed to. She was afraid that if she'd done things wrong when she was little, she'd do it later on." The father beamed in his approval at her brightness and her articulateness, and he did not see anything amiss regarding Chloe's guilty obsession. It was only a part of the package of ego precocity he valued.

Chloe was articulate, outspoken, and highly accomplished in juvenile verbal sarcasm. Her mother said, "She's a little on the antisocial side: caustic about people, including grownups." "She says what she thinks," the father added. Her oneupmanship and belittling of the therapist provided a grating note in what was, otherwise, a productive and smooth therapeutic course. Chloe worked to understand herself, including dreams, with great progress.

Both parents felt expert in their ken of what Chloe's inner world was like. For example, they pooh-poohed the idea that she might have fears of the dark that made going to the toilet hazardous for her. However, when Chloe was seen, in the first hour, she gave this account of her night life: "Every once in a while I wake up and go to the bathroom. I usually carry Leo (a stuffed toy lion) with me. Sometimes I think about Dracula and just go back to bed, I'm scared of the dark. I give a big jump over the rug by my bed because I imagine there are tarantulas there. I'm afraid of tarantulas. Spiders too, but not of Daddy Longlegs though."

Chloe's mask of adequacy, quasi-omnipotency, proved during treatment to be a compulsive replacement for shyness, loneliness, and deep fears of inadequacy. She came to learn why it was she experienced fantasies of superhuman feats (a recurrent dream, and conscious wish, was to fly) at the selfsame time when she felt inferior. She became less grandiose and more natural during treatment. She also overcame her bedwetting. Treatment removed some of her symptoms but, consisting of only 29 sessions, did not totally reverse her tendency to obsessive ratiocination. Little wonder, for her father wrote the following account in a letter to the therapist:

> On the way home today there were some passages you might find significant . . . I told her that even with no deal agreed on I'd like to hear her question. It was, 'What are thoughts made of?' I tried to explain in simple terms that there are several kinds of thoughts but that thinking is a skill of the mind—that a thought isn't made of anything really but is a way we have of bringing memories, questions, feelings into our own attention so that we can use them to solve some problem."

Child #4
CINDY G

Cindy was a four-year-old girl, whose mother was a nurse, aged 27, and whose 32-year-old father was a pharmacist. The mother was pregnant at the time psychiatric evaluation was sought, and although she believed Cindy might be influenced negatively by her pregnancy she attempted to explain and reassure the little girl. The mother also tried to decondition Cindy's fear of policemen by setting up personal contacts. She would, in addition, refrain from harsh verbal rebuke when Cindy made an accidental mess, and introduced the child "to finger paints to combat her compulsiveness." She encouraged water play and sought to bring about more frequent short separations of Cindy from the immediate family. Cindy, though, seemed happiest only when she was on family vacation—in constant contact with both parents.

The mother was, of course, attempting to practice what she had learned as a nurse about obsessive children. Her intervention, however, did not work: Cindy became increasingly fearful of police-men, soldiers, priests, monsters, germs, God, and poison plants. The mother's conviction was that she feared being annihilated or cruelly punished, but she was not certain for what. Nightmares and compulsive acts worsened for a period of about three months, and the mother instigated psychiatric evaluation.

The evaluating doctor, a resident in general psychiatry, found the father and mother both to be "dangerously compulsive" but opined that the little girl was without severe psychopathology that could not be related to her parents. As a result, he arranged for the mother to come for psychotherapy after the parturition with her second child.

Cindy's mother said she had a strict and puritanical upbringing by an intrusive, overcontrolling mother and a father whom she perceived as weak, inadequate, and paranoid. The mother felt locked into a forced repetition of the same things her mother had done to her. The marriage of Cindy's parents was stamped by sexual and other communicative difficulties. The mother, an enter-prising soul, felt she derived benefit from enrolling in a marriage course. But pregnancy with Cindy had brought new difficulties, and the father began rejecting his wife as not sufficiently attentive and tender toward him. She could not find a course to cover this problem, so she threw all her energies into obsessive infant care. She made visitors refrain from touching the baby, and remove their shoes at the front door when Cindy began to creep and crawl. The mother washed and sterilized Cindy's toys until she was exhausted, haunted by an indefinable uneasiness that some lethal contact might befall the child. At the end of the first year of Cindy's life, the mother set out to reform herself and to "stop all that overprotection." She felt she succeeded, but was aware of being insecure and overconcerned about Cindy's health right up to the time of the outbreak of Cindy's obsessive symptoms at the age of four years.

Indirect work with Cindy, through direct work with the mother, was associated with Cindy's symptomatic improvement even as Cindy accommodated to the presence of the new baby. The psychiatrist hoped the mother's own obsessive character would derive surer help from psychotherapy than from the courses and projects she had relied on in the past.

Child #5
JOYCE Q

Joyce was an asthmatic girl seven and a half years old when she was referred for the sudden appearance of an exhausting onrush of compulsions and obsessions. Joyce had her first attack of asthma at age one and, thereafter, had become frightened whenever she was separated from her mother. In kindergarten her mother had been required to stay full-time for a week and for part of the day thereafter.

The 49-year-old mother was a twin who believed there was a mystical bond of identity and telepathy between herself and her twin sister. She found separations of all sorts difficult, but separation from her husband was the skeleton that haunted her closet most.

Joyce was the second of two children, and her 21-year-old brother was away at college. The family was rich, but the money was newly acquired and, apparently, had not brought much in the way of joy or liberation for the family. The father, owner of a mercantile chain, worried constantly about his cardiac health.

Two months before her evaluation interview, Joyce had mumps, a bout of constipation (in a bowel-centered household), and then a severe attack of asthma. Death of two relatives occurred next, and Joyce refused to attend school. During the week before she was first seen she had developed a full-blown handwashing and doubting compulsion, and had begun having nightmares about snakes and alligators. She had been a rather lonely child theretofore, but then she became totally withdrawn, spending her days in anguish or brooding. The acute compulsive picture eased considerably as soon as it became clear that Joyce was bothered by her feelings that she was unclean after touching her dog's "tee tee." She had developed the obsession that she not only had done some grievous wrong but also had somehow gotten "tee tee" on her hands, and this could not be washed away. The imagined soiling of her hands accounted for her refusal to eat, and, consequently, a recent weight loss. She feared that all food she touched immediately became blanketed in "tee tee" from the dog's genital.

Joyce had an underlying obsessive character that was not modified during the brief psychiatric intervention over five sessions. Nourished in a hostile dependency with a mother who, as a therapist expressed it, sent "messages of unnaturalness, of neglect and of rejection," Joyce was an obsessive child whether she did or did not have a handwashing compulsion. Born when her parents were nearly 42, Joyce did not revive an empty marriage. Her negative reaction to all parental guidance; her defiance, anger, coldness, and narcissism; and her sexual preoccupation, her shift from omnipotence to helplessness and from goodness to badness, right to wrong—all reflected a young girl's long experience in obsessive patterns.

Child #6
MARIE N

When Marie was first seen she was a tiny 10-year-old fifth grader whose presenting problems included emotional immaturity, poor peer adjustment, constant worry over her problems, extreme compulsivity, and constant conflict with her mother.

Marie proved to be a severely obsessive compulsive little girl. She was a rigid perfectionist, showing great disappointment if, for school work, she received an "excellent" rather than an "excellent plus." She was stubborn, demanding, bossy, and extremely rivalrous with her six-year-old sister. Constantly concerned with exactness and order, she had become a compulsive clock watcher. She would berate her mother if breakfast was not on the table the instant she was ready to eat.

Marie showed no feeling for her friends, but she soon became surprisingly open in therapy. She reported having power struggles with her father over small things, for example, who would close her bedroom door when she went to bed.

All of these power and perfection problems dated from the

birth of her sister. That event had been accompanied by the onset of severe constipation in Marie. When a proctologist was consulted, he prescribed a special diet and Fleet's enemas. After six months, the crisis had eased although Marie continued to have difficulty in moving her bowels. Following her sister's birth, Marie had also developed a routine of falling out of chairs onto her head in order to get attention. The strategy worked. The practice disappeared fairly soon, but Marie continued to be demanding and selfish.

Marie's mother was a warm, friendly person who became easily upset and was often depressed. She summed up her daughter's problems in the unflattering statement, "She's just like her father." This seemed to be only too accurate, for the father was extremely cold and compulsive. He unflaggingly suppressed all feelings and anxiety. In the midst of situations that would normally provoke fury, he responded with an unflinching smile—a trick he purportedly learned in a "self-improvement" course. He really believed that he could undo the effects of any aggressive speech by smiling. Rather than discuss his feelings, he elaborately depersonalized discussions in terms of "what behavioral science research indicates." Social work with him and his wife rarely progressed beyond the sociological characteristics of the lower middle class or the *abstract* psychology of human development, normal and abnormal. He was rigidly compulsive about order and timing, and minutely attentive to his bowel movements, for which he had purchased a veritable pharmacy of laxatives, and on which he was wont to discourse at length. He felt a need to prove himself intellectually superior to all around him and his superciliousness in therapy made communication most difficult. All marital problems were attributed to his wife, and Marie's difficulties were ascribed to anxiety about her diminutive stature, completely normal in view of both her parents' small size and stature.

Marie's problems seemed to be related to the total lack of communication and the completely unexpressed anxiety and hostility associated with her rigid, compulsive home atmosphere. Insecurities all around became heightened as her parents' marriage steadily crumbled. Marie was unable to obtain any emotional support from her father and she was involved in a tenuous relationship with her depressed mother, not to mention being the recipient of the hostility her mother was unable to express to the father. Faced as she was with parents who projected all blame for her problems onto her small stature, Marie adopted her father's defense of rigid overcontrol instead of her mother's pattern of in-turned anger.

Child #7
MINA C

This girl, whose tenth birthday occurred on the date of her second psychiatric interview, was fourth in a sibling group of five. Her father, age 49, had inherited considerable wealth and also worked as a biomedical scientist, in research and teaching. Her mother, 43 years old, was depressed and had experienced longterm psychotherapy for neurotic and character problems. Mina herself had had a sudden onset, just as she was turning eight years old, of rather exhausting (for her) and disquieting (for others) obsessions and compulsions.

Some of the things Mina reported were rather odd, but nobody considered her psychotic. She shook everything she encountered, large or small, to see if it was hollow or unstable—she hoped for solidity and stability, but even if she knew that a wall or table was unmovable she tried to shake it. She felt compelled to test her environment. She confessed minor wrongdoing endlessly, she said, and gave as examples of this her telling the maid (who toilet trained her) each time she set foot on the floor with only her socks on, or whenever she sat or lay on her father's bed. She was compelled to blow kisses to her toys to prevent their coming alive and either doing her harm or being killed by "someone." Moreover, she said, "If I don't kiss my toys goodnight I feel they'll resent my not giving them any love or attention." Her own craving for real love was almost transparently obvious. She felt driven to lay dresses upside down across chair backs. She also had counting rituals, particularly with light switches: "I have to count two not to go over and flip the switch over my sister's bed. Sometimes I feel guilty anyway, so I count to five, then five and a half, and then one, I do it up to 25. I try hard to make it odd so I can stop sooner. If it's even I have to keep it up and keep it up." Utilizing her verbal IQ of 131, she stated, "My brain says, 'Do it, or you'll have a guilty feeling.'" Mina was well-motivated to get help "in my difficulties—those things I have to do."

She was seen only three times before her parents moved to another part of the country. The mother reported an improvement that was almost magical if true, after only two sessions with the psychiatrist. The girl herself attested to a rapid improvement— meaning great symptomatic relief—after only one session with the psychiatrist, saying she felt good talking to someone who understood how she felt about her obsessions and compulsions which she called "difficulties," her friends, her hated little brother, her asthma, her constipation and bowel preoccupation, her sexual interests and her dreams of spiders. To quote her, "This week I've been able to do my difficulties in an easier way. You know what they are all about, and that makes it a lot easier." Indeed she became more spontaneous, and laughed when at the family table, delighting her parents who had seen her as only somber and unhappy for many months.

Child #8
PATTY S

Patty was a dark-haired, dark-eyed little eight-year-old, "cute in the way Latin children are," brought for consultation by her parents because she sucked her thumb, became upset very easily and was quite jealous of her siblings, a brother aged ten years and a sister aged seven. These problems had existed as long as her parents could remember.

Patty's parents were quiet, restricted people, apparently desirous of relating to each other but frightened to communicate directly. This general inability to communicate, combined with a lack of confidence, showed up in their interviews with the social worker. Their sadness, anger, and guilt over Patty were revealed as an undercurrent by silence and facial expression. Significantly, their relatives had impressed upon them that they had spoiled their son, the oldest child. Hence, in their attempt to do better the second time around, it appeared to them that they had only failed, over-reacting, being overly strict and demanding—hence, Patty's problems.

Patty was quiet, compulsive and meticulous, usually wearing her school uniform. She spoke in an immature, infantile fashion around her parents. She spent a great deal of time talking to the therapist about her religion and her private religious ritual. She appeared to have serious problems in over-control of unpleasant impulses. Her self evaluation was uncomplimentary despite high intellectual ability and superior school performance. She tended to confuse a punitive morality with her angry feelings. Her inability to please her parents satisfactorily gave her a sense of inadequacy and an inability to accept herself as ever doing anything very well. Her parents apparently had brought this on by their determination not to spoil Patty and their inability to communicate with her effectively or affectionately.

Patty in turn was extremely rivalrous of her siblings. She obsessed over her relationship with her mother and constantly tried to prove herself responsible and trustworthy. She felt lonely, insecure in unfamiliar situations, particularly social ones; she felt constantly threatened by her own unpleasant impulses. Patty felt she could not exert initiative without causing harm to, or losing the favor of, her parents. She felt extremely vulnerable and imperfect in respect to her self-image. Consequently, when she was able Patty took advantage of her high intelligence and imagination to structure her world in an artificial, even "bizarre" fashion (revealed particularly in her views of a punitive morality). Related defenses included her compulsive attention to small detail and her employment of reaction formation reflected in her overly ladylike front and her overly affectionate, ingratiating remarks about parents and friends. Patty tended to withdraw, particularly in encounters with peers, and to regress (hence her infantile behavior) in relations with her own family.

Child #9
WENDY C

Wendy was an attractive 10-year-old fifth grader brought in because she had an obsessive fear that she or her mother were going to die of some incurable disease. She felt sick all the time, suffered terrible nightmares and had a number of rituals, e.g., touching a table several times with a glass before finally setting it down, closing doors repeatedly, writing over her "r's" 15 times, and feeling a "thing" spinning in her head and always having to force it to go in the opposite direction. These were matched by a great number of phobic manifestations. According to her parents this symptomatic picture started in the second grade but only burst forth in severe proportions six months prior to the referral. The onset coincided with the death of one of her brother's playmates, whose funeral she had attended. Very quickly she developed a rash, fever, dizzy spells, rapid heartbeat, and abdominal and chest pains. She had two abscessed teeth removed and then mild scoliosis was diagnosed, but it was concluded that her illness was not essentially somatic in origin.

Only a very superficial acquaintance with Wendy's family led to a conclusion of deep pathology. Her father was a conservative man who tended to relate superficially, appeared quite anxious, and frequently covered up his true feelings with a joke. He tended either to deny Wendy's problems as nothing more than "a stage she's going through," or to blame his wife. Wendy's mother was a neat, very proper and polite woman who immediately belied her calm façade by becoming extremely angry with a secretary concerning clinic registration. In interview, the mother was a compulsive talker, often with inappropriate affect; she showed loosening of associations, severe separation anxiety, ambivalence, and continual projection, denial, and distortion of information which made anything she said rather unreliable. She had one brother (of 11 siblings) who was a paranoid schizophrenic. Wendy's family included a 17-year-old sister who showed some of Wendy's symptoms and experienced frequent depression, and a 15-year-old brain-damaged brother near psychosis.

Neither of Wendy's parents had been close to anyone during their own childhood. Her father thus was unable to relate well or to show feelings and this was a primary source of her mother's resentment. In part this was his own compulsive style and in part it was a way of handling his wife's and Wendy's pathology. His wife showed a compulsion to see herself as the perfect wife and mother and to feel intensely needed; and in trying to reach out to the members of her family while satisfying these needs, she had formed hostile dependency relationships. Family pathology seemed to have developed to accommodate this and to handle Wendy's resultant phobic fears and enormous anxiety. Her death obsession was, apparently, an extension of her mother's separation anxiety. Wendy also suffered from acute anxiety about sex, in no small part a consequence of her having been sexually molested by a 12-year-old when she was three.

The development of Wendy's compulsive ritualization had threatened the entire family's equilibrium to such an extent the mother appeared with her for treatment. It seemed that Wendy's rituals were her way of expressing hostility to her mother. Her mother's response was, "Wendy drives everyone crazy with her rituals. I have to shut myself in a vacuum to keep my sanity."

During therapy Wendy was compulsive and perfectionistic, possessed of an overbearing superego, incredibly anxious to please but characterized by a dismal self-concept, absolutely intent on denying her sexuality, and fearful of a nebulous impending doom, whether from threats from without or the threat of being overwhelmed by her own emotion. It was concluded that she had developed a full-blown obsessive-compulsive neurosis.

Child #10
WINNIE A

With a father 44 years old and a mother aged 40, Winnie was 11 1/2 years old when she was referred for psychiatric evaluation at a clinic almost 200 miles from home. Her major problem, as her parents saw it, was that she was "out of it" so much of the time—extremely withdrawn, verbally and motorically hypoactive, and ritualistic in a plodding, unhappy way. If she did become engaged, they said, it was with tearfulness and great displays of anxiety. Both parents and Winnie's eight-year-old twin sibs characterized her as staying by herself but easily upset. When she got upset, she wrung her hands and jumped up and down on tiptoe.

The parents place the onset of Winnie's shyness at age three when her twin sibs, a brother and a sister, were born and she underwent a tonsillectomy. This shy withdrawal remained so pervasive that in kindergarten she entered into psychotherapy. After several years and treatment at two clinics, she was discharged as improved. When she was nine years old, Winnie was "caught" masturbating in class, and the teacher arranged a consultation at one of the clinics where the family had been seen earlier. The father refused to keep any appointments made at that clinic. In the sixth grade at school when she was evaluated, Winnie read below grade level but made superior grades in spelling. Her preference seemed to be for structured tasks calling for memorization. She was fearful of failing at school, and she was extremely sensitive to teasing by her compeers. She was teased a lot, and was a friendless and lonely preadolescent.

Winnie appeared slightly obese and pubescent. She was severely inhibited in many ways. Her walk was stiff with her arms hanging rigidly at her side. Psychomotor retardation was present. She sat tense and still throughout the psychiatric interviews with little change in facial expression. Her responses were brief and colorless. Agreeing with anything the doctor said, she showed no affect. She did, however, disclaim being unhappy, when the doctor said he thought she was unhappy. Although she had taken ballet for four years, she went rigidly through the motions, having acquired no gracefulness of movement.

Winnie was seen three times, as were her parents. A diagnosis of obsessive-compulsive neurosis was arrived at, with schizophrenia considered unlikely. A facility for more hopeful, continued psychotherapy was located in a community much nearer the parental home. Parents and Winnie were referred there and the psychotherapy of her obsessional neurosis continued at least for several months, it was learned on followup.

Child #11
ALEX J

Alex was a 15-year-old junior high student, the younger of two male siblings. His brother, aged 22, was a college student.

The list of presenting complaints in Alex's case was virtually endless: "frequently angry, wets bed, soils himself, has sudden rages, is depressed, has trouble learning, sucks thumb, untidy, lies, bites his fingernails and toenails, steals from other members of the family, won't go to school, hits parents, etc." He was diagnosed as suffering from school phobia and obsessive-compulsive neurosis.

The primary source of Alex's problems was two-fold. First, health problems abounded. He was born without a rectum and immediate neonatal surgery resulted in the deletion of any sphincter muscles and of the function of his colon. Consequently, he could only accomplish elimination by enema and he was obliged to take medication to combat fecal impaction and intestinal infection. He had been hospitalized twice for two-week periods for followup examinations concerning this defect. In addition, prolonged hospitalizations had been required for recurrent kidney infections and an abscessed appendix. It appeared that he might require a colostomy in the near future, and he had received continuing medical treatment for an inflamed testicle. Not surprisingly, he had great anxiety about his physical condition, anxiety which he attempted to hide with a breezy, worry-free attitude. He had substantial problems from his inferior self-image, and he was worried about his ability to deal with, and gain the respect of, his peers. His problems in self-concept were made more pronounced by the fact that his father was a minister, a circumstance which caused Alex to feel obliged to be a "goody-goody." The onset of adolescence only exacerbated all these difficulties.

The second major source of anxiety was his mother. Two years previously she had had a radical mastectomy with subsequent recurrence and presumably successful radiation treatment. In the midst of this, she had a complete emotional collapse—reportedly, a "depressive reaction in a schizoid personality." Alex had observed her steady deterioration, was very anxious about her, and entertained strong guilt feelings because he resented her deterioration and concomitant over-protective attitude to him, and also imagined that he had contributed to her condition through his constant physical problems. This anxiety-laden relationship, combined with Alex's peer problems, was also at the bottom of his school phobia. Obsessive fears of death, both his own and his mother's, added to the general high anxiety, which Alex attempted to control primarily through a compulsive perfectionism, but also through regression, denial, displacement, isolation of affect, and intellectualization. At times, his anxiety burst forth, uncontrolled, in rages. That Alex's difficulty in accepting his own and his mother's problems was not greater can probably be attributed to his high intelligence and to the very strong supportive role his father played in the family. Obsessional defenses did, indeed, seem to spare him—as long as they worked—from a worse fate still.

Child #12
ALFRED Y

Alfred was 12 years old, a red-haired lad, referred by a general practitioner. He had experienced the acute onset of urinary frequency, difficulty in swallowing, and a set of "bizarre" rituals. He incessantly questioned his mother about goodness and badness: "Is it a sin to close my eyes while I sleep? Is it a sin to take my socks off this way . . . to strain to pee . . . to pass gas . . . to step on small rugs? Is it a sin to look at a girl's legs? If I pray for forgiveness and don't believe, is that an unforgivable sin?" He had frequent spells of crying, and sometimes seemed tortured and agitated. He would pace up and down. Part of the time that he was awake he would hold onto his mother's skirt or hand, asking questions about God, heaven, hell, and sin. When he was not restless, he sat mutely brooding . . . "in a deep study," as his mother said. He went to the bathroom to urinate as frequently as every three or four minutes, and between trips he would return to the toilet to inspect it, to mop the floor, and to wash his hands. His mother observed that he was constantly straightening his trousers and picking at his genitals. At times, he assumed a prayerful attitude and said he felt he must keep praying and reading the Bible. His referral was precipitated by his mother's inability to tolerate his questioning and atypical behavior; she felt that unless Alfred changed *she* would suffer a breakdown.

Alfred's parents were separated. His illness coincided with his resumption of school attendance, following his return from a summer spent with his elderly alcoholic father. During school terms Alfred lived with his mother in a small apartment in a lower class, blighted area of a southeastern city. He shared his mother's bed, and his mother bathed him and selected his daily wardrobe. He was not permitted to associate with "roughneck boys" in the neighborhood because of their delinquent behavior, shocking vulgarity of speech, and their untidiness and boisterousness (as appraised by his mother). He rarely played with girls, and only occasionally with boys, mostly five or six years younger than himself. He joined a fundamentalist Protestant church the year before his psychiatric referral and attended four church services weekly. He was in seventh grade and had made excellent grades, devoting from two to four hours nightly to academic preparation. Since his illness, however, his study had become unproductive, and he had begun to experience some academic failure.

Living circumstances were economically marginal, but Alfred had never worked or done anything to earn money. Indeed, when staying with his father (in whose bed he also slept) during the summers, and living at this time in his half-brother's household where there were seven children, only Alfred, like the preschool children, was exempt from farm work. With his father during the preceding summer he had spoken of becoming a preacher. This coincided, as therapy later uncovered, with his masturbation to orgasm and some interpersonal sex play which aroused great guilt.

His mother was in her fifth decade when Alfred was born, her second marriage, and Alfred was her eighth child. She had deserted her first husband and their seven children. She was reared in extreme rural poverty, the third of eight children, and received six years of schooling. She was painfully shy, and spent her childhood and youth terrified of her stern father, who died as an old man in a mental hospital.

Alfred's father had also grown up in an impoverished rural Southern family, but his was a family with relatively higher esteem in the community. The father was regarded as a highly intelligent if uneducated man who had been industrious and frugal in economic matters, but he was penurious with regard to his second wife, Alfred's mother. Only Alfred was the recipient of his generosity, and this was spasmodic in occurrence. With his first wife, the father had been happy, and had three children. She died, and many years elapsed before he remarried. Hence, there were 10 half brothers and sisters who heaped favors upon Alfred, the product of their respective parents' advanced years. In some ways Alfred had 12 parents who were involved in his life.

Alfred's parents were divorced when Alfred was five years old and remarried when he was eight. Their final separation took place the following year. Alfred was always surrounded by parental conflict, and his symptoms at the age of 12 were reminiscent of earlier restless and anxious behavior during times of parental discord and violence. Symptoms, at the time treatment commenced, often reflected the waxing and waning of his parents' continuing battles. Alfred was deserted by his mother for several days at age four, several months at age five, and from age six to eight lived with his mother alone. With the remarriage of his parents, the nuclear family was again together, but the father had now become alcoholic and abusive, chronically accusing the mother of sexual infidelity.

Some further developmental data are notable. Alfred underwent an operation for pyloric stenosis when 21 days old and continued with colic ("stomach spasms") until he was nine months old. The surgeon predicted that Alfred might have *early* feeding problems, but the mother remained concerned with his dietary habits and gastrointestinal complaints indefinitely. He had very strong food preferences and aversions.

Alfred had begun speech with single words at nine months and remained verbal throughout childhood. At nine months he had become so restless and energetic that his mother took him to a pediatrician who suspected intestinal worms, but tests did not confirm this. Alfred walked at age 12 to 13 months and was toilet trained easily and thoroughly beginning at 18 months. He had long red curls, shoulder length, until he was four and a half years old, when his mother consented to having his hair cut. He was always extremely neat and tidy, refrained from "dirty talk," and was ardently moral in his verbalizations. He was companionless and, in fact, unable to play with children even when he was as old as seven years. "He didn't know what to do with children when he started school," his mother said. He was persistently critical of other children's acts and speech, and as far along as age nine he resolutely refused to play with a boy who had said "fuck." Alfred showed no sexual behavior, nor asked any questions about sexual matters, before his illness at 12 years of age. But lifelong, his mother said, he grasped at his penis as though it hurt or disturbed him, and at nine months "had played with his privates."

Alfred was in a societal, interpersonal and intrapsychic bind. He could only be treated once a week for a half-hour. His therapy (50 hours extending over 27 months) was successful in removing his obsessional and compulsive symptoms, and even in some character alteration.

Child #13
ARNIE T

Arnie was an 11-year-old fifth grader. He lived with a younger brother, eight and one-half years old, and with both parents. He was referred to child psychiatry because of facial and voice mannerisms—tics, trouble getting to sleep, problems in school and intermittent problems in getting along with his brother and with peers. The tic, which had begun two months previously, was the most significant factor serving as his "admission ticket."

When we first saw Arnie he appeared as an attractive, freckle-faced, sandy-haired lad who was very intelligent and quite dramatic in his communications. He very quickly demonstrated his determination to control the interview by means of an amazing verbosity and a compulsive attention to detail. He was unwilling to reveal too much of himself, but readily showed his tic which at that time consisted of head jerking, protrusion of the tongue, and a bark.

Both of Arnie's parents were personable, intelligent, psychologi-
cally-minded people concerned with their own personal growth
and their children's emotional health and achievements. Significantly, though, they were both "only" children who had grown to
be tense and driving, pushing themselves and concomitantly setting up an atmosphere of high achievement for their children.
Moreover, Arnie's mother had been reared as the protected, only
daughter of highly conservative parents. She had determined to
give her children that freedom which she had never enjoyed. Unfortunately, she was not able to translate this rebellion against her
own upbringing into effective childrearing practices—so she tended
to be inconsistent by giving choices too soon, expecting too much,
and, in general, responding with uncertainty. Arnie apparently was
not able to hold up under this kind of stress and controlled his
anxiety with compulsive verbosity and attention to detail. Fortunately, his parents were well aware of Arnie's problems, though at
times they intellectualized to the extent that they sounded more
like two verbose but not first-rate therapists than like parents.

Arnie's life had thus been oriented toward his most unnerving
head jerk, tongue protrusion and bark. This was a display of anger
and naysaying for all to see, and persisted until, through therapy,
other happier ways were found for him to live within his world,
seeing himself as rightly dependent upon parents who would protect him lovingly as long as he needed care and protection.

Child #14
BILLY J

Billy was a timid, physically frail-looking, freckle-faced 11-year-
old, who was in the fifth grade. He was brought for psychiatric
evaluation because of a long history of serious difficulty in school.
In fact, his parents were not interested in *treatment* for the youngster but only in our opinion as to whether or not he was educable.

Billy's school problems, a mixture of inability to settle down
and concentrate on his work and impulsive mischief, indeed
bordered on the riotous. He was an obsessive whose outer appearance was of an antisocial child. Notes made by his teacher

over a three-month period included: ". . . he sneaked out of the room and [another teacher] saw him crawling on his hands and knees past the windows . . . Billy got out of his seat, went outside, found a stick and a dog's fecal material which he put on the stick. He returned to the room and tried to poke children in the room with the dirty stick. When they told him to sit down 'or else,' he sat in his seat and licked the stick . . . quiet day! In lunchroom he emptied mustard containers in his hands, spread the mustard all over his face and made believe it was shaving cream. Used his hands to 'shave' and then wiped them on his pants. What a mess . . . tripped two children . . . spit at the windows . . . Billy *knows* a rattlesnake when he sees one . . . found a nest of baby rattlers . . . waited until a group of six or seven girls got near him and then quickly picked up a rattler by the tail and deliberately threw it into the group of girls . . . threatened to stab a child with the *sharp end* of a compass . . . Today Billy started barking . . ."

Billy had a long history of stealing. He had had severe tantrums for the past year and could not tolerate his two sisters (both younger) to the extent that his hateful, sadistic behavior towards them was being extended to include the girls at school. Actually, Billy was showing evidence of a mixed neurotic picture: both acting out impulsively and behaving compulsively.

His troubles centered on his relationship with females. His father, a passive obsessively-inclined man, spent very little time at home and apparently acted almost solely in a punitive capacity with his son. Billy's mother was a fairly dynamic and capable, though nervous, woman who did substitute teaching, led a Brownie troop, sewed, swam, played golf and attended numerous night courses, but felt very insecure in her role as a mother. She tended to set high standards of academic achievement for her children but in Billy's case she gave up, becoming rejecting and non-supportive.

Billy strove for masculinity. The absence of any close human relationships and of a father to serve as a model made his development in this respect highly problematic. He constantly tried to assure himself of his mother's love; this pursuit extended to his relationships with his teachers. The interaction of these two problem areas (with anal problems, such as coprophilia, hoarding, sadism, and stealing, and the compulsive need to manipulate his environment to control his anxiety) largely explained Billy's grotesque behavior and his vicious attitude towards women. Unfortunately, his parents were not able to see his problems as being amenable to psychotherapy. They abruptly terminated therapy after only six meetings.

Child #15
BOB J

Bob, 10 years old at the time of his referral, was brought in because of underachieving in school, hyperactivity, multiple facial and vocal tics, an exaggerated fantasy world with occasionally tenuous contact with reality, and an obsession with death and injury to self, parents, and doctors. He had been diagnosed as borderline schizophrenic in need of residential treatment before he was referred to our outpatient clinic.

Bob had been adopted at the age of four days, an event for which his parents had waited eight years. He was bottle-fed milk until it was determined that his severe diarrhea resulted from milk allergy. Soy product was used until he was 18 months old and could handle a normal diet. This early experience apparently had a lasting impact in that Bob tended to hold back until the last minute when in need of moving his bowels and at times soiled himself or his bed even at 10 years of age. Throughout his life, he had had a chronic respiratory disease and was seldom without a runny nose. He also suffered from ichthyosis.

The issue of adoption appeared to have been handled relatively well by Bob's parents although he still entertained some separation anxiety and a desire to return to his idealized true mother.

Bob proved to be superior in intelligence (IQ-130) and for this reason he was always "one step ahead" of his parents. The parents, and particularly his father, were overly devoted to him and tended to confuse a negligent permissiveness with love. They experienced great difficulty in exchange of tender feelings, and there appeared to be no working through of negative feelings at all. Bob's father, with an obsessive personality, dwelt constantly on his own impending death (he was 60), on the degeneration and stagnation of his late life, and the decline in his family's status. The parents' marital relationship was poor and, coupled with fear of, and for, Bob, had led them to great inconsistency in discipline. Behind closed doors they had engaged in much thrashing out of issues. The origin of Bob's problems was projected by them onto the school, and Bob fulfilled their expectations by a rapid onset of school problems.

Between parental ambivalence, his own chronic somatic problems, and his adoption, Bob had a very poor self-concept and a sense of great insecurity. Overlaid on this was enormous anxiety over any cognizance of sexual and aggressive material. In defending against this, Bob appeared driven. He talked incessantly, always shifting his position, changing subjects, apparently in an effort to stave off a real relationship and always parrying any intrusion into his own feelings. In fact, he seemed unaware of his own feelings until they threatened to overwhelm him. His compulsive manner and his ritualized redoing of things not done perfectly the first time, apparently a main source of his difficulty in school, were only partially successful in enabling him to cope with his enormous anxiety. He showed tics. He lived much of the time in a grandiose fantasy world, at times showing loosening of associations, but in general making a neurotic, obsessive adaptation.

Child #16
BRYAN S

Bryan was an unhappy 12-year-old referred for psychiatric evaluation because he had symptoms of obsessive-compulsive neurosis. The neurotic symptoms began at age nine years with ritualistic hand washing and prominent touching and avoidance compulsions. A 25 percent hearing loss, secondary to a virus infection during infancy, had adversely affected his development. Personality traits observed in Bryan included indifference to things he should do combined with excessive worry about underachievement; temper outbursts; dawdling; and lack of self-confidence.

From the beginning, it was obvious that Bryan's family environment was deeply pathological. Not only were marital relations pernicious but Bryan's father was in need of, and soon got involved in, individual psychiatric treatment. The initial psychiatric interview with the parents seemed to establish the tone of their relationship, as a disagreement quickly developed. The parents' characteristic manner was summed up in his "May I speak now?" and her "Are you finished?" The general mood at home was cold, critical, cautious, and distrustful—over-controlling alternating with acting out.

Bryan's mother appeared to be a very touchy and suspicious woman. In collateral treatment it became obvious she was sexually maladjusted and prone to using sex as a device for manipulating men. She was subject to depression and tended to rely on obsessive-compulsive mechanisms. Her MMPI profile suggested that she obtained vicarious gratification by having one or more of her children act out her hostile impulses. Shy, indecisive, and aloof, she had difficulty in all of her social relationships.

Bryan's father appeared to be very agitated and disturbed. In contrast to his wife, he was active and had a strong need to be with people. He seemed to be psychosexually passive and much less masculine than the typical (though unsuccessful) businessman he presented himself to be. He used repression and conversion as mainline defenses, and, while his reality contact was not badly impaired, he did tend to see himself as different and estranged from people. He had chalked up a history of failures in business and one unsuccessful campaign for public office, all of which had left his family with substantial indebtedness. As matters worsened, he became an alcoholic and at the time of his son's referral he was also in the habit of using drugs ill-advisedly.

Bryan was caught in the middle. He was the recipient of hostile feelings that his mother was unable to express toward his father, hostility engendered by years of the father's failure, drinking, and drugs. Bryan had to cope with parents who were in many ways psychical opposites, and who were both caught facing middle age with a sense of hopelessness, failure, and despair. The parents projected much of the blame for their warring onto Bryan. He recognized the preferential treatment accorded his younger brother who reportedly was normal in every respect. To boot, Bryan was nearly overwhelmed by his developing sexuality, masturbation guilt, and a pathological Oedipal conflict.

Faced with enormous anxiety and unable, because of his mother, to communicate significant feelings directly, Bryan had to rely on negativism, passive obstructionism, and symbolic expression. He used defenses of denial, projection, and avoidance, all in the style of his mother. The result was a severely obsessive-compulsive youngster, plagued with obsessions of death or injury to family members and enacting a variety of compulsive rituals.

Child #17
BURT A

Burt was a nine-year-old fourth grader referred by the family pediatrician because of daily fighting with peers, conflict with his stepfather and stepbrother, and threatened suicide. Burt himself concluded that he was coming in because of "my suicide attempt and ... just going crazy."

Burt was attractive, bright and verbal, very eager to please and to impress others with his politeness and maturity. He willingly produced much verbal material about his problems and conflicts, all the while showing obvious anxiety, manifested in rapid speech and motor activity and occasional trips to the bathroom. Sometimes, he dealt with his discomfort through intellectualization or dramatization, by spinning classic tales of super-heroes winning out over vampires and monsters.

Burt's mother seemed concerned and motivated to help him. She demonstrated some understanding of the family's problems. Her husband was a coldly aloof young man, in stiff control of himself. He was of the opinion that the only way to deal with Burt was through force. Burt's mother, whose background was filled with family tragedy, had married Burt's biological father and divorced him before the child was born. Until five years later, when she had remarried, she and her son had lived with her grandparents. The second marriage brought with it a 20-month-old stepbrother for Burt.

When Burt came for psychiatric services, his parents were having substantial marital difficulty and his mother was devoting herself especially to working things out with her husband. This, combined with her husband's view of Burt and his naturally cold manner, meant that Burt received little or no attention or love—in fact, he was placed in direct competition with his stepfather and step-brother for his mother's love. He found himself in a "can't win" situation. His tenuous role in the family was exemplified by an incident in which he was sent to wait in the car while his parents tried to decide whether they would separate. Burt reported "I sat there two hours and it was dark and cold, and finally I got brave enough to sneak back into the house. Mama was crying, and they forgot all about me. Sometimes they forget I even live there."

Burt felt that he was unloveable and that for that his first father had left him as his second father was about to do. He found it impossible to please his mother. The resulting anger led to anxiety and guilt and on occasion to an overriding sadness or depression. All in all, he felt insignificant, worthless, and inadequate. He attempted to deal with his situation and its attendant anxiety through intellectualization (at which, with his high intelligence, he was quite good) and through a compulsive perfectionism—a constant seeking to overachieve. This latter was exemplified in the test situation. When Burt was asked to draw a person, he complied by portraying a whole family. Compulsiveness was accompanied by an insatiable desire for praise which Burt supplied for himself if it was not forthcoming from others. Failures in achievement only reinforced his already low self-concept.

Child #18
CARL D

Carl was an eight-year-old whose chief complaints were nervousness, jitteriness, talkativeness, poor school work, and, at times, silly behavior. Though this problem had been quite evident in the previous three or four months, he had always been a nervous child and had had many nightmares. He rocked, moved around constantly, and could barely sit still to finish a meal. This distractibility was such that the family physician started him on 50 milligrams of hydroxyzine hydrochloride ("atarax") daily, which helped to calm him down.

Carl's whole family seemed to be suffering from a great deal of unrest and anxiety. His father, with time's passage, had transformed an unhappy youth into a miserable adulthood. An intelligent, personable fellow, he had nonetheless experienced a long series of very bad deals with jobs. While unquestionably he must have shared some responsibility for things turning out as they did, he did appear to have been plagued with misfortune as a sort of "hard-luck Charlie." His relationship to the family was reasonably good and yet he sensed that things were not as they should be. He felt emotionally (and sexually) starved. He and his wife had attempted everything with Carl and were definitely at their wits' end. Because of all this, the father was depressed and discouraged. He tended to project family situations onto the outside world, which he then viewed as hostile and untrustworthy. He became frustrated with his inability to do anything about a world which was in a mess.

Carl's mother felt insecure and inadequate as a woman clearly unable to deal with or understand her family's problems. On the other hand, she tended to handle her anxiety through denial and repression, thus presenting herself as an aloof, not very warm person. This in turn fed neatly into her husband's pathology.

Carl probably sensed the air of discouragement and depression, even despair, in his family and this led to his feeling of basic insecurity. Another factor was an intense and anxious need of the parents to give their boys (Carl had two brothers, both younger) more than they themselves had had—a need so great as to be threatening to Carl. At the same time, the obsessive way Carl's parents had of dealing with their problems laid little basis for communication and exchange of real feeling between Carl and his parents. Of course, his own obsessive behavior only made this worse even though it did enable him to bind and place some of his anxiety. The diagnosis was of "anxiety neurosis with obsessive compulsive features."

Carl himself was incredibly talkative, relating a joke or an interesting (to him) event at every turn, always managing the discussion. He talked compulsively, constantly turning to an unrelated topic, jumping around and feebly trying to rationalize his silly motor behavior. He evidenced great anxiety about his own aggressiveness and hostility, devoting much time to talk of wars, violence, knives, guns and other deadly arms. He had, as a matter of fact, received a large supply of knives and guns as gifts from his father. His fear of sexuality was such that he denied seeing the sex organs on our dolls. Despite an above average intelligence, Carl's school performance was being hurt by his compulsive activity. Overall, his life was hurt by his compulsiveness interfering with free, intelligent choices.

Child #19
CECIL R

Cecil R, a 13-year-old boy, was referred for psychiatric consultation after neurological examination showed no physical defect except a possible slight impairment of hearing. His parents were primarily concerned with Cecil's problems at school, his "nervousness," and his incessant playing of war games. He had a history of hyperkinesis dating back to entering kindergarten, and, according to his parents, controlled at that time with medication.

He had been adopted when he was six weeks old, and lived with his adopted parents until he was two years old, when the wife deserted the family. The only child in the household, he continued to live with the father and a succession of housekeepers until the father remarried when Cecil was ten. Cecil's first adopted mother had made no attempt to see him and in fact never saw him again.

Cecil's hyperkinesis and behavior problems became quite apparent after his new foster mother had borne two children: one 18 months old (a boy) and the other two months old (a girl) when Cecil was referred for psychiatric evaluation.

Cecil's father said he was trying with little success to divert Cecil's conversation and interests from war games to space exploration. He said the only other things Cecil really liked were violent television programs. It was on the instigation of Cecil's new foster mother that first neurological and then psychiatric aid were sought and obtained.

Cecil knew he was adopted but knew nothing about his biological parents. He cried during his first psychiatric interview, saying he wanted to know more about them. His parents said he had first begun asking about his natural parents during his foster mother's first pregnancy.

Shortly before the psychiatric consultation, Cecil had been admonished by his school principal for turning around in class and hitting a boy on the mouth. That evening, the father said, Cecil cried and "came apart," saying that everyone "hates me and thinks I'm crazy."

Cecil was a thin, rather withdrawn, non-verbally oriented youngster who told the therapist his real problem was that, he, Cecil, had "two chemicals in his brain" and they "don't go together." He then declined further conversation on the subject.

In talking a little of dreams, Cecil said he had once "dreamed while I was awake" of a gigantic man, resembling Frankenstein's monster, standing "in my doorway." He said occasionally at night he will still hear heavy male footsteps in his home, but doesn't see anyone.

He seemed most interested in the history of wars and in playing war games. He said he didn't care for space exploration but was trying to like it because his father wanted him to. He shot darts "with vigor and delight" in the therapist's playroom and if given a choice would choose war games.

He invariably looked sad and depressed, and said he had only one friend. His parents said he refused to play with other children unless the others did exactly what he told them to do. Cecil said he wanted to grow up and be a general.

His IQ was in the Bright Normal range. Personality testing indicated he was very dependent upon his parents, but that they were seen as being emotionally remote and extremely demanding. In fantasy, he expressed strong feelings of aggression and anger.

It was noted in early therapy that Cecil, while not openly uncooperative or directly hostile, would behave in a passive-aggressive manner, reluctantly and begrudgingly performing simple tasks.

It was felt long term family therapy was in order because Cecil's feelings of inadequacy and anger were obviously intimately connected with his family relationships. It was also felt he had to learn more appropriate ways of handling aggression and expressing anger.

Child #20
CHESTER E

At age 12 1/2 years this lad had suffered a "breakdown" which, his parents believed, began to build up when he was from 10 1/2 years old back to nine years of age. Certainly, for at least six years (i.e., after his younger brother's birth) he had been odd in his behavior and had had the breakdown only two months before coming for psychiatric help. Chester's breakdown consisted of several things that severely upset his parents: ritualistic dressing and undressing, compulsive touching of doorknobs, refusal to sleep in a bed or in night clothes, saving of his urine and feces, destructiveness and angry obscene speech aimed at his parents, and fear of being "contaminated" by any food prepared by his mother.

His parents (affluent, intellectual, educated) wrote they hoped "that he can be brought to a point of understanding his problems sufficiently well so that, with the practice of proper self-discipline, and with a proper religious orientation, he can lead a successful and happy life."

Defiance dominated the clinical picture with Chester. He dated the onset of his sickness to the previous summer when his parents pressured him into going to a summer camp. At camp he became preoccupied with his underpants, believing they contained, on the right lateral aspect, a spot of poison placed there by his mother, but possibly with his father aiding and abetting mother's black magic act against him. He trusted his five years older sister and six years younger brother, although he had considerable contempt toward the brother. He felt that his mother was a fake and that she did not do enough loving (and babying) things for him; on the other hand, he saw her as domineering and aggressively malignant toward him. His picture of himself was also mixed. At times he was helpless and longed for a happy "innocent" childhood, but at other times he was omnipotent and grandiose, believing himself to have had royal origins and to be the adopted son of plebeian parents. At one point in psychotherapy he asserted that he was, in his secret heart, a barbarian warrior destined to kill off the civilized intruders who surrounded him. Naturalness was equated with murderous lust in his eyes. At times, though, he longed to retreat from civilization, not fighting it but living alone in the woods unbothered by all those people who objected to his "being an atheist and a Nazi."

Antisocial actions (including destruction of property and running away) and his school phobia added to his obsessiveness made his placement in a residential hospital setting imperative after one year of attempted outpatient care. The ultimate outcome was good despite his being adjudged as suffering from a borderline psychosis.

Child #21
CHUCK J

Chuck, a six-year-old chronologically ready for school, was a somewhat rigid, over-controlled little boy who found it very difficult to deal with or express any negative feelings. His parents brought him in because of temper tantrums. During these Chuck would scream, yell, and kick; he seemed out of contact, couldn't be talked to and, according to the parents, often required a shock (generally provided in the form of a spanking) to bring him "around."

Chuck had terrible nightmares almost every night and at times became sick with them. As we got to know the family, its members revealed themselves as almost a classic case: rejecting, compulsive parents generating an overwhelming anxiety in a youngster who then chooses the family style of coping by developing an obsessive compulsive personality structure.

Chuck's parents were young, attractive, personable, and productive people. Both did very well in college, and had been quite

involved in school politics. The father was class president in high
school for three years, and it was through continued political
activity in college that he met his future wife. They were married a
year before graduation, and their marriage appeared to be a highly
successful and happy one. Despite this, the two of them appeared
rigid and contained. Chuck's mother, in particular, having had a
restricted and unhappy childhood, was quite hampered in her expression of feeling and affection. Evidently Chuck's father had
been instrumental in penetrating her defense sufficiently for them
to achieve a happy affective and sexual relationship. On the other
hand, he depended on his wife as the more stable "straight" member of the family.

Of great significance to the compulsive nature of Chuck's parents was their strong involvement with a fundamentalist religion.
Both grew up along the restrictive lines of this faith. They had
been heavily involved with church activities in high school and
college, and indeed Chuck's father had become a leader in a loose-
ly-structured Protestant denomination.

Into this environment Chuck was born as an unplanned and
unwanted child. Not only was he emotionally rejected, but also
for the first three years of his life he was cared for by a nurse and
by friends of the family, while his parents completed their education. At age three and one-half, Chuck had seen a sister born, and
recognized that *she* was definitely wanted and loved. The parents
knew they were rejecting, and they were very guilty over their
early treatment of Chuck. At times they were now overprotective
in compensation, and, in their about-face vacillations, literally unable to deal with him—to play with him, respond to him or love
him in a mutual relationship. His tantrums were to them a desperate conundrum, particularly as they required a quiet, well-
mannered little son for a public-minded father. The imagined
scene of Chuck blowing up in the middle of a church service
seemed to hover over them. On the other hand, Chuck was insecure, felt rejected, tried incredibly hard to please, to always be the
good little boy. The anxiety engendered by his failure to obtain
support from his parents threatened to overwhelm his rigidly compulsive personality structure.

It is of note that his rapid progress in therapy was accompanied by absolute joy on the part of the parents. They seemed to discover for the first time that Chuck was indeed a human being, a person to whom they could relate in a mutually supportive, loving fashion, and from whom they could derive much pride and happiness. As they came to understand Chuck they loved him more, and they found new dimensions of gratification in their family life.

Child #22
CROWN M

When he was referred to the child psychiatry facility, Crown was a 10-year-old boy who manifested "unhappiness, excessive worrying, excessive guilt, and a lack of friends." Neither his parents nor his minister were able to bring him any sizeable comfort.

A slender blond lad with an overly-serious facial expression, his parents proudly viewed him as being unusually honest and fairminded. He *was* moralistic in that he often questioned the rightness and wrongness of things people did. Nonetheless, he was highly sensitive to the slightest criticism of himself and refused to initiate any peer interaction on his own. He had no friends but liked outdoor life and loved horses. He tended to discredit his own capabilities; both his parents and his teachers saw that he needed frequent "ego bolstering."

During most of his psychotherapy sessions Crown maintained his early, blandly unhappy look, but eventually became openly sullen and antagonistic for a time. Still, his "preferred image" was of politeness. He had little spontaneity and no humor. Rigidity characterized his posturing as well as his defensive, stilted relating to other persons.

For his protection during the beginning of psychologic testing he kept up an aloof, uninvolved stance. On the Wechsler Intelligence Scale for Children (WISC) he obtained a verbal IQ of 124, performance IQ of 106 and full-scale IQ of 117. His test behavior showed a slowing attributable to perfectionism and feelings of imperfection. But he was able to think, to solve abstract problems and to discern (almost to the degree of overlearning) the why's and wherefore's of his middle-class Protestant world. Particularly with the Bender-Gestalt reproductions he showed how he was held back by his slowness, sadness, meticulousness, and compulsiveness. He labored for half an hour with the Bender test. On projective testing he showed responses that, by their sequence, indicated he used repression and denial straightway when afraid; then, if that did not help, he resorted to being constricted, compulsive, and highly intellectualized.

Much of his fantasy life and family life came out into the open during psychotherapy. Crown was the eldest of six children, with four younger sisters and a brother. When asked how it felt to have so many younger sibs, Crown answered with a characteristic stiltedness, "Sometimes it is difficult, because one has the advantage over the younger ones, and one must remember that." The mother, in her mid-thirties, was a professional turned housewife. The father, at 39, was a professional also. He was becoming very rich. The boy looked upon his mother as an unhappy, depressed, and emotionally deprived person. He viewed his father as being ungenuine about his feelings, pretending happy moods that he did not feel. The boy's guilt about his parents' unhappiness became conscious in spite of his great resistance to considering why he should feel responsible for parental unhappiness.

Crown saw his world as a place of coldness, filled with impossible demands, and generally unrewarding. He thought he could not trust his parents. The mother was viewed as a partner in an early infantile sadomasochistic relationship; the father was lifelong a hated, punitive figure. Crown had decided that being a boy is "being trouble." He became anxious about sexual lust and actions, and afraid of masculinity. He lived in fear of anger—from his parents and from within himself—and, in fact, almost any strong feelings set his formidable defenses into operation.

Although his parents detected that he was afraid of criticism and terrorized by possible failure, the father frequently "blew up" at Crown about the boy's passive defiance of him, lack of initiative, and need for more self-assertion! In one respect, the mother joined Crown: that is, in feeling that the child suffered from insufficient affection and approval. Both parents believed that, beginning in his kindergarten years, they had put too much pressure on him and had pushed him into an excessive maturity by "laying on" their high expectations. Surely at age 10 Crown still felt pressured, striving to please parents and teachers, and deriving only pain and suffering from school.

Crown's guilty ruminations about religion centered on his recurring thought that really there might not be a God. This thought, hideous to him, led him to extremes of guilt and depression, and mental efforts to rid himself of the intrusive notion. At no time, however, did the unhappy boy report any ritualistic acts.

Child #23
CYRIL T

Cyril was a "little genius," a child of the space age. He was 12 years old when he was brought for psychiatric evaluation and brief treatment in 1962 by his 46-year-old father, an "exact" scientist who had risen to a high post in the aerospace bureaucracy, and by his 40-year-old mother, a housewife. The presenting complaints offered by his parents were, "He is not accepted by other children and his school achievement is below capacity." Although Cyril had a verbal IQ of 130 and full-scale of 120, he was lackadaisacal about daily school work and underachieved. His older brother was more conformist and more pleasing to the parents than was Cyril, about whom the parents said: "He has his own ideas which he stubbornly defends, so much that he seems not to respect parental authority. He seeks too much to be with older people and to get their attention. He seems too bright for his own good. He is cruel to younger children, or at the very least he is bossy, so they don't like him. He seems to be in his own world some of the time." The older brother's alliance was with the mother, and Cyril was said to be "more like his father."

The parents had been both geographically and socially mobile, living with only superficial relationships as a result. A mental health professional said of Cyril's parents, "I predict they'll wake up one day and wonder what their life was all about." Cyril's

stilted conventionality, rectitude, and hyper-maturity made him
seem very much their son. His deepest wish, he claimed, was "to
have the best education of any man in the world."

As an illustration of his association-chain, Cyril was talking,
rather pedantically, when the electric lights in the psychiatrist's
office went dim:

> Oh, there's lightning outside! We were in *some* rainstorms in
> our camp. One time the lightning struck about a mile or a
> quarter mile away. I was swimming but I was the second one
> out. Not that I expected to look down and see my leg fried
> off or anything like that. I saw lightning strike the ocean last
> week and, where it hit, steam rose. A thing like that you can
> expect to boil a little water. My nails are dirty because I only
> clean them when I am bored and want something to do with
> my hands. Do you play chess? Let's play some time.

The therapist questioned his "strange jump from lightning to dirty
nails to chess." Cyril explained that he was a compulsive hand
washer after touching his penis, either "urinating or scratching."
This, he felt, explained the transition from the fear of lightning
damaging him, to masturbation, to water, to dirty nails. The therapist asked further about the jump from hands to chess, and Cyril
said he went from something bad about him (masturbation, fear of
punishment, love of "dirt and germs and things") to something
good (his skill as a chess player). Cyril had a long way to go in
taking life easily and abandoning his compulsive ways of operating.

During psychotherapy from June to November Cyril did loosen
up. He became more boyish. He made friends. He became less
defensive, sarcastic, and snobbish. A sense of humor replaced some
of his pedantry. His schoolwork improved when he went into
eighth grade. His own testimonial to the therapy was:

> I feel I have more friends than I did last summer. I'm in more
> group activities, and people are more friendly towards me. Of
> course, we have our fights some time. I think coming here
> helped me to get along better with people in general. I feel

more at ease now. Before, well, I'm at a loss for words—I was, inside of me, a little shy, maybe. I felt fine with grownups, but I couldn't do things with friends. Now I'd rather go out and do things with my gang. Too, schoolwork has improved. I work harder, and I'm less confused usually now about schoolwork.

Child #24
DANIEL D

Daniel was 14 1/2 years old when he was referred to child psychiatry at the University of Florida, bringing with him the diagnosis of a borderline schizophrenic. He had spent two years of his early life in a residential treatment center. Despite the referring child psychiatrist's opinion that inpatient treatment should be resumed, it was decided to make a trial of outpatient psychotherapy.

Daniel was a large, flabby, and ungainly adolescent male. He spoke in a high-pitched, girlish voice and sat stiffly picking at his facial acne and smelling his fingers. Physical examination, when he was hospitalized for a brief evaluation, indicated that puberty had been reached.

Daniel had a long history of psychopathology, and of intermittent psychotherapy after age seven, but his re-entry into psychiatric care was precipitated by increased tension, an exacerbation of compulsive behavior, and difficulty in sixth grade school work. His mother, a widow aged 57, was concerned about planning for his future and preoccupied about what might happen to Daniel in the event of her own death.

He was the only offspring of the mother aged 43 and father aged 56 at the time of Daniel's birth. Delivery was at term, achieved spontaneously after 13 hours of labor. The mother had enjoyed the pregnancy, her first and only conception. She was a well-educated and graceful woman, having been a teacher many years before marrying late in life. He was a successful businessman, but obsessive. The family lived until the father's retirement in the suburbs of a metropolitan New England center. The father died suddenly in 1962 at age 68 (when Daniel was 12 1/2 years old). The father had been happily married previously to a Swedish woman who died after many years of marriage and three pregnancies, two of which ended in still births and the third in neonatal death. Hence, neither father nor mother was prepared experientially to cope with a developing baby such as Daniel.

Daniel was bottle-fed, but had recurrent constipation and colic from the beginning of life. His mother was highly attentive, and absorbed in the care of the infant child. She eagerly shielded the father from the loudness, dirtiness, and inconvenience of a baby's presence in the household. She consulted a pediatrician very frequently. Yet, when Daniel was a year old both parents left him with a servant while they went on a vacation lasting more than three months. Daniel was weaned at ten months, and when the mother returned from her journey abroad she undertook toilet training, beginning at age 18 months, but not achieving success until Daniel was four years old. The first 18 months of bowel training were arduous for the mother; and Daniel was forced to sit on the toilet for hours. To make this prolonged placement more acceptable to the child, he was given books to look at and toys to play with. He came to accept being placed on the toilet, but he was uncooperative and was adjudged to be chronically constipated. Between age three and four, he passed five days without defecating and was hospitalized for gastrointestinal studies. No abnormalities were found, but the child cried continually while in the hospital. At age 14 1/2, however, the mother still instructed him to go and defecate, periodically.

As early as age four, Daniel had developed tics, a jerky gait, indistinct speech, and a disposition of jitteriness and nervousness. He failed first grade, and was teased by school mates for his ungainliness, his speech problems, and numerous compulsive acts. By age nine he was underachieving academically in second grade, at which time his father had retired and moved to a resort area. This added to Daniel's upset. In third grade, Daniel developed additional symptoms such as eye-blinking, compulsive touching of diverse inanimate objects, tic-like clearing of his throat, etc. At age ten, he was seen by two psychiatrists who adjudged him to be "schizophrenic" and his parents to be "rigid and compulsive" persons who exerted a malignant influence on Daniel's development. His parents then accepted his entry into residential treatment in the northeastern part of the USA for slightly more than two years, but removed him contrary to advice because they concluded they wanted to be with their only offspring while they grew old.

A series of intelligence tests showed a verbal IQ of 104 at age seven, 101 at age eight, 99 at age nine, and 99 at ages 10 to 14 1/2. Nevertheless, all examiners believed that Daniel's intellectual potential was above normal; all were impressed that his fantasies always involved robots, dragons, and royalty.

Daniel, though, having reached puberty at 14 years, was socially, intellectually, academically, and emotionally handicapped. Outpatient therapy provided him with some insight, some relief from his major disturbances, and a modicum of naturalness.

Child #25
DAVID J

David J, a 10-year-old boy, was brought by his parents on pediatric referral for psychiatric evaluation because of his lack of satisfactory peer relationships, his excessive worry over school performance, his often-stated fear of being mentally retarded, and recurring atypical behavior such as extreme fascination with traffic lights and watching windshield wipers.

He had previously undergone pediatric neurological examination on the recommendation of his school because of "apparent hyperactivity." His academic performance was adequate at his appropriate grade level, but, in addition to regular classes, he was attending a special education class at his school four days a week. The special classes bothered him considerably because his regular classmates teased him, saying he was dumb, etc.

His father, a college professor, and his mother, a secretary, appeared defensive and threatened about bringing David to a psychiatrist.

David himself was highly verbal. He said he was "nuts about traffic lights," and wondered if that meant he was "crazy." He asked the therapist if the therapist thought himself "magic." He told the therapist, "I have magic in me," but said he didn't want to talk about it. He occasionally accused the therapist of asking him "dumb questions," and, watching the therapist's note-taking, asked if "secret symbols are being used to grade me."

He was aggressive with consultation-room play materials, pushing in a doll's head and running over others with a car. He was quite anxious during his first sessions, but became less so, although both his anxiety level and his thought sequence fluctuated considerably during therapy. When he became anxious there would often be a veritable flight of ideas with David jumping continuously from one subject to another. At these times, he could not sit still. He was also frightened by the possibility of unlikely or impossible events, such as worrying without respite during one session over whether the clouds (of a rainstorm outside) would collide with nearby buildings.

During psychological testing, he had great difficulty keeping his attention focused on the tests, regardless of environmental circumstances. He couldn't sit still unless he had a play object in hand or close by.

His full-scale IQ (WISC) was 90, but his "inquisitiveness, interest, and sporadic samples of higher ability" strongly suggested to the psychologist "his cognitive development is hampered by emotional factors." Rorschach testing suggested he organized his thoughts in rather peculiar ways at times, but that his unusual responses evolved from "emotion laden elaborations of conventional percepts" rather than from any inability to conceive correctly. It was felt these distortions centered about close interpersonal relationships, and were evoked especially when David was somehow threatened by thoughts of change.

According to David's parents, he was "always high strung and needing to unwind." His birth and developmental milestones were normal except for speech. When two and a half years old, he would sing along with records but promptly become quiet if he thought he was being overheard. He didn't carry on simple conversations until he was three.

His mother said he "scared easily"; and he had separation problems when first beginning school. At home during this time he would "scream with fear" if his mother left him to go a few feet away in their yard. He then became fascinated with traffic lights and automobile windshield wipers and would play "for hours at a time" with the wipers. He was said always to have preferred solitary activities and to have avoided play with other children.

His dog died when David was eight years old, whereupon David became "obsessed with death," and began rituals of prayers and blessings at meals.

His parents appeared to have their own rather consequential problems, especially the father who acted extremely anxious during psychiatric consultation and, according to the therapist, "became somewhat loose in his thinking at times also." Both parents were overwhelmed with the question of how to rear David. Both said their household is run "democratically, with no limits." This "democratic" structure of the family apparently confused David, and a concomitant family emphasis on intelligence and achievement seemed impairing. It became clear during therapy that David tended to turn more and more to his mother in an unhealthy dependent way, that she might be fostering this, and that the father quite definitely felt "out of the picture."

David was the youngest of four siblings. His older brother was in military service, one sister was married but living at home while her husband was in the National Guard, and the other sister was away at college.

The parents, though wary of psychotherapy, began weekly sessions along with David who also began remedial tutoring with a special education teacher, outside his school.

Child #26
DON D

Don was an appealing 10-year-old, bright, engaged in a wealth of activities, and enjoying many friends. He was brought for psychiatric services by his parents because of school problems which had been occurring on and off for a period of about two years. As it turned out, Don's "school problems" were not highly unusual. They were mostly "boys will be boys" sort of things. His appearance for treatment was actually a result of an idiosyncratic teacher's recommendation *and* of his father's oversensitivity to Don's possible need for psychiatric help. The latter stemmed from the fact the father's first wife had committed suicide during a post partum depression after a long history of manifestly psychopathological behavior. Father was vigilant, particularly where the pathology of other people was concerned.

On the whole, Don's parents were pleasant, intelligent people, unusually candid about their feelings and perceptions, and nicely attuned to each other. They, their oldest son, and Don shared a basically healthy family life. Problems resulted mainly from the fact that both parents, particularly the father, were rigid perfectionists, highly self-critical, obsessively concerned with the consequences of any "slip up," and highly demanding of others. Don was internalizing this value system and encountering severe difficulty in meeting the perfectionistic standards which were now his own to a degree. At the expense of freedom and spontaneity he was becoming better and better at controlling his frustration and approximating his ideals. This, however, did not spare him from the self criticism characteristic of a perfectionist. In addition, Don experienced anxiety about badness in himself which he sensed his parents were searching for.

He appeared well on his way to developing a relatively severe obsessive-compulsive character structure. He dealt with problems and situations with an orderly, thorough precision that is rare for 10-year-old boys. Only too frequently he would become so utterly lost in minute details and nuances that he'd wind up missing the obvious. He also tended to ruminate on what people were thinking and on the enormous number of possibilities inherent in situations. With his highly cognitive manner of dealing with living, Don was not very sensitive to the *emotional impact* of his environment. His neurotic conflicts centered on control of aggression; they were still relatively accessible but it appeared that he would soon bury his conflicts beneath an elaborate and sturdy defensive structure bleached of affective impact. Don's sturdy ego equipped him to employ a highly ideational defense. It seemed that Don would become an unfortunately "successful" obsessive, rarely in touch with his feelings.

Child #27
EARL G

Earl was an attractive, intelligent (IQ 141) 14-year-old in the ninth grade, who presented himself as a sad youngster with an air of hopeless defeatism. The basis of his referral related to school phobia. Indeed, he had attended only three days of the current school year, then nearly two months along. Evidently, Earl had always had difficulty with social relationships although the school phobia dated roughly from the time of his father's death a little more than a year earlier.

Earl's mother was a petite, delicate-looking woman who related well but whose emotional stability was as tenuous as her physique was fragile. Her husband, a mental health professional, developed cancer and died very quickly, leaving her little time to prepare herself. The father, apparently, had been possessed of a cold, sardonic personality and had shared few intimate feelings with his wife. As long as he was alive, though, he was able to provide the emotional support required by the family, and things worked out reasonably well in spite of the wife's helplessness. His death precipitated the latent crisis.

The overprotectiveness and weakness of the mother coupled with an adolescent need for an ego ideal had pushed Earl toward his father. His father's general demeanor had engendered much resentment in Earl, who consequently felt guilty over responsibility he assumed for his father's "magical" death. As a result Earl had never really faced this event and resolved his own guilt and anxiety over it. His mother's helplessness, her inability to turn to her own mother, an essentially hostile woman, and her view that Earl was brilliant caused her to turn to him as truly to head man of the family. At the same time she projected her own weaknesses onto Earl, maintaining that he was "too weak" to handle school attendance. This acute dependency relationship, coupled with the fact Earl had a younger brother and sister who looked up to him and garnished with constant reminders by relatives and friends that he was now "the man of the house," placed incredible demands on him Moreover, because his mother resorted to projection, denial, and flight from her own feelings, Earl was unable to communicate with her and resolve family problems, or to count on her for any emotional support. His mother not only claimed that she did not believe in discipline, but refused to show anger, or for that matter any other feeling, to the children. Her brand of permissiveness was an abdication of parenting. Understandably, Earl felt inundated. Add to this the normal problems of sexual identity and conflict over dependency needs and desire for freedom at his age, and it is a wonder that he held up as well as he did.

Aside from denial of feeling for his father's death, and his school phobia which constituted essentially a withdrawal from a threatening situation, Earl used obsessive-compulsive personality mechanisms to cope. He was superficially polite, restrained, manifested little or no affect and yet showed a capacity for biting sarcasm. He was highly competitive and domineering, and he resorted to elaborate intellectualization to deal with his anxiety.

Child #28
ELVIS K

Elvis was the seven-year-old eldest son of a professional family. He came to the clinic accompanied by his parents and a history of unsatisfactory peer relationships, temper tantrums, poor school performance, enuresis, and a compulsion to construct machines. His parents felt all these problems became truly severe when Elvis entered the first grade of school.

Elvis was the product of a normal-term pregnancy. At the time of his birth his father was completing work on a Ph.D. in one of the natural sciences and the mother in another. Both parents came from rigid family backgrounds and had developed obsessive character traits of their own during childhood and adolescence. This led to some insecurity for Mrs. K in her new role as mother. Elvis was described as an irritable, demanding baby. Three years following his birth Mrs. K had twin girls and post-partum depression.

With this, family life became chaotic. Elvis's toilet training was haphazard with rigid demands one minute and no demands the next. All the children remained enuretic until Elvis became a psychiatric outpatient.

Elvis's peer relationships had been fraught with temper tantrums and fighting. By age six he was a neighborhood isolate. At this point he began identifying with robot-like computers that he fashioned from his father's computer cards. His world became peopled with friendly machines that he constructed, for people were regarded as dangerous and destructive. If his manufacture of machines was interfered with, Elvis would fly into an hysterical rage. This general behavior continued in the first grade, and Elvis quickly became an isolate in his classroom At this point he entered into individual therapy on a twice-a-week basis. His parents were seen conjointly once a week. Over a period of 30 sessions Elvis developed several close friends and much of his compulsive behavior ceased. He was also able to deal with anger more appropriately. The parents were able to reduce the chaos in the home and to set more consistent but not overly rigid limits for all of their children.

Child #29
ERIC D

Eric was a cute five-year-old boy who had big brown eyes and a rare and tentative smile. He was brought in by his parents because of his inordinate immaturity, short attention span, fear of separation from his mother, and a forecast made by his kindergarten teacher that he would encounter difficulty in first grade.

Possessed of average or slightly above average intelligence, Eric's main problems were in the area of interpersonal relationships. He employed compulsive mechanisms to control his aggressive, hostile feelings, but these were not always adequate. His obsessive preoccupation with prehistoric animals (saber-toothed tigers, for example) appeared to be one way of intellectualizing his primitive, aggressive impulses, of withdrawing into a fantasy world where his angry feelings could be contained. In general, he related more easily to animals than to people, particularly the people within his own family. During psychological testing he was withdrawn, nervous, defeatist, and compulsive, in an apparent effort to control his anxiety. He showed signs of resenting his only sib, a younger sister, on both testing and interviewing.

Eric's problems appeared to be a direct reflection of his parents' difficulties. His father, a doctor, found it difficult to handle negative or angry feelings. Consequently, he expended great effort at maintaining a laughing "hail-fellow-well-met" image, and laughed loudly *and inappropriately* in an attempt to make light of serious, affect-laden areas. The father was a compulsively high-pressure individual, always going "full speed ahead," explicit, and both rigid and demanding of the very best in performance in all areas for both himself and his entire family. His obsessive-compulsive, perfectionist manner and his effort to maintain an adequate front at all costs precluded any acceptance of weakness in himself and led him to vehement rejection of his own strong dependency needs. Eric's mother appeared cold, distant, hostile, suspicious, and was often sarcastic. It later developed that this was a defense against her own poor self-concept. Moreover, she was locked in a struggle with Eric who appeared to be the recipient scapegoat for her curbed negative feelings toward her husband. Her feelings of loneliness and inadequacy were exacerbated by her uncontrollable rage at Eric, her resultant overcompensation and spoiling of her son, and her unhappiness with herself and her marriage. She complained frequently and "made life miserable" for the family. She constantly "swallowed" her feelings toward her husband and suffered from stomach spasms and headaches. The parental sex life was a shambles because of his reportedly excessive demands. He needed constantly to prove his own sex performance adequacy, but she wanted—in the days before oral contraception—not to have another child.

Eric simply could not cope with this incredibly obsessive-compulsive situation. His problems were substantially alleviated by the treatment, and subsequent great improvement, of his parents.

Child #30
GEORGE D

George was a shy, constricted seven-year-old. He had received some treatment (involving hypnosis) from his family's physician without success. Two psychiatric consultants suggested schizophrenia as the proper diagnosis in view of his gesticulations. His parents felt that he was severely disturbed and pointed to a peculiar behavior they termed "butterflying" in which George would stand on his toes and rapidly flap his arms. This he had done since he had begun to walk.

George was extremely reserved and unnatural, almost totally lacking in spontaneity. He also appeared to be ungainly and retarded in motor development, but minimal expressions around his eyes and mouth indicated that he was very alert to social situations and his general conversation showed he was of at least high average intelligence. His general demeanor was not that of a schizophrenic but rather of a very frightened, cowed boy with compulsive mannerisms.

George had three younger brothers, twins aged six and a "baby brother" aged four. His father was a tall, slim, intense man who tried hard to be polite and cooperative, but indirectly communicated hostility in everything he did. The father appeared to be obsessive and defensively intellectualized, but relatively naive. He ruled the family with an iron hand and demonstrated impatience with his children's behavior. The mother was attractive, dependent, and deferential, giving the impression of shyness and extreme helplessness. She seemed depressed, on the verge of tears, and, at times, nearly beside herself with unexpressable hostility. She clearly identified with George. She appeared to be quite schizoid, also naive, and disarmingly open in expressing adoration of her husband. He, in turn, seemed to accept this godlike position which his wife ascribed to him as being only his just due.

Despite the fact that George's father was proud of his ability to "understand the situation," this family exhibited extraordinary blindness concerning the father's problems. On one thing they all appeared to be in agreement and that was that George was the source of their discomforts. It became clear that George was a scapegoat and a recipient of hostility which his parents were not able to express towards each other. Both parents harbored great guilt concerning George, particularly the father who had maintained forced feeding and strict regimentation for George as a young child. Even George's mother felt some resentment and hostility toward her husband for this. Apparently this early brutal treatment had made George "peculiar" enough for him to become the natural "odd one out" and the scapegoat in a family of six that was unable to look at itself closely and honestly.

The resultant paradigm of rigid demands given without emotional support produced sufficient anxiety for George to develop a severely obsessive-compulsive life pattern. His unutterable rage at parents who were rejecting, and who frequently violently lost their tempers, became unbearable. He responded with his "butterflying," a grotesque communication of his dehumanized chaos. In responding to his fearful, rejecting world, George had become a shy, mincing, compulsive and very sad youngster.

Child #31
HANK W

Hank was a rather slender, appealing, blond, blue-eyed 10-year-old. Physically small for his age, his facial expression connoted a "little lost boy" look, while his loneliness, shyness and general appearance suggested an obsequious quality of personality. His father was a doctor. He had one sister, aged 11 years, and two brothers aged six and one-half years and 21 months. The parents' main concern about Hank was his increasing trouble with school work and difficulty in keeping friends. They saw him as immature (he had given up baby talk only two years before). Hank also seemed too clinging, particularly to men and older boys, they thought.

His parents admitted that they placed a high value on academic achievement, and there is no doubt that Hank himself recognized a great deal of pressure in this direction. Hank, however, was found to be of normal intelligence in a family where substantially above the normal was the standard, and he had a learning disability in Automatic Sequential functioning. Most significantly, the fact that Hank did not have superior intelligence apparently had resulted in his parents unconsciously disvaluing or rejecting him, and consequently, offering him little affection and support. These emotional sustainers, indeed, were scarce even for the other children in this family. Hank was unable to experience sufficient feelings of self-fulfillment and achievement. He had developed a deep-seated sense of insecurity, even of worthlessness.

He expressed a good deal of hostility toward his older sister and he felt—and later articulately commented upon—the substantially hostile undercurrents in the family, particularly in his mother. In the face of his anxiety, Hank functioned in a passive controlling way, at times showing considerable stubborness, repressing in the style characteristic of the rest of the family. His dreams carried themes of combat between a small but powerful boy hero and various and sundry monsters.

Quite clearly, promise for Hank lay in special tutoring for his mild to moderate learning disability, and in greater understanding and support by his parents. With this help, there was no doubt that he could perform up to his potential. Indeed he did, as therapy freed up his motoric, cognitive, and emotional life.

Child #32

HARRY J

Harry J was an outgoing, somewhat immature eight-year-old referred because of his reading and learning difficulties and his tendency to be a loner. Upon testing he proved to be low-normal in intelligence and to have some perceptual-motor difficulties. There was also slight but possible evidence of minimal brain dysfunction. All of his reported problems were of long standing. He had had a complicated birth with substantial difficulty in breathing. According to his parents, Harry almost-died, for he had developed hyaline membrane disease.

Harry's parents were intelligent people who evidenced a strong competitiveness in their interaction. The father was generally prone to rambling, philosophical statements; the mother was highly verbal and assertive. A three-year-old adopted sister rounded out the family circle. Harry's parents showed some anxiety about their own roles, about their social and educational status, and demonstrated that they were striving quite hard to improve themselves in these areas.

Harry's problems seemed to stem primarily from the excessive demands of his parents, particularly his mother—demands which because of his deficiencies Harry was unable to meet. As a result, he had a defeatist attitude about school. Because of his problems in self-concept, he always tried to secure center stage and to deal on an adult level, despite his patent immaturity. He demonstrated marked anxiety about his own worth and identity, and he seemed focused on authority figures' reactions to his behavior. He tried to be "as you desire me." Evidently this stemmed from his confused relationship with his mother who carried out all the discipline and made demands of him, while at the same time she offered him little affection. Harry, besides, was confused about his sexual role, probably a consequence of his parents' somewhat tenuous relationship with each other, and Harry's Oedipal overtones added into the mix.

Combined with Harry's compulsive, center stage, rigid and structured dealings with adults was his refusal to divulge himself (evidenced, for example, in a refusal to discuss dream material) and an almost complete inability to play with peers. His long periods of solitude were filled with obsessive playing at doctor or priest. His religious preoccupation was so great and enjoyment of the fantasy priest role so thorough that his mother—who derogated the Catholicism of his father—made him vestments and a chalice, unaware that this was odd behavior on her son's part. Harry was excessively concerned with death, darkness, sin, what happens to bad people, etc., and preoccupied with contamination with infections or illnesses. The doctor and priest play could not quell the demons that pursued him.

Child #33
HENRY B

Henry, oldest of four children, was a 14-year-old Catholic junior high school student who was referred for psychiatric treatment following a stabbing incident. He had observed a neighbor appear at her window in a nightgown in response to a car which had honked while turning around in her driveway. Henry took an ice pick, put on some cotton gloves and went over to ask her for some sugar "for his mother." When she turned to comply he stabbed her a dozen times, threw her on the floor, mounted her and proceeded to "feel up" her body. She managed to escape and get help. Henry was incarcerated, hospitalized for tests, sent to a juvenile center followed by a foster home, and finally back to his own home pending psychiatric examination. The whole affair greatly surprised all who had known him.

He'd had a normal birth but at two weeks of age nearly suffocated and was only saved by his father's artifical respiration. When he was two years old, his family moved from the northeast to the southeast. He was very close to his paternal grandparents who essentially served as his parents, and the traumatic separation caused him to change from a happy, outgoing child into a quiet, morose one. When he was five, a friend died of suffocation after a sandpile tunnel caved in. Henry's efforts to dig him out were futile. When Henry was 13, his beloved grandfather died.

During this period Henry's siblings were born. He had never been prepared for their arrival. And at the time of his referral he had not been informed about sex. His mother's response to a question about sexual intercourse was: "Horrible, dirty, bad." He had demonstrated no feeling for his siblings although he evidently harbored a deep resentment, for after the stabbing he began to express resentment by yelling at them.

He did very well in school where he was also a superior athlete. However, with the onset of adolescence he had used his athletic endeavors as a compulsive means of driving himself to exhaustion. He was enuretic to the age of seven, and until the age of 14 (when his mother "put her foot down") Henry kept a "Linus" blanket which he cuddled while making clucking noises with his tongu_ Shortly before the stabbing, he evidenced some adolescent rebellion, expressed outwardly by his adopting long hair and mod clothes. Both of these precipitated a violent reaction from his father.

Henry's father was a compulsive, hard-driving man who tended to be a tyrant at home. He was away at work, however, much of the time. He had a big temper, which made its appearance periodically in the form of rage outbursts during which household items were smashed. Henry's mother was a meek, harried-looking woman, so contorted with nervousness as to appear deformed at times. Yet when she relaxed, she was seductive. She resented her husband's lack of attention to her; she used Henry as a major emotional support and to aid in substitute satisfaction of her sexual needs. She resorted to use of guilt to discipline Henry. The children in general were indulged with plenty of material possessions, but with little love, and there was little evidence that any direct feelings were expressed in the family.

Henry apparently lived in a restricted, deprived world thoroughly laced with violence, pressure, anxiety, and exogenous sexual stimulation. With little or no emotional support available to him, and called on to be supportive of others, he developed an obsessive-compulsive personality structure in seeking to contain his anxiety. He resorted to denial and repression as defenses, and he also attempted to exhaust himself physically. All this proved unsuccessful and he "blew," expressing his aggressive and sexual feelings in an exceedingly destructive fashion. Henry's parents insisted—with some coolness—that he was normal and had simply made one "big mistake." They meant that neither they nor Henry needed any depth probing.

Child #34
HERB M

This odd-appearing young man had just turned 15 years old when he was referred to the clinic. He was the second of three children, with a normal younger brother and an older, adolescent

psychotherapy for a severe obsessional break-
onspicuously was an obsessive character with
v symptomatic obsessions; his mother was an
..en obsessive who was also seen in prolonged
..apy. The family kept up a good front for the outer
..rid but were an unhappy lot. The family's economic status was
that of the top 10 percent of the population nationally.

Herb displayed obsessions, compulsions, tics, grimaces, a "nervous laugh," and crying spells that were forced by him "to relieve
tension." He looked eccentric and professorial when he said in the
first hour, "It's hard to keep going. I have this constant battle
between recreation and study. I work hard to get grades instead of
information. Another thing I worry about is God. Off to myself I
vow to be nice, and then when it gets down to it I'm not nice . . . I
get to feeling sorry for myself. I feel compelled to keep on going
and drive myself nuts . . .Even my recreation is tedious—reading
chess books, and collecting shells, and stamp collection . . . My
father is the way I am: hard-driven, doesn't enjoy his work, and
stays tired an awful lot of the time."

His basic difficulties were attendant upon his low self-esteem
handled compulsively. His main battle was for autonomy, especially against his mother. He was identified with his compulsive
father. He had poor relations with his peers and disclaimed interest
in dating girls. He felt manipulated by his older sister (blaming her
for "involving us too deeply in psychiatry"); he was suspicious
that his parents talked about him "behind his back." He had nobody for a friend. He told the therapist, "As soon as you say
anything I reject it just because you say it."

His impulses to rebel, get angry, talk sarcastically, feel sexual
arousal and to tend to be lazy were all unacceptable to Herb. He
saw himself, awake and in dreams which he reported reluctantly at
first, as a puppet and as a mechanical man. He was immersed in
self-pity, brooding, doubting, fatigue and easy irritability. He
strove to be super-Christian, super-altruistic, hyperserious, overly
studious and elaborately planful—to make up for what he saw as
profound inadequacies and defects. He stated, "Even my enjoyment is controlled."

Shortly after treatment commenced it became clear that his father's employment would require the family's removal to a distant city. As a result, Herb was seen only 15 times, once weekly, but he achieved considerable improvement and an introduction to psychotherapy—and to detecting and understanding his resistance—which proved beneficial when he resumed treatment after the family move was completed.

Child #35
HILL A

Hill was the 13-year-old only child of a New England family who had moved to the South. Hill presented himself at the clinic with a two-year history of extensive compulsive rituals, obsessions, and increasing social isolation and withdrawal.

Hill's mother and father were Protestants who were closely tied to the paternal grandparents. The mother's pregnancy was a long sought-for event and the newborn Hill was described as a perfect, happy baby. This description continued to be an apt one throughout his toddlerhood. Hill's mother made perfectionistic demands during his toilet training, particularly concerning his cleanliness, and this marred her earlier warm bond with Hill.

By school age Hill was not able to be a part of any group of children, and all of his interests continued to be directed to his family of origin. Most of his life centered on his mother. The father was absent frequently on prolonged business trips. Hill continued friendless until the fifth grade of school. When taken to play with the children of his parents' friends, Hill played in one room alone and the other child or children in another room. Every emotional tie, and all energies, remained invested within the family circle. He experienced some ascendancy within the family, however. He liked to manage the family affairs, so he took over the function of completely planning and preparing for family trips. He made the most detailed arrangements and preparations for these travels.

When the family moved from New England, transporting the paternal grandparents to live adjacent to them, Hill was taken by surprise. That trip was one that he did not plan for, and one that he resented sorely. Arriving in the new home at age 10 1/2, Hill began to display a series of compulsive rituals. Most of these revolved around religiously watching all news programs and having severe bouts of anxiety and hysteria if news programs were interfered with. The most important events were wars, disasters, and political news. Hill created elaborate displays of current events occupying the entire living room. The mother and father were not allowed to touch them because that would contaminate them. Hill isolated all his possessions, eating utensils, clothing, etc., from his parents and "purified" them. He referred to the parental bed as "the most poisonous place" in the entire house. Hill's manner became increasingly that of a little old humorless man with all spontaneity and joy completely squelched. If the family interfered in the increasingly elaborate and extensive rituals, Hill would lapse into hysterical rages. He frequently threatened the mother with scissors. This series of events led the family to seek help from a variety of agencies. After a diagnostic evaluation at our clinic Hill's therapy was continued at a site some 150 miles nearer to his home.

Child #36
HOLT A

Holt was referred to the child psychiatry clinic, at age 10, because he was unable to sleep alone at night. Six months earlier Holt, who had slept in the room with a younger sister, had been assigned his own room in the family's new house, but unfortunately it meant that he was alone not only in his room but also on the first floor—for the rest of the family slept upstairs.

Pleasurable physical contact was important for Holt, and at times he seemed infantile in his seeking physical contact. He obtained a back-rub at bedtime every night, from his mother. He persisted in thumb sucking on into his eleventh year of life.

In the past the child had shown some difficulties. Between age four and six he had night terrors, but his parents did not think that he was afraid to be alone (in his bed) at that earlier age. Also, between ages five and seven, he suffered from severe asthma and when he began psychiatric treatment he was getting desensitization injections and taking prophylactic medication (by mouth) against asthma. Despite these problems, Holt's parents perceived him to be an intelligent child who was low in frustration tolerance, and a slightly overactive boy but with a pleasing sense of humor.

Holt's parents were in their forties. The father was a successful professional person whose facial expressions were frequently misperceived by Holt. Holt imagined his father to look angry, to be scowling or menacing, when indeed the examining psychiatrist saw no such clues on the father's face. The mother, also well educated, was a professional woman turned housewife. The eight-year-old sister was not as involved in the familial tensions as were Holt and his parents. The family of four lived in affluence.

Holt's activities during interviews were corroborated by the results of his psychologic testing. He reported his terrible nocturnal fears, recognizing that they had emerged only when he moved down to his own room. He knew it was silly but, when afraid, he said, he kept thinking somebody would stand outside lying in wait to break into the house, to rob the family of its belongings and to kill him. Trying to control his panic—he literally believed he was to die—Holt invented certain ritualistic mentation designed to ward off disaster. For instance, when lying in his bed at night he could only diminish the threat by controlling his breathing to put his heart beat into synchrony with a ticking bedside clock. Or he would be driven to repeat sequences of numbers forward and backwards. Testing showed a full-scale IQ of 128. Only on picture arrangement did he fall below his age level, results reflecting, usually, a distorted perception and prediction of how social events are ordered.

Projective testing further revealed what Holt was like. He was highly intelligent. He had a very active fantasy life with recurrent angry and sadistic thoughts. He perceived violence everywhere, even in the mildest and most peaceful scenes shown to him He showed obvious enjoyment, and little guilt, in describing most situations of fighting and destruction. He evidenced fear of his angry thoughts about violence *he* directed to his mother, father

and friends. He felt rejected by his family and friends and perceived himself as basically undesirable. Themes that pervaded his
responses to projective testing were: parents try to dispose of their
son, mother and son fight and employ lethal tactics, boys fight
with each other, big boys bully the weakest member of the group,
a son becomes violent when kept separate from his mother, and,
generally, boys fare ill at the hands of others.

Holt's undeniably rich and colorful, and brutal, fantasy life did
not make him happy and did not reduce his state of anxious
tension.

Child #37
HUGH D

Hugh, a blond-haired boy eight years old, was brought for
psychiatric consultation by his family on recommendation of a
child psychiatrist practicing in Hugh's hometown.

Hugh was referred because of cursing at school, exhibiting his
penis to his classmates and teachers, alternately throwing temper
tantrums and withdrawing from all contact with his family at
home, and enuresis.

He was extremely talkative but not hyperactive, appearing sad
and depressed. An adopted child, he readily described his hostile
feelings toward his parents' only biological child, a seven-year-old
boy, whom Hugh saw as "stupid, idiotic, and a tattletale." In fact,
he would become so anxious he would lapse into baby-talk while
continuing to detail the deficiencies of his brother.

During the initial interview, Hugh appeared very serious and
pseudo-mature most of the time. He said his teachers were "crum-
my," his parents weren't much better, and he enjoyed "throwing
cups of water on my mother and her friends." He asked the therapist to bring his parents back into the room, and let him hide
behind the door and ambush them with a dart gun.

In later therapy sessions, he built intricate towers and buildings
with building blocks, insisted his "creations" were special and
could never be duplicated, then wrecked the structures by throw-

ing blocks and aiming darts at them. He described his creations as defense places impregnable to enemies.

His parents, who had adopted Hugh when he was only a few weeks old, said he'd had behavior problems since beginning school. They said he didn't like other children, and other children didn't like him. His teachers were quoted as saying he took great pains to devise long, intricate methods to solve simple problems, and that he generally refused to do anything he didn't want to do.

The father called his home life and marriage "miserable," and said he stayed away from his house as much as possible. The mother said she felt resigned to an unsatisfactory life, and that she was probably "too strict and nagging" toward Hugh. She felt her husband was "too passive and permissive" with Hugh.

In psychological testing, Hugh had on WISC a verbal IQ of 135, performance IQ of 121, and full-scale IQ of 131. Peabody, Bender-Gestalt, Draw-a-Person, Rorschach, TAT and Sentence Completion were also administered. There were no indications of perceptual or motor difficulties. It appeared, however, that he found great difficulty coping with affects. It was also apparent in projective testing that he saw the world as threatening, dangerous and hostile, and that he himself felt extremely hostile and was having considerable difficulty in controlling angry "explosions" toward the world.

Hugh's conflicts revolved around feelings of rejection and strong needs for nurturance, partially expressed in intense sibling rivalry and acting out behavior at school. His trouble was labelled as "overanxious reaction of childhood with obsessive-compulsive features." Both Hugh and his parents went into therapy.

Child #38
MEL G

Mel was the first-born son of a 19-year-old mother and 21-year-old father. He was referred at age six because of tantrums that he had displayed since age three, extreme hatred of his younger sister who was born when Mel was four years old, bedwetting, and obsessive questioning and worrying about money and parental death. He was an expert in dawdling and other passive-aggressive tactics, and showed some rituals. He suffered from frequent asthma. At age five he was hospitalized, but he claimed that he enjoyed the separation from his mother as well as the surgery he experienced at that time for urethral stricture.

He had spent six months, from age 18 months till two years, with his paternal grandmother because his mother, depressed, was hospitalized. When he was in first grade, his father was drafted and sent to Viet Nam. The boy asked to sleep with his mother, and he did so frequently, although the mother wondered about the propriety of this. He became preoccupied with familial money troubles as well as with the meaning of death—these were his mother's realistic worries, but they appeared bizarre when voiced by a young child.

At school Mel appeared more feminine, or at least less mature, than other boys his age. His mother did not like his practice of kissing his boy friends, and she thought his poorly disguised genital fondling and manipulation excessive. She summed up her worries about him when he was entering first grade: ". . . apparently he is overcome by his emotions. His learning block and disruption in the classroom are the immediate problems, but his Oedipal tendency and lack of masculine identification are more important but less urgent." The boy was not seen for therapy during first grade. During that year the fatherless family moved to a new city, got adjusted to the father's absence, and established some familiarity with their new setting. Actually, besides, the child did well academically in first grade despite the ominous warnings of the kindergarten specialists.

When the father returned from his military service, the parents discussed Mel's problems and decided together to seek pyschiatric help for Mel. At that time the boy was seven years old, and eight and one-half when termination of therapy came, after 50 sessions, one and a half years later. The parents were helped by a psychiatric social worker who saw them once weekly over this time.

All of Mel's problems (asthma, bedwetting, sadism, tantrums, bisexual leanings, indecisiveness, preoccupations with death, dirt, and money) were part of an obsessive style that passed beyond being a mere stylistic variation on healthy childhood. He was so devoid of naturalness, so steeped in unwelcome obsessions and compulsions, so confused and, although verbose, so unclear in his messages, that he was adjudged to be suffering from an obsessional neurosis of moderate severity. His parents, observing his brittleness and attuned to mental illness, believed he might be psychotic, but they accepted the notion that Mel was *not* psychotic, however necessary treatment might be. The child was wary of psycho-therapy but ultimately trusted the therapist, reported a few dreams although he defined dreams as "family secrets," developed warm feelings for the therapist, and came to have realistic expecta-tions of what treatment could do for him. He learned that his bladder was his, not his mother's, property. He learned to trust the parents to take full responsibility for the family finances. He came to understand that his mother had problems and that she was not a lethal figure—although in his therapy session number 37 he dic-tated the following statement of his world view:

"Happiness is hitting your girlfriend.
Happiness is having the children take over the world.
Happiness is choking your mother.
Happiness is killing your sister with a knife."

He worked through some of his earlier puritanical constrictions about death and duty too: "I hope life is not made too easy. It is bad for our bodies if we don't do some work and keep active." His asthma did not improve during therapy, although much work was devoted to his early separation from mother, his fears of death and abandonment, and many pediatric and allergist interventions. As his unwelcome thoughts abated, he became more outgoing, more spontaneous, and this change was reflected as well in greater motoric gracefulness.

Child #39
MILES C

Miles was 12 years old when he came in, supposedly schizo-phrenic when he was seen the day before by a psychiatrist in his home city. He was worn out by compulsions and obsessions, the latter looking to some observers as if they were "delusional." Miles was on the rack, pulled between thoughts of murdering and surrendering, good and bad, omniscience and stupidity, autonomy and total dependency. His being betwixt-and-between mentally reflected, to some degree, his being the middle son with brothers aged 16 and five years. He was trying at the moment to work out a perfect family budget, but he was not able to concentrate because of his "worries" and his elaborate touching and handwashing rituals.

The entire family was caught up in Miles's obsessive-compulsive symptoms. The father, a 45-year-old retired sergeant, was upwardly mobile in aspirations and advocated the virtues of obedience and diligence in order to get ahead. It was hardly in his heart to derogate Miles's bookworm inclinations. The mother had little emotional contact with her husband, but she tuned in and resonated to Miles's rigid ways, for she was a 39-year-old working-class "mom" who was an overly meticulous housekeeper. She left all things other than domestic routine to her Man. The parents had no social life whatever. Miles, therefore, as a precocious and omnipotent male, had assumed with ease a tyranny over both parents. Relinquishing that tyranny was not easily wrought during therapy, even when the symptoms showed dramatic remission after only four weeks of once-weekly sessions.

The therapist wrote, when discharge was effected on parental insistence after ten sessions:

> The patient has become relaxed. He socializes easily with family members and doesn't feel required to spend all his time with books. He seeks outside pleasure and has begun generally to enjoy himself in such activities as bowling with some of his friends. However, he has never become completely free of guilty thoughts of having masturbated and taken part in genital play with other boys in early childhood.

Four years later, Miles returned because his problems with lust and rage had blown up again, worse than ever. He had demonstrated rage attacks; he had threatened his mother with violence and rape, including "lewd advances." All these things suggested to the general psychiatrist who interviewed Miles "schizophrenic reaction, catatonic type" and at least six months of hospitalization was recommended. Luckily the parents could not afford schizophrenia and its treatment. The young man benefitted again from outpatient psychotherapy for obsessive-compulsive neurosis. Once more, however, the treatment was stopped against psychiatric advice.

Child #40
MILTON C

This nine-year-old boy gave a longstanding history of personal difficulties in a family of difficulties. His troubles included asthma, poor coordination, babyish immaturity, numberless phobias, and troubles with peers who found him inordinately bossy. More recently, Milton had developed compulsions—frequent hand-washing, touching especially of furniture, and looking for fire under furniture. The situation, in his 46-year-old mother's testimony, was that of "the most disagreeable child I ever saw." Although his unhappy life pre-dated it, his "disagreeableness" increased after his little sister (father's prize possession) was born when Milton was four years old. From that time on he became asthmatic, perfectionistic and an incessant talker to get attention. All of these features showed through on psychologic testing. He talked on and on, showed a superior intelligence, and although anxious, compulsive and phobic, he was, the psychologist believed, barely staving off a schizophrenic illness.

His mother did not hold him or touch him at all until he was several weeks old—she had a respiratory infection. She became an heiress during the years Milton was in treatment but she never got from under the shadow of the Great Depression and the downward rush of family security that had resulted during the 1930's. She remained "compulsively planful" and penurious, swearing never to be in want again. Milton too was a budget maker and put his oar in as a manager of the family finances! Mother, after marriage, spent 13 barren years so she was elated when Milton began gestating. She wanted a baby and it seemed that she yearned to keep Milton as her long-awaited baby forever. As her marriage waned she clung all the more to Milton, who secretly nourished great retaliatory rage toward his mother.

The father thought Milton was effeminate and undisciplined. He, aged 53, was a Depression product himself, rigid and insensitive, authoritarian, tending to project and be suspicious, an extreme racist, argumentative and unloving toward his wife, and overinvested in breadwinning. The social worker who labored for and with Milton's parents described the mother as an introjecting obsessive and the father as a projecting obsessive.

During two and one-half years of treatment the mother and Milton (more than the father) made symptomatic improvement. However, two years later the family returned at the request of Milton because of recrudescent obsessions about physical harm and school failure. Milton said he knew his "worries" were "silly" and hoped "since you helped me before you might again." Treatment continued, off and on, until Milton completed high school. Gradual improvements came for the boy, but scarcely any boon to the parents, and the younger sister moved into the spotlight as the most unhappy family member, occupying the role of patient.

Child #41
MOSES X

Moses was an 11-year-old boy of German and Hungarian derivation. He was the eldest of five children born to a Roman Catholic couple in their mid-thirties at the time Moses was seen in psychiatric consultation. When Moses was three years old his mother, having had her third baby, attempted suicide.

Moses impressed the examining psychiatrist (who treated him in 22 psychotherapy sessions over a period of seven months) as an obsessive-compulsive lad whose major "hangup" was along the omnipotence-helplessness axis. In his mother's words, "He's sad and sees no joy in life. He prefers making up stories to being with people looking at a sunset." Moses called his fantasies "my private enterprises."

He strove for perfection, claiming his religion disallowed anger, but his recurrent fantasies had to do with murdering others. He

came to acknowledge some of his anger—toward the maternal
grandfather first of all, then toward his father, his 10-year-old
brother and finally his mother—and it was the latter with whom he
struggled for his autonomy and his very life, as he saw it. He was
not well motivated for independence and emotional growth, seeking only intellectual development and the outward mannerisms of
a grownup. His father expressed it as Moses' living as a social
misfit.

A chronic bedwetter, Moses stopped wetting during the brief
treatment although the subject was not emphasized at all. Also, he
became less stuffy, less the "little old professor" which was the
label his schoolmates had applied to him. Some of his fears of the
dark, deep water, staircases, etc., abated during treatment. The
therapist lamented, after the 19th hour, "Moses needs to be seen
three or four times weekly, but the family can manage to bring
him for such a long distance only every second week." Within a
month the treatment stopped abruptly when the family moved to
another state where the father had obtained a better job.

Therapy was rocky because of the boy's hyper-moralizing discussion of the counsels of perfection, of racial segregation (he was
for integration), of politics, of cigarette smoking, of birth control,
etc. He was ever vigilant to find himself one-up morally with respect to his parents and his therapist, and this made for some
"interpersonal disjointedness" in his relation with the therapist.
The therapist advocated letting up and the boy advocated perfection, and it was difficult to adjust their clashing viewpoints when
the sessions were two weeks apart. The boy said it in these terms:
"The main thing wrong is that you praise me for being natural, but
I feel like I have to put business before pleasure. I need to get
more exercise in self-control . . . my mother can't get the picture
the way you do. They look blank when I say what you say. And
they really need to know your ideas about me. I don't know why
they don't get your ideas. If you could hand over some of your
ideas to Mommy it would be better for me." Left to his own
resources within the family culture, Moses made only innovations
such as "giving up for Lent" a handclapping compulsion (his
abstinence, moreover, was fairly successful). "I clap my hands

because they're stupid and don't know what to do. They're clumsy little hands. They're rebellious and do what I don't want them to do. They don't know who's the master." He knew that his mother cultivated his preoccupation with control and domination but that it had become internalized, incorporated as a part of hiumself: "Sometimes I think I have a right to my own feelings. I am a harsh criticism of myself. I have a bad stern thing down there (points to chest) that says I can't have my own feeling and be good." Yet he located his perfectionistic motor between his eyes: "It causes me to get all nervoused up. It is in control of my nervous system and my waterworks (tears). It's between my eyes. It has a nice location near my brain, but a very bad disposition. I'll get rid of it one of these days. It calls me stupid, ignorant, weak, a coward. It expects me not to exercise but to be strong and have no fears. It tells me because he (the 10-year-old brother) does it I gotta do it. It's got control of everything. It's vicious. I hope I can overcome it someday."

Child #42
NED C

Ned was nine years old when he first came to child psychiatry clinic. At that time he felt inferior, appeared hyperkinetic and was said to fly off in anger too frequently. He was the second of three boys and compared adversely to his older and younger brothers. Since birth, he'd suffered colic, asthma, frequent diarrhea, allergies, and nervousness. The parents, a 38-year-old father who was a doctor and a 37-year-old emotionally disturbed mother who was a longtime "friend and supporter of psychotherapy," feared Ned might be autistic. The examining team recommended family therapy lest the boy develop along the lines of anxiety neurosis and hypochondriacal reaction. They commented upon the mother's anxiousness and confusion, and the father's aloofness from vigorous, affective participation in the family's life. The team also noted a "double bind" or two in the family interaction. The boy's worries, preoccupations, and diphasic speech and thought, did not warrant the diagnosis of obsession *at that time*. He harbored but was afraid to show his hatred of his mother.

The advice for family therapy did not take. The mother, though, continued with individual psychotherapy. Two years later Ned returned to child psychiatry clinic (and a new evaluation team) presenting many of the same traits (to which had been added a fear he was homosexual)—but seen in a new light on the second appearance he was regarded as obsessive-compulsive. "On projective tests, his approach reflects an obsessive style of perceptual organization which accounts for a surface appearance of calmness and competence. But the intensity of his concerns betrays this facade and shows his troubled, preoccupied, confused, and highly ambivalent inner world."

His outer world was no bed of roses, either. During his weekly and twice-weekly therapy, race riots occurred at his junior high school. His mother, who took up an extramarital affair, became psychotic and was hospitalized for several weeks in a distant state. Hence, Ned was called upon to face many stresses and strains in reality, as well as in fantasy. He did become more natural, more outgoing. He made friends and in his words, "I used to be shy and withdrawn. I was a lonely person . . . I had few friends, and I complained of little unimportant things. Now I feel better. Sometimes I could run away from home, and I think about it, but I'd remember to call you first."

Child #43
RALPH L

Ralph was an extremely well-mannered, ingratiating, rather good-looking 10-year-old, brought in by his mother because of his learning problems at school, excessive daydreaming, inattentiveness, and a mutual difficulty in mother-child communication. His mother viewed these problems as a prelude to later, possibly more serious difficulties. Indeed Ralph showed signs of incipient neurosis and not of any fixed pathology.

Ralph's father experienced an unexceptional childhood although he did seem overly dependent on his own mother who had pushed him intellectually. His marriage to Ralph's mother lasted 18 years and terminated in divorce two years before Ralph was seen for treatment. During the entirety of their marriage he was an alcoholic. His abusiveness when drunk and overattentiveness when sober was a primary source of marital difficulties, exacerbated by financial problems resulting from the alcoholism. Ralph's maternal grandfather had been killed when his mother was six. His maternal grandmother had been domineering and an alcoholic, as were six or seven other members of his mother's family. During the course of two marriages the mother had six miscarriages, followed by the successful (although complicated) delivery of Ralph and, four years later, a girl. She had received a partial hysterectomy for cancer, and surgery for double hernia. She was allergic to a wide variety of substances. Four years before she brought Ralph for treatment, she had a "nervous breakdown" from which she was still recovering at the time of Ralph's treatment. She tended to work until she was "stupid" with fatigue, both to alleviate her financial difficulties and to escape her problems. Her work reputation was that of an effective office administrator.

Ralph had a history of hospitalization for tonsillectomy at age four, surgery for hydrocele and hernia at age five, and hospitalization, and prolonged separation, with pneumonia at age six. Both he and his mother were constant victims of flu.

Ralph was of above average intelligence with a breadth of interest and a rich imagination. His basic anxiety revolved around fears of survival. His woes were existential—the world appeared to him to be unsafe and unpredictable. In view of the family's incredible difficulties, Ralph's view was plausible! He used a crisp manner, deriding humor, sarcasm, compulsive constraint and silence in an attempt to control, and he tended to give minimally of himself. Ralph was unable to accept angry feelings towards his mother, and all who saw him believed he definitely needed a father with whom he could identify and who could aid him in separation-individuation. Neither Ralph, his mother nor his father had completely accepted the divorce and all had strong feelings for each other.

Child #44
RUFUS T

This 10-year-old chubby lad, addressing all adults as sir and ma'am, was referred because the family's pediatrician found him to be too constricted, too compulsive, and too panicky about failure at school. The parents (father, aged 50; mother, 35) were worried that Rufus, the eldest of their three sons, had become more like a robot than a boy, seemed unhappy and to be withdrawing increasingly from any trust or enjoyment of his family. He struck the examining psychiatrist as "overcorrect, pseudomature, and like an alienated automaton." The psychologist's observations and test report consisted of many of the following terms to describe Rufus: guarded, constricted, vacant, anger undone by compliance, compulsive, bland, denial, mechanized, and unnatural. His intelligence quotient was in the normal range, and it was speculated that, even without the neurotic interference, he would have scored no higher than about 110 IQ.

Rufus appeared to the therapist to be in need of loosening up, accepting his natural feelings, and dispensing with his undue tidiness. What was early appreciated as virtuous—his constant cleaning of ashtrays and arranging of magazines, books, etc.—had come to be an irritating thing for his parents and his brothers. Rufus suffered from tension headaches, and this brought some indulgence of his controlling behavior. But his general state of being "nasty nice" rankled, and his parents were overtly angered by his frequent repetition of everything the parents said, but, as if in an attempt to agree with them and please them, the echolalia was done sweetly.

During treatment, his fears of separating from his mother came to be seen as part of his sadomasochistic bonding to her. His sexual problems were found to be extreme, with Oedipal longings and castration fears near the surface, and with much ignorance and factual confusion concerning genital, gestational, and parturitional matters. The affect most pervasive of all the treatment interchanges was *hatred*, and Rufus came to do better both at home and school after sorting out some of his justifiable anger from his inappropriate anger. His learning problem at school improved apace, and his compulsions and rigid demeanor let up.

The mother herself was constricted, "should oriented," conventional and eager to please. She seldom talked about her husband, and seemed to have set up an emotional life in which the significant others were her sons only. The father was loath to be involved in the psychiatric treatment of his son, but with insistence he did come for sessions with a social worker and proved to be a father and husband who could change, when help was made available to him. He and Rufus became closer love objects for one another, and the father helped Rufus out of the intense, ambivalent attachment to his mother. Both the mother and the father complained regularly of the long trip required to bring Rufus for treatment, and on two occasions they stopped for several weeks and then reconsidered. The boy, then, was not alone in indecisiveness and resistance to change.

Child #45
SAM M

Sam was referred for psychiatric evaluation because of his inability to sleep by himself, his school difficulties with an IQ in the dull-normal range, his tantrums, hyperactivity, perculiarities about all odors, and constant smelling and washing of his hands. At the time of the referral he was nine years old. The most notable occurrences in his development were a history of colic until he was three months old, caretaking by several maids while his mother worked until he was about three, and finally the adoption by his parents of an 11-year-old mentally retarded boy when he was three. Because of his colic, Sam was rocked constantly for his first three months and this appeared to be the start of a lifelong history of slavish attention provided him by his parents. His father refused to discipline him at all and Sam threw tantrums when his mother attempted to limit him. The adoption of an older brother (in Sam's eyes) was a tremendous slight and he remained resentful and hostile to this new brother.

Sam was enuretic until five years old, and, while then successfully toilet trained, he "refused to wipe himself" until he was nine years old, just one and one-half months before the beginning of therapy. All attempts to get him to take care of himself only resulted in fecal smearing. His parents bathed him and dressed him until he was eight. When he was referred Sam still would not put on his own shoes and socks. Domestic life for the family was complicated by a "musical beds" routine. From the age of three, when Sam first indicated he was scared of the dark, of shadows and "boogey men" that might creep in the window, Sam would not sleep by himself. He would move in with the parent nearest him, eventually displacing him from the bed. Shortly after the parent left, Sam would awaken and go hunting for an occupied bed.

All his life Sam had been excessively sensitive to smells, screaming in response to cigarette smoke, perfume, hair spray, etc. Six months before the referral (age eight and one-half), he began obsessively sniffing his hands, constantly washing them, and he refused to do chores which would bring him in contact with things that smelled offensive. This defiant behavior essentially replaced his more passive complaining about smells.

It became apparent that Sam's father was an immature man who would rather spend his time working, or in obsessive pursuit of his hobby, collecting data on state political figures and surmising about their political machinations. The father also tended to be passive-aggressive, sly and secretive, and used Sam to act out his own resentment of his wife. The father encouraged Sam to hit the doctor, too, if the latter asked him questions he didn't like. Sam's mother was unable to cope with both Sam's and his father's behavior, particularly since she received no support in discipline. She, also, used Sam to satisfy her sexual needs. At times she stroked Sam, and attempted to kiss him on the mouth. Her sexual life with her husband was essentially nil. All in all, both Sam's parents had stormy childhoods of their own and their approach to their own marriage and to Sam was consequently adolescent. Both appeared to be physically and emotionally afraid of Sam.

In this atmosphere Sam discovered that the only way to win love was to act like a baby. His parents' total lack of control left him completely in charge and the resultant anxiety and guilt threatened him. Sam responded with regression, obsessive-compulsive smelling and hand washing, denial, repression, and a phobic fear of the dark. He tried to cope.

Child #46
SAUL C

Saul was almost 13 years old and in the seventh grade when he was referred for psychiatric services regarding his "immaturity and compulsive behavior." His mother was a 32-year-old Roman Catholic who had guiltily and reluctantly divorced his father when Saul was four years old. Saul's only sibling, a little brother, was then two years old. Their mother had later remarried, and had a three-year-old daughter by her second husband. In this family the mother stayed on the defensive. Her husband, Saul's stepfather, portrayed himself as a 36-year-old New England Brahmin who felt he "could get by with murder" because his wife would never bring herself to divorce a second time. In return for his exalted style, he demanded nothing more than order, logic, and perfection! Marital conflict raged. The stepfather's insensitivity and disrespect for Saul, for the mother, and for the younger boy were really the final straw that brought Saul into care although he came ostensibly for tics that had existed "since very early childhood" (that is, since the mother's divorce). Divorce was made into a capital plague within the family values.

Saul was not an ordinary boy, and assuredly not an ordinary tiqueur. His head and upper extremity tics said symbolically: "Take it away." They worsened when he was fatigued or nervous. His eyeblink, however, was not quite like the other tics. It had the quality of a compulsive act to ward off murderous anger toward members of his family mainly, secondarily toward his age-mates outside of the family. Saul considered all of his "twitches" embarrassing but the eyeblink seemed particularly nonsensical because he felt he *had to* do it.

Familial patterns were complex. Having attempted suicide when Saul was six years old, the inconsistent and guilt-ridden Catholic mother felt morally blackmailed by the stepfather. She came out of a family of alcoholism, and violence, and divorce. The stepfather in effect did blackmail the mother, and the mother in turn blackmailed Saul and his brother. The little girl, almost everyone's darling, was resented sorely by Saul. All the family members were experts in "fighting dirty."

Saul placed himself, in fantasy, in the noble position of fighting on behalf of his mother and of being able to preserve or break up his mother's marriage—almost accurate but a slightly grandiose assessment. At one point, after seeing a movie about the life of Freud, he identified with Freud's affectional preference for mother, not father. "Freud liked his Mom much more than his Dad. Still, the only time I felt jealous of Mom not loving me more than anybody was when [little half-sister] was born, she stopped paying attention to us." He had a shifting hero identification with great men and felt that only his age and his twitches prevented his own achievement of superlative fame and fortune. He resented that "in Boy Scout troop those fools all call us *the Catholics.*" He envied his stepfather's taking any patriarchal and sexist prerogatives, and stated his resentment generally in the fifth session, "Adults are so crazy. They enjoy life themselves, but they won't let kids have any of it." Envy, resentment, and hatred went on unabated until the boy became involved in psychotherapy for about five months at age 12 to 13 years. His compulsive eyeblinking disappeared fairly early and his tics seldom flared up by the time he was removed by his stepfather from association with what the stepfather called "your mother's damned psychiatrist." He was more relaxed and less perfectionistic. The family needed to travel 150 miles to get to the psychiatrist and the parents—perhaps understandably—opted to stop when symptoms were relieved.

Saul reported six dreams during the ten psychiatric sessions, and his dreams along with his recounting of his "biggest emotional time since last here" provided the major content of the therapy hours. His dreams were steeped in fear and murder, monsters, snakes, bugs, and spiders, "Japs" and blacks. He told the doctor, "I know why you think my dreams are so important. A dream is a picture of something in your subconscious: a figment of the subconscious imagination, sometimes fact with real people and sometimes fiction." The therapist expressed regret at the unavoidable early termination of Saul's treatment.

Child #47
STAN C

Stan was the eldest of four children, and the only boy in a family which began with the marriage of two professional people. Treatment was undertaken when Stan was 11 years old because of a year-long flurry of phobias, obsessions, and compulsions. Stan called the compulsions "promptings." He was preoccupied with germs, dirt, danger and bodily harm, sexual unrest, insomnia, and mounting compulsive rituals. School phobia had kept him at home for four months. Both parents had yielded to some of Stan's efforts to "boss" them. Not so, his sisters. He fought with any and all; however, his battle with his mother was for him the most captivating and had the most far-reaching roots. During his second therapy session, he responded on Sentence Completion test to the stems indicated in italics: *If I only* "had a mother." *Mother should* "not switch me." His first dream was of a battle with a queen leading each army. In the first hour he identified the interpersonal significance of his compulsions in this wise:

> I can't tell you what my troubles are. I can tell you what I do that's objectionable to my parents, especially Mama, and to me too, and probably to anybody else: I do things like if I see a spot on the floor—one that I imagine—I wanta keep from stepping on those dots . . . and if I do step on a dot I have to go back and step on it again. It hasn't happened here but it does at school and at home. I been outa school nearly four months and I wanta go back. I quit because I wasn't getting along well with other children. I do better whenever I am with my mother right there with me. Maybe my trouble is some feelings I don't understand. The spot is like feces, or dust maybe. Sometimes I backtrack and do things by threes [he smacks his lips and supinates his outspread hands]. I go back and add two to make it come out five or ten. Sometimes I'll intentionally trip, just so's to have a minor to ward off a major.

He confided rather readily, although he said, "This talk embarrasses me and makes me nervous and my explanations are not logical. Why I do things is silly, so that gives me a headache." He feared "something will go up through my anus." There were other signs of his "anality" as he talked of pleasurable, however sinful, enjoyment he derived from varied anal manipulations.

Stan made drawings in and out of the therapy sessions. He was a prolific dreamer who did insightful work concerning his dreams of queens, monsters, shepherds, petrified cavemen, deformed torturers, biting snakes, tigers, giant frogs with monkey faces, the sun exploding, and so on. He talked, and talked, but more easily and naturally with less of the intonation of a Southern belle as therapy progressed. After 35 sessions spread over 50 weeks (this boy had to travel 200 miles each way to participate in psychotherapy), Stan was virtually symptom free and termination occurred. Five months later he returned for two more interviews because of a very dramatic *délire de toucher*. He was masturbating with both enjoyment and guilt at that time, and he smiled when he understood what was going on.

Once again, when he was 13 years old, he came one time, and then again at age 22. As a young adult he was rather deeply involved religiously with a fundamentalist group and looked like a very savvy but finicky obsessional character. He disclaimed having any outright obsessions or compulsions.

Child #48
WALT B

Walt was an eight-year-old son of a physician. His parents complained of his poor relationship with peers and teachers, that he was a poor sport and a consummate teaser, though prone to explosions when the tables were turned. According to them, Walt's problems included speech trouble, poor comprehension, talking incessantly to himself, having many temper tantrums and being chronically angry over the previous two years. They said he was too close to his maternal grandmother who "spoiled him miserably," that he was intensely rivalrous of his older sister, that he was very domineering, immature, extremely competitive and generally difficult to get along with. Their description of his personal qualities was unfortunately borne out during the therapist's interviews with Walt.

Walt's parents seemed to be basically good people. However, their generally negative appraisal of Walt, while largely accurate, also tended to sum up their own feelings about him. Both parents seemed to have rather rigid personalities, handling their feelings secretly, so much so that one of our social workers felt moved to describe them as a "contemporary reissue of Grant Wood's *American Gothic*." They did not seem to like Walt very much and showed ambivalence toward qualities and behaviors they complained about. For example, the competitiveness that was very highly valued by the father was viewed as a fault in the son. The boy's acting out of parental attitudes and wishes seemed to be a real possibility. Walt's maternal grandmother was the sort of person who was at once desperately in need of warm affection and physical contact and absolutely repellent in her personal manner of constantly striking out for gratification of her selfish desires or in retribution for perceived slights. A most difficult person to live with, was this maternal grandmother. She had attached herself to Walt, an unhealthy relationship for him, and he had become the unfortunate recipient of much of his parents' hostility (felt but not expressed) to his grandmother.

Walt's feeling of rejection by his parents, his awareness that his less stormy sibling was preferred, and his desperate need for controls, all led to a very shaky ego strength. Related to this was a general approach to tasks that was impulsive, careless and error ridden. He showed, besides trouble in concentration and difficulty in persevering, continual use of denial and projection as defenses when he felt threatened—frequently he would strike out critially at the examiner when pressured in the testing situation—and a tendency to collapse in tears when his feelings were approached. Walt showed himself to be unable to read his mother. He was preoccupied with power struggle. His grandmother's tendency to dwell on crime, violence, burglars, "what is this world coming to" sort of things, was associated with a definite obsession with these ideas on Walt's part, accompanied by a ritual of door locking and checking. Walt used compulsions, and obsessive ideation and ritual, to handle his enormous anxiety about himself and his place in the world.

Child #49
WILL S

Will was an attractive but rather sullen looking nine-and-a-half-year-old third grader, initially evaluated for psychotherapy because of his negativistic behavior at school. This consisted of dawdling, not getting his work done on time, being generally disruptive, openly defiant of his teachers, and persistently ridiculing toward peers. His behavior at home was sullen, whining, brooding, and generally unsatisfactory to his parents. He was withdrawn, very guarded in any expression of affect, and, in general, miserable.

It was quite clear from the beginning that his behavior at school was a direct displacement from his conflict at home. His paternal grandmother, a domineering old lady, was an integral part of the family. Will's father, a doctor, harbored deep resentment of the paternal grandmother's behavior toward him personally, and had not been able to resolve his relationship with her. Will's mother became the unfortunate recipient of the father's resulting hostile feelings. While his wife was an alert, normally aggressive woman, she responded in a compulsive way to this, knowing that anger would not be tolerated by her husband. Will's father appeared to be the dominant member of the family. His personal qualities seemed to be those of exactness, high expectations, and good intellect: he was somewhat compulsive and had little time to give to his family. With respect to Will, and Will's younger sister and brother, both parents were highly critical, judgmental, quite moralizing and, in general, unaccepting and manifesting little tolerance for honest expression of feelings. Will's mother, in particular, at once suppressed her own feelings of anxiety about Will while tolerating "absolutely no sass" from the boy. In an environment where very little expression of aggression or hostility occurred, Will could only act out these feelings in school.

From the beginning, Will exhibited, as a result of all this, a strained, "hyperdeveloped" conscience. This was evidenced in his preoccupation with cleanliness, his stringent restrictions on any expression of anger or assertiveness directly toward his parents, his apparent contempt for his peers, his complete intolerance of his own imperfections, and his externalizing and projecting these onto all authoritarian figures. His superego was shown also in his inability to accept his own mistakes and shortcomings, and, hence, in his reticent and guarded attitude toward any risk or trying anything new. All this seemed to be responsible for his depressed demeanor and his generally compulsive behavior, rigid control of feelings, and failure to express himself intimately or warmly. Hostility towards parents, guilt, threats of sexual lust, anger with siblings, all served to provide the underlying anxiety to keep him going in an obsessive-compulsive type of adjustment. The pattern of adjustment was of course founded in the obsessive-compulsive nature of Will's parents. There is a Southern saying when children are like their parents, "The child didn't suck it off his thumb."

5

Pathogenesis and Etiology

THIS CHAPTER WILL DEAL with matters known commonly as etiology, pathogenesis, pathodynamics, and predispositions. Occasionally, we will touch again upon some of the substance that arose in earlier discussion of the child, the family and the clinical picture. A survey of child psychiatric theory and research on the topic of how obsessive children come to be ill is, however, definitely in order.

Causes. In an earlier scientific era, a more deterministic age, it was required that the psychiatrist search out *the causes* of any disorder he wished to discuss. Conversely, today, after quantum theory and discontinuity have had some influences on our thought patterns, the *Zeitgeist* no longer requires a last word about "final causes." Experience has shown that similar outcomes of mental deviance or illness emerge from different circumstances—that is, the same disorder can be generated in diverse breeding grounds. Oftentimes, a notion of complementarity is required, and either of two (or more) alternative or complementary views can hardly be

191

avoided if we wish to explain the genesis of disordered behavior. A physicist can conceive of waves and corpuscles as alternative or complementary views of energy and matter, and he does not apologize for his imprecision. The important thing for him is to get the job done in that way which includes as many observed events as possible. The physicist does not make a fetish of his working hypotheses and theories. In a spirit approaching that of a Zen master, the modern physicist is content with workable paradoxes and negotiable dilemmas.

In child psychiatry, as in the behavioral sciences generally, we must content ourselves with conclusions that involve *multiple causation* and *mutual dependence*. The certitude that comes from isolating *the* pathogenic agent in infectious disease is not for us. Indeed, with a modicum of political sophistication, today it seems almost simple-minded to think that parasites or bacteria (and not poverty or lowered host resistance or unsocialized medicine) are *the cause* of many infections and infestations. In child psychiatry, when we do find a one-cause "explanation" being palmed off, we have learned to regard it suspiciously, as wishful thinking, or as dogmatism, unwarranted by reality, by the actual experiences of children in complex interaction with their family members, with their own self concepts, and with their own bodies.

Yet child psychiatry is not totally empirical, for we do seek after general rational principles that aid us in our problem-solving operations. We do, therefore, wish to find those general forms of biosocial conditions most frequently correlated with the origination and development of neurotic disorder in children, including obsessives. Whenever possible, we would like to demonstrate *causal* connections among correlates. Our intellectual curiosities crave some kind of intellectual satisfaction. We want to know how the problem starts in order to control it and prevent it.

The job of making dynamic assessments of complex interpersonal situations is indeed an important part of the child psychiatrist's task, and one he cannot shirk if he is going to help the children and parents with whom he works. As a clinician, he must size up the situation and move on toward solving problems. The solving is what matters most. Theories of mutually dependent correlates certainly have no intrinsic merit simply because they are more complicated—that is, because they initially appear murkier and more difficult—but instead *specifically* because they do fuller justice to what we *can* say (backed up by some rather hard evidence) about the pathogenesis of childhood obsessions. When simpler but untenable explanations have great allure, I think—in the interest of intellectual integrity—we must acknowledge that that is just the way it is. Our "simple truths" are often untrue. Even if a one-cause, one-effect explanation gains votes or sells books, it "prevents a rational conception of interdependence and cumulative dynamic causation" (Myrdal, 1944, p. 1069).

Simple, linear cause-to-effect reasoning was carried, in the first place, into science from folk thinking. Everything is either a cause or an effect. This way of reasoning has had a very important place in fundamental biomedical research and theory. It has not only been "satisfying" cognitively to the biomedical scientist but also has been *fruitful* in controlling infections, parasites, tumors, and metabolic "errors." On the other hand, in the mental health fields, including child psychiatry and child development, cause and effect reasoning has *not* been fruitful. It is *only*, as the middle class Britishers say when their enthusiasm peaks, *"Thought provoking."* Mutual dependence theory, however, *is* fruitful for child psychiatry. Mutual dependence thinking has both logical and empirical advantages over simple cause and effect.

Mutual dependence theory contrasts with cause-effect thinking in the following way. Obsessive symptoms, in accordance with one example of cause-effect reasoning, develop in a child because the child undergoes harsh toilet training. Harsh toilet training is of course the cause; obsessive symptoms, the effect. According to interdependence and cumulation thinking, however, harsh toilet training may be elicited in the mother by a child who already shows some obsessive and overly defiant features; it may also appear in the early lives of children who *do not* develop obsessive symptoms, or in obsessive children whose harsh toilet discipline is an apparently conspicuous variable; or in other obsessives where it seems relatively insignificant. Wherever it occurs, harsh toilet training acts as any other variable: it behaves in an inseparable, cumulative, interactive, and interdependent way as part of the entire dynamic system. But alone it does not explain obsession.

Cause-effect reasoning in the foregoing example reflects a sampling bias (too fragmentary observation of unrepresentative cases), of course, but even more basically it reflects a craving to "explain" things simply. For scientific work, the more useful imperative would be to explain things *accurately*. There is a concrete consequence of choice of viewpoint. LaBarre (1945) chose to consider harsh toilet training as causally related in a linear fashion to obsessive disorder; Sandor Rado (1969) chose to impute causal status to a more inclusive interpersonal style, namely, the autonomy battle between mother and infant. Rado's view seems to me to be superior to LaBarre's merely because it explains a greater number of obsessive cases actually seen in treatment. Rado's more comprehensive view is, then, more fruitful than the one-cause, one-effect viewpoint.

Another example might be illuminating. It points up some of my own deficits. My views, borrowed from Fromm (1944), of the authoritarian family atmosphere as a precondition for obsessive illness in the child, tend to lump a range of variables together as if they were one generic "cause" of childhood obsession. The risk again is one of oversimplification of a complex and dynamic set of variables. This is what Bingham Dai (1972) objected to when he argued his viewpoint that the basic precondition is not in a specific family order but instead in a tendency of parents to stress *any* or *all* cultural elements in such a way that the child's "nature" is interfered with. A concrete consequence of this further differentiation of viewpoint is that the one-cause (authoritarianism) approach is overly specific and, therefore, less fruitful than the perspective of Dai which defines conditions that run transculturally and refer to a lack of parental empathy.

Nonetheless, some move toward simplicity and specificity holds great attraction. Without some effort at assigning weightings to the variables and to nailing down the more important conditions, we may become lost in concepts of such generality that they do not help to explain childhood obsessive disorders. What is involved in the genesis of obsessive illness specifically and not in neurosis generally is what seems important to search for. More-over, some specification, according to an older terminology, of the *necessary conditions* as distinguished from the *sufficient causes* for generating obsessive illness is also quite in order.

Necessary conditions are those elements which we abstract from a field of forces, singling them out because they provide the *sine qua non* for precipitating obsessive illness in children. Without these conditions there could be no obsessional illness, but, still, the occurrence of these conditions does not guarantee that the illness will occur. *Sufficient conditions* or sufficient causes, how-ever, do *guarantee* the occurrence of obsessive illness and also guarantee that the obsessive illness will not occur when these causes or conditions are not operating. At least, then, we should strive to weigh and measure our interdependent variables to *that* extent—that we parcel out some grades and differences among the sets of variables, such as distinguishing the *necessary* from the *sufficient* ones. By the end of this chapter we will have made some attempts along this line, based upon the study sample of 49 child-ren, but, first, we must consider some of the literature dealing with the etiology and genesis of childhood obsessive illness.

Viewpoints on Etiology and Pathogenesis. The study of child-hood obsession's pathogenesis—referring specifically to the origina-tion and development of the illness—has intrigued some leading theorists and clinicians, from Freud onward. Often, those who write about pathogenesis are "imaginative and global." Therefore, not all who have written about obsession's pathogenesis have given clearcut and systematic presentations, but there are seven "camps" which seem to have said enough about pathogenesis to warrant our consideration. An eighth camp exists but appears to have ex-empted itself from consideration, and I refer here to behavior modification. Spokesmen for this viewpoint assert that etiology and pathogenesis are irrelevant to the work at hand; changing behavior, whether the behavior is respondent or operant, is what counts and is *all* that counts, they insist. Therefore, while not generating etiologic concepts, the behavior modification theorists have served well as incisive critics of those who have been more "conceptual" in their inclinations.

Describing most child development concepts as imaginative and global, Bijou and Baer, in Honig (1966), commented that many traditional concepts "remained comfortably located in areas where no experimenter had the competence to manipulate processes: in the child's genes, for example, or in his state of neuromuscular development, or in his intelligence, or in his ego." Their perspicacious criticism I believe, applies in some measure to each of the seven camps briefly described in the following paragraphs.

1. *Genic programming: exemplified in the view of Woodruff and Pitts.* Deducing incidence chances for obsessive illness from the concordance of an identical twin pair—and considering the very slight probability that this could occur by chance alone (one in 600 million)—Woodruff and Pitts (1964) built a case for some "common determinants" of the concordance. They zeroed in, both cautiously and judiciously, on the likelihood that these common determinants lay in the hereditary or genic programming of the identical twins. They concluded that genes and heredity account for obsessive illness, in twins and others, but through extremely complex mechanisms not presently accessible to analysis.

Woodruff and Pitts were careful not to go beyond the data except by adhering to the most sober and safe statistical inferences. Because they were so careful, their example of the geneticist viewpoint is especially trenchant. Like some of their more speculative colleagues in genetics, they appropriated evidence from family studies—on the rationale that obsessions "run in families." Moreover, they referred to early onset of the obsessive-compulsive symptoms (at 2 1/2 years) as being indicative of the hereditary preprogramming of obsessional illness—on the assumption, presumably, that whatever happens in infancy is hereditary.

Other advocates and aspects of gene hypotheses are discussed in Chapter 2, but for the present we need to acknowledge only that there is a strong genetic thread woven throughout the literature on pathogenesis of obsessional disorder. The genetic camp warrants our serious regard.

2. *Psychosexual genesis—sexual trauma: view of the early Freud.* Sigmund Freud (1896, Part II) in his early years leaned heavily upon the belief that childhood sexuality (so-called child-

hood immorality) caused later neurosis, whether the neurosis was hysteric or obsessional. He held that neurosis, generically, was caused by "passive genital experiences during childhood" (that is, seduction by older persons) and that what distinguished obsessional neurosis was that the child enjoyed the seduction, and, subsequently, "committed sexual aggression against the opposite sex." Thereafter, until the outbreak of illness following sexual maturation, Freud reported, symptoms of conscientiousness, shame, self-distrust and doubt mark a phase of successful defense or "apparent health." The final stage, said Freud, was that in which repression failed, self reproach flared up, and obsessive symptoms appeared. The conscious obsessions, according to Freud, operated as "stand-ins" for infantile memories of the sexuality experienced. The conscious obsessive ideas and affects, Freud stated, are "compromise-formations between the repressed and the repressing ideas" so that by looking closely at the obsession's content the analyst could receive clues to the partially-repressed childish sexual activity which gave rise to the obsessional illness.

Freud's description in 1896 was lucid and forthright, although based upon a small number of cases. His study population of hysterics at that time numbered 13 and his obsessive patients were fewer still, or so one must surmise. The sexual aggressors against the children were mainly nursemaids, teachers and older brothers, Freud observed in a diatribe bordering on puritanism. Still, he retained his conviction that children were innocent until seduced by older persons. That seduction constituted what Freud called quite clearly "the germ of later neurosis."

It is worth emphasizing that Freud did not, in 1896, include the possibility of *childhood* obsessional illness, for he postulated the onset of the neurosis only after sexual maturation had occurred. One year earlier (1895), however, Freud had reported his acquaintance with an obsessive niece, aged 11 years, of one of his male obsessive patients. We do not know if this young person was sexually mature at age eleven. But we do know that Freud, in the last decade of the nineteenth century, concentrated his speculative gaze upon post-pubertal obsessives and he believed their neurosis traceable to childhood sexual "traumata." These simple formulations underwent considerable revamping toward complexity in the later writings of Freud and the Freudians. Nunberg (1955), though, did some orthodox and fast footwork when he wrote:

> "The 'traumatic' theory of neuroses thus, by and large, remains unchanged. It merely has to be extended to cover the fact that while there need not always be an external trauma, there must be an inner one in the form of an instinct danger."

3. *Psychosexual-aggressive genesis—anal sadism: view of the later Freud and Freudians.* By 1907, Sigmund Freud himself began to stress *the repression of current instincts* as the basis of obsessive disorder and to lessen his earlier stress on "childhood sexual immorality." In his discussion of the Rat Man, however, Freud (1909) again emphasized the patient's infantile sexual life as a psychogenetic condition of the adult obsession. The early view persisted at the same time that Freud stressed both the "pleasurable anality" of this young patient who had worms, and his anal *sadism* as displayed by his fantasy of the rat boring into his father's and "lady friend's" anuses. (See Appendix herein, Notes toward a Psychiatric Chronology of Obsession.) By 1913, though, in "The Predisposition to Obsessional Neurosis" Freud stated more openly and directly a changed perspective—now, not childhood genital criminal pleasures but anal eroticism was given top billing in the genesis of obsessive disorder. This anality, moreover, was based upon "regression from a higher state" as well as upon a persistent fixation at the anal sadistic stage. In either event, anal sadism was at the forefront. This, in its interpersonal setting, was primarily a question of "hostile impulses against parents"—a wish to have them die.

By 1923, with *The Ego and The Id*, Freud had begun to subdivide all the drives into Death Instinct (or *mortido* or *Thanatos*) and Eros, and saw the defect in obsessional disorder as either an un-fusion ("defusion," diffusion) or an originally inadequate fusion of the two sets of drives. For the rest of his life, Freud adhered steadfastly in his publications to the view that hatred and sadism—as expressions of death instinct—play the crucial role in obsessive neurosis.

Freudians such as Nunberg (in English translation, 1955, p. 57) hewed quite literally to this line in attributing to destructive or death instincts all drives which resist change and novelty, and seek the past ("eternal rest"). Melanie Klein was ultra-Freudian concerning death instinct. She went the run-of-the-mill Freudians one better when she stated in 1932, "It seems to me that obsessional neurosis is an attempt to cure the psychotic conditions which underlie it." Betty Joseph (1966), a Kleinian, saw obsessional neurosis—in a child under four—as an improvement upon his paranoid psychosis. The child, she notes with approbation, "progressed from a paranoid organization to an obsessional one during the first two years of analysis." This Kleinian view assuredly does not disclaim that human infancy is steeped in malevolence and death instinct.

Otto Fenichel (1945) and almost all North American psychoanalysts have played down the metaphysics involved in death instinct conceptions of obsessive illness. Indeed, many Freudians rejected Freud's view on this matter. An optimism of *Weltanschauung* prompted some of them to hold onto libido theory but to throw out *Thanatos*, and still others to throw out *libido* as well. Some other "Freudians" became exquisitely selective in an effort to keep a psychoanalysis that was more in step with behavioral science theory. That, at least, was the attempt made by Hartmann (1964) and the analytic ego psychologists.

4. *Drive/ego/objects—comprehensive metapsychology: view of Anna Freud, Nágera and the Hampstead Clinic group.* Nágera (1966) and A. Freud (1965) can be regarded as the foremost spokesmen of the Anna Freud group which developed a "psychoanalytic ego psychology" and brought the ego out of the psychoanalytic limbo into a zone of some worth and autonomy. Having recognized the ego, they moved on to articulate a "developmental psychoanalytic psychology." This latter phrase refers to their effort to assess the drives (both aggressive and libidinal), the ego, and the superego, as well as "object relations." Their assessment is dynamic, not static. They see children's behavior and intrapsychic life as well as interpersonal relations as occurring along a temporal trajectory. A child's biography is viewed along a pathway in time—

that is *the developmental perspective* of Anna Freud and her co-
workers. They attend to *developmental disturbances, developmental conflicts, neurotic conflicts* and *neurosis proper*, but they
insist it is not only pathology but also normal adjustment (con-
flict-free, phase-specific coping) which is of great concern in their
comprehensive "metapsychological assessment." The Developmental Profile is the concrete, practical application of the concep-
tualizations made by the Anna Freud-Nágera group (see A. Freud,
1965, pp. 138-147).

From their metapsychological standpoint, what do these
authors say about childhood obsession's pathogenesis and etiology? Virtually all that they report is within familiar fixation-
regression theory.

(1) Anna Freud followed her father's formulation (Freud,
1913) in contending that obsessional neurosis can be traced back
to the anal stage, at which time "the precocious ego" reacted
against the anal instincts, but she sees a causal role in anality *only
if* there were fixations such as those arising from "undue environmental interference with the child's anal impulses" (the words of
Nágera, 1966, p. 66).

(2) Phallic oedipal conflicts may emerge and promote regression to anality in "a child with constitutionally strong anal component instincts" (Nágera, 1966, p. 66), but "the ego will object
to the ensuing regression to the anal phase, and now an obsessional
neurosis could possibly develop if some other factors not always
clearly discernible are concomitantly present (strong ambivalence,
et cetera)."

Sandler and Joffe (1965) declared with a bit more firmness
(seemingly) that the role of the ego, and especially the "functional
regression of the ego," merits considerably more attention in
psychoanalysts' discussions of how obsessional neurosis emerges in
children. They consider "on the side of the ego" such matters as
the increase in magical thinking; the "aggressive cathexis" of
thinking; the defensive maneuvers of intellectualization, rationalization, isolation, undoing, reaction formation and displacement;
and (also an ego function, for them) the regression of object relationships to an "analized" state. Yet on p. 427 there appears the

caution that regression is not literal: "Indeed, we hardly ever see a complete and simple regression to the anal phase but rather see a regressive analization of Oedipal relationships and conflicts, so that masturbation conflicts, for example, may be a dominant feature of the clinical picture." Sandler and Joffe even wind up by noting that the proper approach is to evaluate id, ego and superego in the case of an obsessional child. Hence, they stress ego because ego has not been given enough emphasis, but not because they think ego regression stands in a special place. Sandler and Joffe worked in the Anna Freud group. When they wrote of obsessive defenses against psychotic disruption of the ego, they referred not to Melanie Klein's work but to the work of Ismond Rosen (1957) and E. Stengel (1945).

After all is said and done, Anna Freud's group have hewed to a fairly orthodox Freudian line, omitting, however, Freud's explicit notions about sexual crimes, anal sadism and death instincts. Any eclectic leanings away from Freudian orthodoxy, including the leanings of Anna Freud, seem to have a taming and moderating effect.

5. *Mother-child battle—omnipotence, autonomy and authority: view of Rado and the neo-Freudians.* Developing out of their respective Freudian pasts, the neo-Freudians have done some far reaching revisions of Freudian metaphors such as "anal libido." Rado (1959, p. 330) extended the net of "anal stage" referents to include the child's "entire behavior."

> ... one sees obsessive patients whose bowel training has been uneventful, but they are nonetheless marked by the same severe conflict between guilty fear and defiant rage; it orginated in other behavior areas. The future obsessive patient's emphatic obedience and stubborn defiance, far from being limited to his bowel responses as a child, are spread over his entire behavior.

In Rado's neo-Freudian formulation, it is not anality *per se* but the *mode of enraged defiance*, alternating with *guilty fear*, which stamps the obsessive's neurotic style. This stylistic mode is considered by the neo-Freudians to be "what Freud adumbrated" or "what Freud really meant" or the "interpersonal essence of the Freudian insightful metaphors." Their idea is that some children fight about anal training and become obsessive as they become locked into the cycle of defiant rage and guilty fear, but that other children without any bowel training struggles get locked into the same obsessive cycle. The interpersonal setting is what counts, the struggle between mother and child, and the cycle of defiant rage and obedient fear. Rado (1969, p. 229) wrote:

> Fear of conscience and guilty fear rest on the belief in inescapable punishment. The belief is basically a dread of the omnipotence which has been delegated to the parents, and now the organism is terrified to discover that the parents can turn his own omnipotence against him. We must assume that stronger-than-average residues of primordial omnipotence are a factor in the predisposition to obsessive behavior.

Rado (1959, pp. 332-333) rounded out a plausible account of the genesis of obsessive behavior with its typical admixture of pride, fear and rage:

> The outcome is a tripartite motivating system: restored pride over repressed guilty fear over more strongly repressed defiant rage . . . now proud of its virtuous conduct, the organism does not choose to remember that it has been forced into morality by its guilty fear of inescapable punishment.

Khan (1971) came to similar conclusions but used the terminology of Melanie Klein, Winnicott and Bowlby. Khan cited "dread of annihilation" as the relevant infantile anxiety which drives obsessive children into a "compliant false-self organization."

Rado distinguished between obsessive attacks and obsessive traits, showing with case material how both the attack and traits reveal the core dynamic of "the infantile conflict between the child's over-strong tendency to self-assertive domination versus his still stronger clinging to the security of being loved and cared for." Rado took the orthodox Freudians to task for overrating *anxiety* (guilty fear, *Angst*) and underemphasizing *rage*, even after Freud had postulated the death instinct. Rado contended:

Beyond a shadow of a doubt, in the etiology of obsessive behavior the ultimate psychodynamically ascertainable factor is rage. (p. 338)

Rado had, in his mind's eye, whenever he encountered an adult obsessive, a picture of a biting, naysaying infant who overvalued his teeth and arms and legs—body parts, Rado insisted, which epitomized autonomy even more than the anus did.

6. *Learning negative feelings—rage and rectitude: view of Henry Laughlin.* The eclectic psychiatrist Henry P. Laughlin (1967) picked up on the more general and commonsense aspects of psychodynamicists such as Rado in his effort to evolve a summary statement about the etiology and genesis of obsessions. Laughlin's statements are astute, fair and highly sensible. Rado himself (1959, p. 339) had written this down-to-earth reminder:

The primary task of education is to domesticate the infant, to make him fit for social life by taming his rage. If this process miscarries, the child's inadequately controlled rage will cause behavior disorders. Trapped for decades in a labyrinth of misconstructed theories, it may well be that we are at last finding our way back to the obvious.

By attending to basics and, being post-Freudian, heedless of orthodox conceptual constraints, Laughlin could attend to the obvious, as Rado had enjoined. Laughlin's statements on the etiology of obsessional neurosis are made as if in answer to the question: *What real circumstances can stack the cards in favor of a child's developing an obsessive disorder?* Laughlin's responses to such a question encompass an understanding not only of the infant and the parents but also of their intrafamilial relations, and, to a certain extent, the values of the larger, surrounding sociocultural milieu. His is a comprehensive and humanistic viewpoint.

Laughlin (1967, pp. 342-343) labelled these conditions as *predisposing factors* for obsessional neurosis:

1. *Parental insecurity*
2. ... *rejection of the child*, with the struggle of the parent at concealment of this through the maintenance of an opposite or different outward facade.

This results in outwardly unreliable expressions. The child comes to doubt, and lack faith and trust. . .

3. *Parental overambitiousness* for the child's success and maturity.
4. Early overindulgence . . . succeeded by later stringent and contrasting *demands for responsibility and maturity.*
5. *Obsessive traits in the parents. . .*
6. Parental, social, and/or religious *condemnation of negative feelings.*
7. *Rejection . . . of spontaneous demonstrations of affection* by the child. *Curbs on spontaneity* of any kind.
8. *Familial, social and cultural premiums placed on obsessive traits. . .*
9. Overdeveloped *conscience*
10. . . . unresolved *Defiance-Submission Conflict*
11. Primordial infantile rage, from whatever source. *Discharge of rage . . . blocked.*

Beside listing these interlocked factors, Laughlin (1967, p. 325) underlined that the key problem in generating an obsessive illness is *the mother's rejection of the child's negative feelings.* Again, to quote him (p. 321):

Rage and its vicissitudes and resulting conflicts [more than sex] are often crucial in the psychodynamic elaboration of obsessional defense systems.

The final effect of Laughlin's consideration is to spotlight *rage and rectitude* as the most telling concerns between mother and child. Nothing could be put into a more convincing interpersonal framework, or could be more accurate, in my opinion. Laughlin acknowledged that *both* rage and rectitude *are learned*—although they are deemed by infant and parents to be contradictory—*during infancy*, in the intimate mother-child relationship as it is influenced by a broader culture that prizes and reinforces certain obsessive traits in both adults and children. It is difficult to imagine any formulation except one derived from careful empirical study that could go any further in giving an etiologic statement than does that one made by Henry Laughlin.

7. *Going against nature—parental empathy deficit: view of Bingham Dai and Leon Salzman.* Dai and Salzman did not disagree with any of the etiologic tenets put forth by Laughlin. They did, however, emphasize a particular aspect of parental behavior that put them into the mainstream of the non-libido theory (or theories) of Sullivan, Horney, Thompson and Fromm. What Dai and Salzman chose to emphasize most keenly was *the obsessive child's sense of being out of phase with the parents,* and of not being understood and loved. The parents are overly ardent in their efforts to mold, or control or shape, the child; the child feels he is "bad" as he innately and naturally *is.* Salzman (1968) referred to this in these terms:

> . . .the outside world may make excessive or extreme demands in terms of fulfilling the cultural modes . . . tending to promote or accelerate any already-exising doubts and apprehensions about oneself. (p. 88)

Further, on page 90, we read a concise etiology as put forth by Salzman:

> The history of obsessional development is as varied as one's environment and the personality of one's parents. The consistent theme in all obsessionals is the presence of anxieties about being in danger because of an incapacity to fulfill the requirements of others and to feel certain of one's acceptance.

What the parents ask is not what the child has to give. Hence, it is the child's dread of being on a different wave length, of being misunderstood and rejected, of lacking the parents' empathy, which is accentuated by Salzman, and also by Dai (1972). When parents do not "read" the child and respond aptly, trouble starts. Dai stated that he believed "any cultural emphasis which goes against the child's inner nature . . . leads to an obsessive disorder." Hence, Dai looks particularly to *over-constraining socialization (or enculturation) pressures, exerted on any aspect of a child's life,* as being the key conducive to obsessional illness. In this etiologic formulation, a deficit in empathy associated with infantilization or

overindulgence by parents—not solely irrational primitive authority—can set the stage for obsessional illness of a child. Certainly,
some of Dai's cases in China (1957) reflected a cultural emphasis
on overindulgence, not harsh training. If a child's inner longings
are not accepted by others, then the child becomes frightened
(anxious) because he senses that he is not accepted and he won-
ders, as Salzman said, if he *can* fulfill the requirements of others.
Obsessive doubting is established, and ambivalence toward others,
and the complete clinical picture ensues.

Onset. The psychiatric literature has been devoted to adult obsessives, by and large. One of the persistently argued themes has been
the age of onset for obsessive disorder. (See Appendix.) The question of onset has high relevance to etiology.

Freud (1913) contended that obsessive illness could occur as
early as six to eight years. Freud's placement of the disorder back
into childhood went against the grain of Legrand du Saulle (1875),
and many others, who contended that such a brainy and patrician
illness was for adults only. However, Séglas (1894) asserted that
obsessions often begin before puberty. Pitres and Régis (1902)
found onset as early as age five, and Janet (1903) presented a case
of a five-year-old obsessive. But many continued to assert that
there was no obsessive disorder before puberty.

By 1937 Woolley could declare, "The age of onset in cases
reported in the literature ranges from 18 months to 88 years, the
majority occurring before the age of 25." In 1942, though, Berman found a group of obsessive children with an onset age between 10 and 12 years, an age congenial to the Freudian requirements. Einar Kringlen (1970) found that one-half of a group of
adult obsessives had seen the illness commence before age 20 and
one-fifth before puberty. Many writers would incline to agree with
Woolley that onset can occur below age two, but some (Gesell and
Ilg, 1943; Bakwin and Bakwin, 1953; and Piaget, 1962) would say
that when it occurs at age two or three it is "normal" or "physi-
ologic." That is certainly the view of Anna Freud and her group.

Many non-Kleinian analysts today follow Humberto Nágera
(1966), insisting that onset during the anal stage is *not* an obsessive neurosis but merely normal anal behavior. Their contention is

that a true childhood obsessional neurosis cannot arise until the phallic Oedipal phase has been reached.

Perhaps a commonsense approach dictates that we set the age of onset to comply with patients whom we know and not with our *a priori* theories. We can do as Kringlen (1965) did, or as Pitres and Régis (1902) before him, and question adult obsessives. Or, with the aim to acquire fresher data, we might study children who are obsessive. Judd (1965) found an onset age-range in his group of children between six years four months and ten years two months. Not one child reported in Chapter 4 was under six years of age when seen, although six of the children were considered by their parents to have shown pathology—tics, tantrums, panic, restlessness, being upset by slight changes, etc.—dating back to age one year. The average age of onset, it was found, for the 49 obsessive children I surveyed was 5.8 years (standard deviation 3.5). The range of onset age was from one to 14 years. Exception may be taken because we saw no obsessive child younger than six years old, and accepted at face value some parental reports of earlier onset. As a rejoinder I would ask, "Who better than a small child's parent can answer queries as to *when this trouble began*?" Six parents of the 49 children studied had no hesitation in recounting examples of behavior of their preverbal children age one (that is, in their second year of life), evidencing the very trouble from which the children suffered when they were referred to psychiatry. Two children were said to have begun their obsessive problem at age two (third year of life); and seven at age three (fourth year of life). One could probably surmise, with safety, that obsessive children can have shown early signs of upset that did not abate after age one. It may be that some obsessive children give aberrant responses very early, responses that continue but solidify into unmistakable neuroses only by age six years. This way of looking at onset would be more compatible with geneticist views, or Kleinian, or my own, than with several others. But it would not really conflict with most of the etiologic theories, in fact.

6

Treatment

TO LEARN HOW malaria sickens and kills (and to understand "unexplainable," permanent cures which appear spontaneously), biomedical researchers needed to study malaria in untreated cases. In that way knowledge was gained concerning the *natural history* of malaria. Only against this background of malaria's natural history were investigators able to institute effective measures. Similarly, they are now able to evaluate the various anti-malarial treatments which appear from time to time. Like malaria, childhood obsession would be understood more logically, and a more rational treatment devised and evaluated, if we knew the longterm outcome of untreated cases of obsessive disorder in childhood. We would be able to test alternative treatment approaches, following the accepted canons of biomedical appraisal, and make conclusions about the respective approaches' efficiency and efficacy in controlling or curing the disorder.

Alas, as we have said, childhood obsessive disorder is not comparable to malaria or any bodily illness—for we know less precisely in the case of obsession about the relevant features of the pathogen, vector, milieu, and host. The simpler biomedical model is not applicable to a spectrum of problems, all of which we label *obsessive*, and the pathogenesis of which, although not fully settled, appears to pertain to a systematized biosocial network of interactive and interdependent variables. To add to the difficulty, obsessive disorder, far more than malaria, involves the critical doings of *selves*, not machines or brainless animals.

Natural history studies of obsessions in adults and children have been few in number and uneven in caliber. John Pollitt (1957, 1960), Ingram (1961), Kringlen (1965) and Rosenberg (1968) are the outstanding exceptions. Taken as a whole, their work affords the best review of outcome studies that has been made. Some of the studies span many decades and go rather far, though without being definitive and final toward achieving a "natural historiography" as Pollitt (1960, p. 94) himself defined the term.

> ... the natural history of a mental illness consists of the detailed development, course and decline of that illness in the lives of individuals in the mass, the characteristics of those individuals, the social effects of the illness, and the factors affecting the pathological process."

Edith Rüdin (1953) found that 39 percent of her 130 obsessives (both adults and children) showed a good prognosis, being followed from two to 26 years. She surmised that 30 percent got neither better nor worse, and 30 percent worsened—a few became schizophrenic or otherwise psychotic; but alcoholism and drug addiction were rare.

To be fairly restrained about it, I would suggest that the natural outcome of untreated cases of obsession in childhood is good if the illness basically only reflects an underlying mood disorder (depression) which is relieved. The outcome is bad if the obsessive picture indexes a schizophrenic process or a psychopathic bent. The outcome is highly uncertain for untreated cases that reflect an obsessional character or obsessional neurosis. In general, those untreated characterologic or neurotic cases in which sexual problems are outstanding are likely to have as poor an outcome as those in which problems with domination or hatred are outstanding. The situation is altered, I believe, when the children are treated, but this will be discussed in the section assessing changes with treatment.

STRATEGIES AND TECHNIQUES

In this section I will not make allusions to the technical literature on psychotherapy, but, instead, I will simply give a rather biased and personal view of what I think works best in psychotherapy with obsessive children.

Concerning duration, one expects to have the psychotherapy span from one and one-half to three or more years. The average is between one and one-half and two years for the majority of cases I have seen personally. For the cases seen by my colleagues and students, the average duration of treatment was 11 months. But this included very brief evaluations, with no therapy, along with some very brief therapy cases. With the "Rat Man," an adult, Freud, a genius, spent approximately one year.

I do not know how to hasten good results and, for that reason, would forecast to the child and his parents that a commitment of 24 months in treatment ought to be anticipated. Some time is taken in building a helpful relationship between me and a child— my luck has been poor in "relationship at first sight." I believe I can lop off a few months of treatment's duration by seeing a child four times weekly instead of three times weekly, but the span of time stays at around 20 months because the ones I arrange to see more often are also sicker. Older children also require a longer span of time in treatment, in my experience. With these children, I console myself that what took years to develop can take a couple of years to eradicate without my feeling too much a bungler.

To state it contrarily or provocatively, I *do know* how to lengthen, or prolong or delay, treatment with an obsessive child. I am of course against using these stratagems because I want the child to stop suffering as soon as possible, but here they are, capable of dragging out a miserable illness:

1) non-directiveness, including both the Axline/Rogers style and the noncommital, classical psychoanalytic approach. (I advocate, on the contrary, greater openness and interventionism by the therapist.)

2) attempting to find the unconscious symbolic meaning of each obsession or compulsion. (I advocate instead an invitation to greater naturalness, and even a "promise" that relief will come when the symptoms are not idolized as having an intrinsic, special, superhuman merit.)

3) offering obsessive advice to the child—on how to obsess, or on how to make rituals—as in the case of the behavior modifier who instructs a child to check only three times and then leave the room, etc. (I advocate letting the child remain the expert in obsession while I try to assist him in trying out non-obsessive ways.)

Concerning frequency of sessions, I find that practically nothing of merit can be done in less than one session weekly. It is not therapy if it can't be at least once a week. In Alfred Y's case, however, for reasons of geography (his home being an uncommon distance away) we got together for therapeutic work on two consecutive weekend days for one-half hour at each session; and that worked adequately. In general, the treatment "intensity" should be more than once weekly. I would prefer at least three times weekly, and I'd like to have the hours staggered throughout the week. In Daniel D's case, the morning sessions that we began having after several months of only afternoon sessions showed him less constricted and driven than the previous sessions, all of which had occurred at hours later in the day. I have repeated this with other obsessive children and I am half-convinced that regularity and routinization of scheduling can be de-emphasized with a salutary result. Of course, an obsessive child, as any other child, deserves a therapist who is serious, punctual and conscientious. If I am late for an appointment, I apoligize to the obsessive as to any other, and as with any child patient I make up *my* lateness but do not make up his. This is a fortunate policy to enunciate, for obsessive children are notorious foot-draggers and procrastinators. They are late in order to get their parents' goat and to try to get themselves presentably perfect, but I don't encourage them to do either

—not at my expense! On the other hand, if I do have the time, I tell the obsessive child that I can give him "some more time today," as a matter of fact. It is a good object lesson in doing what another needs, irrespective of a rigid schedule.

Certain child psychiatrists will insist that the obsessive child's parents must pay to show their earnestness, to manifest good motivation, and to make realistic provision for the need (or greed) of the child therapist. I have charged dearly for each hour, and I have charged not a penny. As a result, I know that payment is an irrelevancy when obsessive children suffer and are engaged in psychotherapy. In "welfare states" this is taken as axiomatic, and I believe in it. Suffering gives adequate motivation for cure and paying or not matters naught.

About hospitalization, which is often recommended in Scandinavia and England, I take a dim view. A child belongs with his family not with hospital staff members, however enlightened or humane the latter sometimes can be. Naturalness can best be achieved in the child's *natural habitat* of home, school and neighborhood, I insist. Parents often crave hospitalization for the child and, although I wouldn't hold out stubbornly against all odds, I'd prefer to try to convince them of the greater wisdom (on my side, of course) of having the child relearn and release in a more homelike setting. Some obsessive children can get very wild—runaway, destructive, and transiently psychotic—so it is best not to dogmatize and to keep open the alternative of hospitalization while insisting that outpatient care or day care is best for the growing child.

Concerning drugs to tranquilize, sedate and energize, my conclusion is that they have virtually no place in the psychotherapy regimen for the obsessive child. They can, when prescribed, muddy the water, distort the treatment relationship, and create dependencies and resistances that hinder more than they help.

I observe, despite the dogmatism just stated, that I do write more—if anything—prescriptions for obsessive children than for others. The prescriptions, though, are for antihistamines when they have colds, Lactinex for herpes, stool softeners for constipation, etc., the kind of attention to general medical needs that, so far as I can tell, does not impede psychotherapy.

Why should I compulsively refrain from touching an obsessive child? from doing physical examinations for school and summer camp? from suggesting and prescribing drugs that may be supportive and relieving? I am glad I found out, by going against some of the hallowed principles that I was taught, that being a doctor does not render psychotherapy ineffective. I might even, as time and learning continue, give up my reluctance to use psychotropic drugs with obsessive children.

I will not set out to condemn the child psychiatrist who is even more pressured than I by demands for services and who decides to take short cuts, intervene only in urgent crises, employ psychopharmacotherapy, etc. His style is not mine, yet if he is trying to be of aid to masses of suffering children my hat is off to him. It is, however, my job to teach what I know and do: psychotherapy with little utilization of psychotropic drugs. It is not my job to knock others who are trying to serve and are forced (as I) to practice an imprecise art.

Concerning the therapist's psychotherapeutic maneuvers:

1. *"For instance."* I convey to the child that I am not pleased with his general verbal formulations that only block his living. I am interested in real examples of his life experiences. I want to see, and help him to see, *events in context.* This provides him with a magnificent opportunity for "cognitive repair"—it encourages straighter thinking than the child has ever done as he moves from global-range statements to middle range and finally to an adequate empirical summation of particular events and situations. I butt in and ask the child to recall a concrete instance of some generality that he has uttered. I let him know that his behavior is tied to context and situation, and that we are intent on "freeing him up" by helping him to understand what is going on in his life.

2. *"Here and now."* It is daily life that we work with in psychotherapy. It is today (the day before, the day after) that we can scrutinize most accurately and in which changes can be most readily initiated. We do not place a high value on the search for origins

(although some obsessive children adore that search), but instead on a search for contemporary patterns and habits—interpersonal and intrapsychic. Nevertheless, obsessive children do have a history, and infantile patterns were stamped in the obsessive mode. Some illumination of the sickness is derived from "la recherche du temps perdu," and I do not rule out some attention to earlier childhood. Besides, interpretation of present symptoms as echoes and reflections of infantile insecurities (or conflicts) is appropriate in child psychotherapy. But I try, in the main, to let the child live more comfortably in his contemporary daily existence and to focus on the real present.

3. *"Thou and I."* I value the psychotherapeutic relationship with a child. The child knows I do and that he has, with respect to me, both professional claims and non-professional ties based on longings and cravings. He learns that his longings and cravings are always demanding to triumph over a realistic, professional relationship with me. Whether he calls me doctor, Paul or shrink, he knows that something out of the ordinary goes on between us. He also learns early that ours is a relationship that can be talked about, discussed and questioned ... while it occurs. He learns early that our relationship will end.

The therapist-obsessive child relationship is very much on the conscious agenda. Examining it has many advantages. A conscious and therapeutic relationship really occurs and hence is good matter for consensual validation. It is the foremost example we have of the present, the here and now. We can observe obsessive children at school and in play groups, if any, without the cramping presumably required of a therapist with adults. That gives us added grist for the here-and-now mill. We can make home visits, have family therapy sessions, even pay semi-social calls to camps, etc. More grist for here-and-now, more elucidation of I-and-thou.

Mel G, aged seven years, showed how a child wants the relationship to become non-professional and to serve some of his distorted object-needs. He had entered a time of some greater comfort, fuller expressiveness and naturalness, and seemed more "with it" (more eye contact, freer talk, less stilted body habits, etc.) during the sessions in my office. He asked me if other children come to see me—how often, how many, boys and girls, what they did. I had said something about his wondering if I had "other patients." I thought I might ferret out some competitive feelings and his wish to an exclusive title on me. Thereupon, Mel said, "Please, Dr. Adams, don't say 'patient.' I want to think of us as *friends*—not a doctor and a patient. The reason I come here is to help me, and you, from being lonely." Clarifying his competitiveness had to wait until some of his "do-nothing transference" first had been clarified. How can I work if he expects the sessions to do nothing about his problems, to be only innocuous visits to fend off loneliness?

The obsessive child discerns that I am not as a parent or relative. I am not a "real object" who will tie him up in my own unanalyzed cravings, for to the extent that I am engaged in something helpful with him I am being a doctor not a relative. That won't mean that I am aloof, trying to be dispassionate, neutral or Olympian (all somewhat "obsessive" virtues, after all). It *will* mean that I am very much myself, engaged and committed but striving to be a psychotherapist, not a love object. To use the technical jargon of many therapists, I would say that I do not strive to promote a passionate positive transference, to induce a transference neurosis. Instead, I strive to use our examined and open relationship as a vehicle for achieving the obsessive child's cognitive and emotional progression.

4. *"Feelings are 'in'."* Affects must be identified and clarified. The child's isolation or dissociation of affects from his total behavior is discouraged, even though his inclusion of affects makes him more scared (anxious) at first. I have to admit that the child is right when he tells me, "You make me talk about things that cause me to get worse." He thinks the therapist is supposed to make him feel good in spite of his madness. He claims he expects never to be jarred or stirred by therapy. Not so, because bad feelings cannot be isolated, denied and purged. They are there. And they will obtrude willy nilly. We will recognize the child's feelings. And, as he comes to know them better, he will be able to live with them in their full impact and significance. By that time he will have learned what Barnett (1966) called "experiential" as opposed to "essen-

tial" concepts. He will live with experiences *whole* not just in their cognitive and categorical aspects.

The obsessive child often tells the therapist that some identification of affect is "interesting." The obsessive child only values the cognitive aspect of his psychobiologic functions. His belittling of affect and feelings *is a part of his disturbance.* I make it a policy to confront the child in this way: Was what I said *interesting* or did it hurt? Was it "interesting" or did you feel scared when I said it?

In my trying to emphasize feelings and encouraging the child to express his feelings as they are felt, I make it a point to use words such as "feel-fear-hate-upset-love-crave-long for" in preference to words such as "think-idea-thought." The obsessive child is a poor thinker but does not know it; he is a strong feeler but does not know it. For that reason I prefer to stress his feelings and to uncover a strength he did not know he had. He takes heart in the process of coming to see himself as a feeler, who is improving as a thinker too.

5. *"Honesty pays."* The obsessive child is given to compulsive honesty, as befits any person who has some of the makings of a first class liar! He hems and haws, does and undoes, but he is ever prone to be "brutally frank." He will not hesitate to hold you up indefinitely while he obsessively weighs the pros and cons of an issue and strives to be fully, nit-picking truthful about something that is not all that important, whether true or untrue. He is a past master at deception and even when he is rewarded for it, truth telling is not easy.

Because the therapist knows his soft spot, I have found myself saying, more than to any other, to the obsessive child, "Tell me *truthfully* what you felt." Or, "Be very *frank*—tell me how you feel about her." Speaking very *honestly*, what are you feeling right now?" These simple statements appear challenging, and one might think they would induce an augmented doubting on the child's part—but I find they do not. Instead, they seem to elicit much more direct, simple, "honest" responses.

6. *"Keep it clean."* The obsessive child spins webs like a spider on LSD. He can turn a clear issue into a turbid doubting fit. As

Adler said, he emits smokescreens and fights only fake battles. He will go on and on, agonizingly for himself and the therapist, with doubt and counter-doubt about the angels on the head of a pin. Literally, he wears himself out about the insoluble and untestable "problems" that come to his mind. All this verbosity is most unproductive, so I have learned to stop it short. This talk is only, as an obsessive adolescent told me, "mountains of bull-shit." It serves no constructive purpose except to play out repetitively the obsessive illness. I would rather turn the child mute (temporarily) and make him aware of what he is doing than honor his obsessive unending talk. Maybe the general idea I am propounding is that I'd rather encourage or be a part of the solution than be a part of the problem!

Some ways in which I try to help the child to make his communication more effective and relevant—that is, to "keep it clean"—are to restate simply what the child has said obsessively, to recognize that declarations and pronouncements are sicker than to-and-fro discussion/dialogue, to show my puzzlement and befuddlement at his inability to talk and think straight, to interrupt his compulsively playing out his problems through chatter that is relatively low in either affective or cognitive meaning, to compliment him for his naturalness and directness when these do occur (especially if his spontaneity flew in the face of his customary anxiety), to assert my values (whenever he asks me what I stand for) without engaging in legalistic hemming and hawing, and to "replay" parts of our conversation. The last may merit fuller description, and an example.

> *Child:* The thought has occurred to me that there might be something wrong in it.
> *Therapist:* You feel uneasy about going in swimming?
> *Child:* The thought comes to me sometimes that there might be something wrong in it.
> *Therapist:* I don't get what you are saying.
> *Child:* If you maybe committed the unforgivable sin, and tricks were played on you and traps set for you every-which-a-way you might turn, you feel nearly everything

you might do could be a sin and that if you commit one more sin it might prove that you are sure-enough *the* unforgivable sinner. One more sin and you can never take it back. You worry and have thoughts about everything you get ready to do.

Therapist: You even feel uneasy about going swimming?

Child: You worry that you might have to look at a girl or think about sex.

Therapist: Aha! Let's replay that. I'll ask you what I did, and you give me the shortest answer that pops into your head. *Are you telling me you feel uneasy about going swimming?*

Child: It ain't natural, it ain't easy: I *am* uneasy. I may be tempted to think about sex.

Therapist: I get your message!

This adds up to some rather explicit "cognitive repair"—but it is warranted if the child is to overcome his thought-and-language distortions.

7. *"Take the chance."* The obsessive child needs more encouragement and reassurance than hysterical or phobic or delinquent children require. He is shaky and uncertain because, for example, of early unpredictable behavior from the mother. Especially in taking risks, the obsessive child needs prodding. I remember telling Daniel (Child #24), soon after I had first met him, that I wanted to urge him to ride a bicycle. He disvalued feeling and physical movement of all sorts, and idolized obsessive thought exclusively. I wanted him to know where I stood, and which side I was on. I told him, "I want to urge you to keep riding." He countered that, because he was not perfect, it was not only "chancy" but outright dangerous. Obviously, only perfection warranted his even attempting it. But how could he achieve perfection without any prior practice, trial and error? I knew, or guessed, about some of his mental circumventions and quandaries so I hit the nail on the head early by defining perfect bicycling as I said, "Gee, on a bike, perfection is getting where you want to go." My definition, along with other measures, helped Daniel to decide (with obsessing, doubting and hedging, of course) to enter an alliance with me

against his tension sickness and in favor of his being more "at ease." I had to admonish him to take risks (for example, to ride the bike) when there were no ironclad guarantees and, moreover, only a *chance* of his deriving relatively greater comfort and enjoyment. He may never be a world champion but he can probably get where he wants to go.

8. *"At ease."* Words to describe the obsessive child's misery are *uptight, can't let go, feeling driven, trying to be perfect, worrying all the time, unnatural, forced, false,* and so on. Words to describe what he needs in order to be cured are these: *at ease, tension free, spontaneous, natural, straight, direct, freedom, letting go, letting loose,* and so forth. I use these latter words liberally. I encourage the child to use them. Unabashedly, I encourage, cajole, and reassure. I admonish him to try new ways, I even hold up, as a goal of our work, for him to be at ease. Both at the precise moment during the hour when he shows some spontaneity, and again at the end of the session, I compliment him for his being so very natural. I think it is a sensible technique. Like the others I have cited, it is *not* classically psychoanalytic.

In general, I take a stand in favor of "at ease" and against "bending over backwards." When a child gets alarmed about his sadistic fears, that he will kill a parent, etc., I have found the Sullivanian technique (White, 1951, p. 136) a profitable one, that is, to tell the child that his fears *may have to intensify* as long as he keeps on fighting to stay unaware of his conflicts, and of his "natural feelings." Likewise, when a child stresses his rugged independence I try to indicate amazement that "anybody needs to be all that strong." If he is extolling orderliness or cleanliness, I come forth with a mild advocacy of the obverse. I do this because I know he is bending over backwards in reaction formation. This is not therapist oppositionism, repaid in kind against an oppositional patient, when I ask about what he felt originally. It is an attempt to *call* obsessive undoing or evasiveness into question, and to show the child what he *is* doing. It is a tactic to help the child to become aware that when he felt himself originally as a helpless baby he became "anxious," and *then* began to propound *compulsively* his great strength. I want him to have his real strengths and weaknesses, in balance. Only by advocating balance and by examining his compulsive swaying from extreme to opposite extreme do we get along with the real job of psychotherapy and put the uptight child at ease.

Concerning play and largely nonverbal therapy. Nothing is more practical for the obsessive child than to be taught to let go and play. Not that play is something done at the height of relaxation. Play requires considerable drive and zest, and that shortage is what makes the obsessive child so un-playful and so lacking in the spirit of commitment one sees in a playing child. The therapist, without making himself into a ridiculous clown, can not only show some lightheartedness and good spirits generally but can actually serve as a model for the obsessive child to imitate. If the therapist enjoys physical play, all the better. Many of the 49 children reported here were ungainly and poorly coordinated, and one of the consequences (not totally unanticipated) of treatment was that the children became less stiff, less awkward. Chess and checkers should not be in sight in the psychiatrist's playroom when he has an obsessive patient among his patient group, for these are games that feed and play into the child's obsessive ways. A rambling walk, a game of catch ball, something simple that facilitates directness, is what I would recommend. Even providing unstructured play materials such as drawing and painting supplies is risky with an obsessive child: he will do time consuming, meticulous and ornate (but not very creative) drawings, such as that in Plate I. The therapist sits idly by and sees the child controlling the hour, or, on the other hand, the therapist tries to be active, urge the child to be talkative, and the child responds by ignoring the therapist and going right on with his obsessive hemming and hawing, erasing continually, as he draws. Play to be therapeutic is accompanied by talking to the doctor, so play therapy is not necessarily nonverbal at all.

Play with animals, water, clay, dolls and guns is to be encouraged and Llorens (1963) has made a good case for fingerpainting as a releasing experience for the young obsessive. Perhaps readers who are war weary wonder why a child psychiatrist includes guns in what is literally the "therapeutic armamentarium," so I will

PLATE I.

digress to say a word or two about the question. Children do not make international wars. They do not vote. They are not even accorded the legal identity given to that mythic entity, a corporation, namely, to be a person, and to have guaranteed rights protected by legal sanctions. Adults had better busy themselves in building a warless world. Adults are the killers and the militarists, not children. Hence, because of my pacifism, I might advocate that adults not use real guns but I must insist that children need augmented ways for expressing anger and hatred. Meeting this need in play therapy and providing "war toys" is one manner of releasing and knowing the rage that drives the obsessive child in the first place.

I hope to have made it clear that play—as a non-functional action and as grist for therapy—and physical activity are to be encouraged during therapy sessions with an obsessive child. Thinking of play not purely as a nonverbal activity, I see it as an integral part of the relating done between child and therapist. I do not see it as a deadly serious activity on to which the therapist focuses himself as a neutral onlooking critic (Kleinian fashion), making heavy footed interpretations of everything the child does. The obsessive child needs a fuller cathexis of his body and he does better in life when he plays, in and out of the consulting room.

Concerning the parents of the obsessive child, my preference is to have them work with another therapist, or two others, and let me work with the child. It is indispensable that their therapist(s) be excellent and collaborate easily and freely with me. A gifted psychiatric social worker is my favorite collaborator. I'd prefer one who is not too doctrinaire, someone who can let the child and me join with the social worker and parents occasionally. It works pretty well with adolescents for me to meet *with the parents and the obsessive youth* once weekly, the remainder of my time is with the child alone. Working with the parents automatically enhances the focus on the present. The parents are changing here and now and, even if they cannot take back what they did in the obsessive child's early infancy, they can "say they are sorry," and they can initiate changes in the family patterns in the present.

My finding has been that the parental empathy deficit is crucial. The parents are, to oversimplify, obsessive characters who breed obsessional neurotics. They do not do this out of purposive malevolence but, out of their system of modern values, show a failure to understand the child, to see things from the child's perspective. They are unable to take up the child's role in imagination. Instead, they cannot imagine the child having idiosyncrasies, seeing things differently from them, being "his own man." These parents look highly complacent initially. Indeed, the parents are downright smug in their being effective, productive, verbose and conventional adult North Americans. They are inclined to see themselves as exemplary models for all humanity to copy, and they are more than *impatient* with rebellion; they cannot "feel for it" at all. So from his early age they categorize all of the child's defiance as wicked, and all of his conformity to parental wishes as the index of goodness. *To be good*, then, according to their upbringing, is to do what parents want—never to be oneself exploring life's delights. To be good is not its own reward, does not enhance the enjoyment of life, etc., but is purely instrumental—i.e., a set of ways to survive, to get ahead, to avoid parental denunciation and so on. This is a morality with a price tag on it. To reverse these patterns, to alter a life style that gratifies because it helps the parents get ahead (although it sickens the child), and to undo their "virtues," their character armor, requires artful and timely work by the parents' therapists. Social workers are often adept at doing this kind of ego work, cracking up ego syntony and scratching out latent parental identification with their offspring. The parents need to change toward fuller lives of their own. If psychiatrists could do these tasks as well as the social workers whom I have been privileged to work with, I'd welcome psychiatrists for collaborative work with parents. I have nothing against psychiatrists. The important question is not about the special discipline of one's training but about getting a difficult job done. The job is one of sensitizing grownups, changing old patterns and opening up new vistas of self-regard and self-conception.

TRANSFERENCE AND COUNTERTRANSFERENCE

I have already discussed the day-in, day-out scrutiny of what is happening between the therapist and the child. In fact, a transference neurosis is not sought and is not allowed to develop unexamined. This is general technology when we work with children but especially apt if the child is obsessive. We do not want to stand in the place of the parent, to supplant or to compensate for the child's actual parent. We want to come into the child's life for a time, do some professional work on basic problems in the child (and family), and then bow out. The *real* family relations exist and a transference neurosis (like a "play family") is an inappropriate state to aim for. The obsessive child has usually been deceived or hoodwinked quite enough, has distorted enough already and lived in quite enough illusory relations. Hence, a passionate, distorted and unprofessional attachment to his therapist is of no constructive use in his life.

But one should not be too idealistic or grandiose about minimizing transference by continual scrutiny of it. Obsessive children do love us and hate us, and we cannot be neuters in their love-hate network, even if we try hard. Moreover, the costliest and best personal analysis is no sure protection against our developing, as therapists, strong negative and positive feelings toward the obsessive child. The older I get, the more I seem to accept certain of the limitations of my therapeutic zeal and skill. My kinship with my child patients is always there and sometimes it is in the way, leading me into both positive and negative (that is, unprofessional) attitudes toward the children. Countertransference of the negative variety has been a special difficulty for many in their working with obsessive children. Even a cursory reading of Adler, Sullivan, Rado, Freud and Nunberg will cue the reader that *most therapists do not love an obsessive.* Of all the prominent writers, perhaps Salzman (1966) is least negative in his stance regarding the obsessive. Hence, somebody may love an obsessive. For anyone who finds himself in battle with an obsessive child, Stolorow (1970) makes a revealing point, or at least inspires some soul searching. Stolorow sees both the therapist and the (adult) patient enshrouded in myths, each about himself. An obsessive patient has a myth about his personal magic omnipotence that clashes, quite expectedly, with the therapist's personal myth concerning his healing powers. This produces what Stolorow calls "mythic dissonance," whereas with an hysteric there is consonance.

When I find myself in a struggle against an obsessive child, I have to ask myself, *what am I doing this for?* What about me makes me feel as if I am against this child? And what can I do to correct my distortions of the professional relationship with this child? Sometimes I feel overly like an authoritarian parent, or overly opposed to the "bad" child in myself, and I need to get myself restored to the job of helping by being a doctor.

When I find myself too preoccupied "positively" *between* sessions with a particular obsessive child, I have to question myself thoroughly about the cause of the positive projection or identification, and the reason for this deviation away from a professional stance as a therapist. At times, I still feel competitive toward the real parents and at those times I need a reminder that the parents have, and deserve, a place in the child's life that I shall not aspire to, all in the interest of the child.

ASSESSING CHANGES WITH TREATMENT

Most of the 49 children improved after outpatient psychotherapy of varied duration. Exceptions were Chester E (#20), Hill A (#35), Miles C (#39), and Winnie A (#10). Some of this group needed inpatient (or residential) care—they had to be hospitalized. Although hospitalization is not considered the treatment of choice, and is usually contraindicated for children with obsessive disorders, it is a boon without a doubt when home care is out of the question. Certainly, we need good residential treatment facilities available. Some of this group, children of mobile professional families, did not remain in outpatient care longer than five or six sessions before their family moved to other geographic areas and new therapists. Still, of those staying in outpatient treatment for longer periods (more than 30 sessions), there was improvement universally.

The judges of improvement were the therapists themselves, but corroboration by child and parents is cited in all of these medical records. In a predesigned study, ideally, a group with a fully stand-ardized or uniform treatment approach would be compared to a group receiving no treatment at all or a very different kind of treatment. Only in a minority of cases did I collect video and sound recordings or have psychologic testing before and after therapy. However, granting the imperfection of any assertions I can make, I feel there are some practical—if informal and imprecise—ways in which the psychiatric clinician can assess many of the *changes made with treatment*.

First, there are *symptomatic decreases*. After treatment carried out along lines described in the foregoing, the children are less tortured by obsessions, rituals, compulsions, phobias and tics. Their schoolmates, teachers, neighbors, parents and siblings can tell this difference rather readily. The oddness, and the anancastic, slave labor aspect, are gone from the child's demeanor. He is not as plagued by upsetting symptoms, and that is a veritable triumph from the perspective of both child and parents.

Second, there are *behavioral modifications*. These are amenable to documentation and, in principle, to quantification. In this study, only approximations, "dynamic assessments," were accom-plished. Some of the case vignettes in Chapter 4 specify some of the behavior changes accomplished by therapy. These modifica-tions consist of *gross motor activity* becoming more fluid, resilient and graceful; *play* becoming more absorbing of the entire body and less stilted; *talk* becoming less longwinded or circuitous and more direct, explicit and "engaged." Verbal undoing (pendular shifting from weak to strong, brave to cowardly, bad to good, etc.) is lessened conspicuously. Stuttering diminishes or vanishes. Academic learning improves. Smiling increases. The child more accurately observes what is going on around him, refusing to play family games of duplicity and deception. His thinking becomes more pragmatic and syntactic and less literal or concrete. He notices when and where, and why, things happen in his life.

Third, there are *changes in feeling tone concerning the self*. More imagination and zest were reflected in post-treatment psychologic test scores in cases where retesting was accomplished. These are the changes Szasz (1967) commented upon as showing an augmented "sphere of autonomy" and as unrelated to symptom alleviation. The child reports his sense of increased well-being. He comments upon the augmentation of his feeling free, on his increased naturalness and spontaneity. He says he enjoys an increased sense of clarity; he displays an increase of productivity. He attests to having gained a fuller sense of self and others.

Fourth, there are *changes in ego structure or ego strengths* (Kluckhohn *et al.*, 1954). These are *conative* (having to do with such features as willpower, initiative, decisiveness, and freedom from perplexity and brooding conflict). Ego strengths are also *intellectual*, or cognitive, of course, and these too can be measured or assessed. Daniel D's (Child #24) intelligence testing showed an increase in performance IQ and full-scale IQ following psychotherapy. The same was true of Alfred Y (Child #12), Stan C (#47), Rufus T (#44) and others, all of whom showed increased IQ scores after psychotherapy. Improved concentration, improved communication, and better problem-solving in general were all in evidence in the post-treatment children. There is a *perceptual* dimension of ego strength also—accurately perceiving or sizing up of what others are like, what situations are like and what oneself is up to.

In all of these signs of "ego strength" the post-treatment children as a group showed considerable improvement. "Ego functions" may seem nebulous but Coddington and Offord (1967) showed that four child psychiatrists showed higher agreement on ego functions even when they were informally assessed than cardiologists showed on electrocardiograms, or radiologists on chest X-rays! That means quite high inter-rater agreement, both in biomedical and behavioral science.

At the mid-point in Daniel D's psychotherapy I tried to write up a progress summary, and concerning his ego changes that seemed to me to be connected to his therapy I wrote some notes that I will repeat here:

Among the changes toward health that were observed during the middle phase of Daniel's psychotherapy are:
On the side of the Ego

slackening of defenses against hate, love and lust—an easing off in their rigidity. This gives more defensive flexibility and hence fuller mastery.

increased initiative, self-sufficiency and responsibility. He is no longer a lesser satellite of his mother to the degree he was.

increased ability to express some impulses directly and spontaneously

increased ability to make decisions

increased ability to persist when frustrated moderately

increased ability to think about real issues. For Daniel this is coupled with a decrease in preoccupation with unreal issues such as magic and the unknowable.

increased ability to say what he is thinking. He has lost many of his original verbal taboos, fortunately, and can say words such as hate, death, etc.

increased ability to concentrate on problems until they are solved. He shows a much better carry-over from one interview to the next, and he recognizes what some of the issues are that require more prolonged work. He says himself that he needs to do more to work on his lack of friends, for example.

increased ability to see reality without distortion

increased ability to see himself realistically, without being Mr. Pendulum, swaying from helplessness to grandiosity

increased ability to foresee the consequences of his actions. He is less literal, more subtle and does not try to hang me because of something I said which he misconstrued, etc.

Fifth are *changes in the superego* of the obsessive child following psychotherapy. My clinical impression holds that children after treatment develop their consciences, in conjunction with an improvement in all their reasoning. This development is consonant with, and may consist mainly of, a development in their "cognitive capacity rather than in the substance of values" (Aronfreed, 1968). But the content of their moral valuations does change. In other words I do not believe that the change in conscience is associated solely with the child's becoming a year or so older—and unfolding conscience changes purely because of his maturation. That is to say, the child's ways of reasoning and thinking and feeling about moral issues become altered in a healthier direction. And, of course, I can only make remarks about the children I have studied, and not dogmatically because of the narrow distribution geographically and subculturally of the 49 children. Yet it appears that these children not only develop a different cognitive manner but also a different thought content. They change their consciences or superegos both stylistically and substantively—all within the confines of their family's and subculture's values, naturally. But psychotherapy too becomes a part of their learning and their conduct change.

The treated child progresses toward a more autonomous or personal set of values, ceasing to be so dependent upon the judgments of other persons. He is more astute morally, for he can second guess his parents and psychotherapists better and make provisions for their insistence, at least until adolescence gives him a fuller reprieve and a more autonomous conscience of his own. The treated child, then, seems to become a better operator when it comes to avoiding punishment of adults. He knows which adults to steer clear from. He is more sensitive to what adults will clamor for; he also seems to have incorporated a more comfortable set of values within himself.

The child, to put it in a zealot's terminology, becomes less corrupt, more honest, shunning duplicity and pretense and moderating the anguish of being unloved for the least transgression. He needs no longer be compulsively honest, insulting people and making himself a pain in the neck in the name of his scrupulosity (Weisner and Riffel, 1960). To the degree that he has let up, learned to tell others honestly what he thinks and feels, developed greater skills at pragmatic and syntactic communication, etc., he has acquired a more useful conscience. To some extent, the more he has been changed by the goals and tactics of psychotherapy the better off he is with respect to his conscience or superego. I think it is only because he has a better conscience that he is less afraid of life and death, and more prepared to undertake risks. See Henrikson, 1962.

A related conscience change in the child who has experienced psychotherapy is mellowing and muting of the ferocity of his self-criticism. Instead of the either-or, black or white, moral reasoning he had before treatment, lacerating his own pride and self esteem continually, the treated obsessive child shows less striving to be superhuman morally as his guilt is dissipated and his self concept improved. Perhaps we could say this in this way, that the child comes to have a conscience that is more appropriate for his developmental stage.

Sixth, there are *changes in interpersonal relations*, or object relations. These changes have already been mentioned when I considered symptom behavior, self, ego, and conscience changes after treatment, but there ought to be more mention of how the treated child's interpersonal relations change. (I would hope to sound more like Harry Stack Sullivan than Dale Carnegie in this discussion!)

After psychotherapy the obsessive child broadens his circle of friends. Many more people than the mother or the family of orientation become meaningful figures to the treated child. He feels closer, more intimately bonded, to his peers, a frame of mind that is a very special boon when he nears the end of elementary school. He displays less shyness, guardedness, and sarcasm in his relating to others. He is more realistic (that is, less magical) in his assessment of the merits and faults of other persons. I have been impressed with how much better judges of others these children become.

The treated child is less hung up on power relations in dealings with others. Although that is a hard nut to crack in lower middle-class family life, where bossing and obeying are so much in the air, the child stops exuding his fondness for sadomasochism. He becomes open for other values and a richer life in human relatedness.

Changes accompanying treatment can, therefore, be assessed in ways that range from crude impressionism to rather precise quantification. The changes in symptoms and other behavior submit to measurement, more than do changes in ego, self concept, and superego. Yet the easily measurable is not always of most value. But the good clinician has to recall that it is the parental opinions that have the most clout, even more than the more or less objective changes listed in the foregoing. The clinician always takes care to arrive at consensus, with both the child and his parents, about what the changes are and about the desirability of terminating treatment at any particular point in the therapy.

7

Obsession and Society

OBSESSIVE PROBLEMS OF CHILDREN, we have seen, have familial and social roots. In earlier discussion I tried not to be totally mentalistic. So, I have never suggested than an obsessive disorder is only an intrapsychic state. Children do not suck it off their thumbs—they come by it from their experience in their families. Psychopathology occurs in the milieu-experience of organisms, and is always context bound. Psychopathology has no independent existence apart from human relations. We have been looking at the contexts in which obsessive children become obsessive and can review this quickly.

Whenever sociocultural pressures, mediated by the child's parents, reinforce the child's unnatural behavior and extinguish the child's easy, natural, "operant" behavior, there will be an increased likelihood of obsessional neurosis in the child. Let me say it at first in a mental way, and then more social or political. Whenever parents impose their wills, demanding obedience to *their* valued overt behavior, the children learn to obey compulsively the

232

letter of the law, and to obsess about the spirit. Whenever in early childhood the parents require rectitude at all costs, failing in empathy with what Bingham Dai calls "the child's nature," and especially where defiance and rage are disvalued or tabooed, the incidence of childhood obsession can be expected to rise. In whatever society the child is made to feel ashamed of his natural feelings and lusts, there obsessive disorders will increase. Whenever parents hate their children to a murderous extent, but deceitfully speak of their love, there obsession will be on the upswing. In short, in any culture area there will be an increase in childhood obsessive disorder if the parents engage in these four categories of behavior toward the child:

1. attempts toward overenculturation
2. lack of empathy
3. disapproval of spontaneous, free field behavior
4. masking hate with a loving exterior.

Obviously, there is wide latitude in all these matters, for obsessive disorder is infrequently found around the world, while *obsessive maneuvers* are very common. Regardless of the culture area— Japan, China, USSR, India, Britain, Latin America, USA, France, Turkey, etc.—the foregoing generalizations would seem valid and applicable. Let me expand briefly on these four generalizations with a more social slant.

Attempted overenculturation was very much in evidence among the 49 subject children and their parents, and I conclude that it may be productive of childhood obsession in any culture. The parents themselves (in some cases) were highly literal in *their* conformity and demanded strict conformity from their offspring "trainees." Some of the parents were deeply committed to (adult) values, the observance of which they rigidly imposed upon their children. Others of them lacked deep conviction and commitment to any kind of values, or were so deeply ambivalent they displayed what might be called "internal polarization and paralysis," but the effect on the children was the same, or similar. The children felt that ritualistic outward observance was the name of the game, that their parents were determined to extract automaton-like obedience, without regard for what their children did, felt, or understood. Often, the children were outwardly copies of their parents. The boys were trained (often by the mother) to be overly correct, giving a result which their peers regarded as sissy or effeminate. The girls were joylessly prim-and-proper, and inflexible. The boys and girls seemed overly "straight," pseudo mature and often anxiously rigid and driven. Appearing older than their actual ages was the result of their being too socialized too soon. The Freudians were onto something correct about too early training of the anal sphincter. The little professors and eggheads were numerous among the obsessive children. In some instances, the children truly went their parents one better, being more grownup, more perfect, than their parents and mentors. They were caricatures of straight-laced adults, hypercorrect on the outside, but deeply resentful and hateful below the surface. The children had obeyed and formed pseudo selves. The children by their tense psychopathology gave back to their parents the fruits of too much filial obedience and conformity, and of overenculturation. Indeed, children's wills *can* be broken—rather easily at that—and children's behavior can be shaped in rectitude, patterned and reinforced to adults' hearts' content—but an obsessive disorder is the potential by-product, if it is not the desired goal. Anyone who has seen at close range several obsessive children living in their conjugal families wishes for "more Spock," not less. A lot more of genuine permissiveness would help them, for the attempted overenculturation has aborted and missed its aim whenever a pseudo self is created.

Psychiatry is a politically relevant field, and Spiro Agnew, the John Birch Society, and even some right-leaning psychiatrists would avow that overenculturation could not play any part in psychopathology. They, and I, can have our divergent opinions in these matters until the final word has been spoken. Until we *know*, though, we can all have partly-open minds, and allow each other the privilege of honest disbelief, belief, and commitment. No matter how dangerous I believe some ultra-conservatives to be, I am happy to let them live! I demand the same liberality of spirit from them in return.

I concur heartily in the view reiterated by political conservatives that there are more "unsocialized aggressive," more delinquent and under-socialized, children in North America than there are inhibited, obsessive children. The mass problem is one of anti-social conscience decrement and of impulse ridden deviance, not of obsessive pseudo selves and pseudo consciences. The big pathology in North America is *not* the Jungian "unlived life" or middle class *ennui* and "inner conflicts." In fact many more children need tightening up than loosening up. Obsessive children, only a tiny minority, do need loosening, however, before they can ever have a life of their own.

Parental *lack of empathy* is a term that includes many "sins" of omission and commission. Deficiency in empathy for children, or for childhood, is the variety that has appeared over and over in my own work with disturbed children and their parents. The parents are not able to take up in imagination a child's role. They never stop to think what life is like from the child's standpoint. They tend to see child rearing as a mechanical, bitter chore and look at it solely from the standpoint of an animal trainer who does not particularly like his job—and may not like the animals at all.

Now, what kind of parents show this empathic deficit to the greatest degree? In those families with obsessive children, we found mostly middle class professionals, the ones who were most verbal, most "intellectualized," and who had "only repressed but not worked through" their own childhood lusts and rages. If they didn't like a human trait they tended not to approach it, not to accept it, and not to make any accommodation to it, but to "stamp it out" by punishing it and outlawing it. I have described this earlier, following Laughlin and others, as the parents' *passion for rectitude* and their disvaluing rage and defiance.

Empathy of a parent is related to that parent's capabilities in living for others, to his (or her) diminished transference distortions, generally, but, particularly, in relation to his children. If a parent equates, in his heart, a defiant, no-saying two-year-old son with a criminal adult relative, the parent is so blinded by this "negative identification" that he cannot put himself into the child's shoes. He is responding to an unreal object, instead, because the child is *not* the discredited relative of the parent's transference onto the child. Further, empathy flows most naturally out of an alloerotic orientation—a perspective, a life style, in which one truly lives "for others," providing others with emotional and material supplies, being fully genital and "mature" in character structure. A consumer of security is oriented toward getting what he can from others, but a giver of security can envision others and put himself in their place, imaginatively. Empathy is also a function of true, constant object relations. It varies inversely with narcissism and self-absorption. The narcissistic parent simply finds herself (or himself) unable to view the child as a separate emerging organism and person. She views the child as if the child were herself, with her cravings and preoccupations, or a competitor for security. And security always seems to be in too-short supply for self-centered people all over the world.

When the parents of children *disvalue, disapprove, and punish their children's spontaneously held and displayed feelings*, the breeding ground is prepared for emotional illness generically and for obsessive disorders as a specialized variant of emotional illness. To be made ashamed of one's own naturally-occurring sexual lust, for example, is a cramping and crippling circumstance for a child to grow up with. Likewise for his anger when he has been thwarted, deprived, frustrated, and hurt. Parents who forbid these and other spontaneous feelings are promoting obsessional neurosis, whatever the culture. Taboos against spontaneity set the necessary but not sufficient conditions.

Who are these anti-feeling parents? Again they are likely to be parents who are themselves overly strict, overly proper and correct, overly concerned with traditional ideologies, and whose being straightlaced has been rewarded emotionally and materially. In brief, they are people who feel rather successful and fairly well-established in their society. As a footnote, I might add that they are the ones who benefit most from sensitivity group, encounter group, experiences. They sometimes like to learn from direct involvement that they are alive, that their batteries are re-chargeable, so to speak. They also have the most meaningful encounters, ultimately, in casework and psychotherapy, even though they arduously resist change.

Masking hate with a loving exterior is the trait of a person who is truly afraid of his hate. As a parent, he feels hate toward his child and he tries to cover it over. He covers it over, only to find as William Blake suggested, that it waxes into lethal proportions. Instead of simple rejection it becomes transformed into murderous hate. The parent now wishes the child dead. Death wishes now burst out as the guilt-inspiring expression of a stifled natural anger. The child senses the hate but learns to play the game, pretending love alone obtains. An obsessive, sado-machochistic relationship has flowered. This seems to be a nearly universal recipe for creating the obsessive character, and perhaps the obsessive neurotic as well.

The Home Scene. Within the U.S. some statements with a considerably narrower swath can be made. We know in our own society what the special forces and fakeries are, and to some extent in what classes and groups they are most concentrated. Boldly stated, obsessive disorder is largely middle class. It has an affinity for the middle class ethos.

The 49 families who provided the empirical base for this book came from the southeastern part of the USA. Many had been born in the North but were bringing up children in the South, an economically depleted or underdeveloped area which came into some of the affluence of the rest of the nation during the past twenty years. Thanks only to war and cold war, aerospace enterprises and a host of capitalistic industries with federal government subsidies, military encampments, and the almost colonial attractiveness of the "American South" as a source of cheap unorganized labor, the southeastern U.S. had become more "prosperous." If anyone needs proof that industrialization in and of itself, without regard to who owns and controls the industries, is an unqualified blessing, let him look at the South's modernization and industrialization! Ambivalence and impermanence grew. The "solid South" disappeared.

Also, the cost of living inflated and spiraled. Consumption of consumer goods mounted, as did installment buying and family indebtedness. The new prosperity had a tenuous quality for many families during these 15 years from 1957 until 1972. A short-lived and inadequate war on poverty did not work, for soon it was sold out, and was handed over to control by local power cliques all across the South. The area and the epoch had its own characteristic qualities, some conducive to breeding obsessive problems in children, some not at all.

Our sample of obsessive children and their families was not truly representative of the Southern region because, first of all, all the children were *clinical cases* seen mainly by physician referral. The children and their families were, therefore, life's (that is, society's) casualties and not successes. Our current dispensation in the health field does not furnish us with representative samples. Our unsocialized medicine removes and conceals many people from a child psychiatrist's range of enquiry, from his field of vision. The poor are not found in representative numbers by our customary methods of case-finding wherein we wait for referrals from other agencies and professionals. Blacks too are hidden from our traditional outreach, relatively, along with the poor of all colors.

The situation with blacks deserves a special word, and a slight theoretical digression. Following the suggestion of Abram Kardiner (1945), I would like to stress the ubiquitous interlocking of myths and childrearing. Acknowledging the human gift of both fantasy and reality principles, Kardiner showed how myths, dreams, etc., were parts of *the projective system* whereas the work patterns, basic institutions and childrearing patterns, etc., helped to make up the reality system in which human culture bathes all of us. All serious students seem to be agreed that racism infuses both the reality and projective systems of people living in the United States. We have our racist views and ideologies; we also have our racist institutions and practices. Kardiner's theoretical concepts are reminiscent of an older Marxist distinction between the *substructure* (material, economic) and the *superstructure* (ideational) but the Kardiner terms may lack some of the pejorative flavor of the Marxian terms. In any event, racism—both as ideology and as institutionalized norms and overt practices—was rampant during the period from Eisenhower to Nixon. Race exploitation or discrimination was, at least in the economic field, as surely entrenched under the latter as under Eisenhower. Blacks lacked equality of results.

The state supported schools were desegregated in the South, to be sure, and that lessened racism as an *ideological* force bearing down both on Southern children and their parents. White or black, Southerners experienced racism's loss of some of its ideological power for justifying the whites' exploitation of blacks. The rationale for slavery (the progenitor of discrimination) slipped, and the prejudices that gave support to slavery's offspring, namely, segregation of and discrimination against blacks, diminished considerably. Racism as a state of mind showed rather great decline. At times the rate of decline became astonishing. Yet *institutionalized* racism—palpable, recurrent, real, predictable—continued with only slight alteration. Southern blacks in the mass remained exploited, disadvantaged and different. By 1970, three-fourths of U.S. black families still earned under $10,000 per year. With integration many black professionals lost their Jimcrow advantages, and sometimes their livelihood. Black school principals, notably, were reassigned, relieved of duties, sent to the boondocks, and otherwise removed from their posts in the wake of school integration. Many blacks moved North and met an economic and social discrimination that was almost equally as implacable as the Southern kind. Hence, in both North and South, a militant black liberation movement found ready adherents.

Obsessive children whom I studied were immersed in racism. They and their parents constituted a racist force, by and large, more often through an economic and institutional complicity in the *status quo* than by overt action or declaration in support of exploiting the blacks. Some of the children and their parents were openly racist and, as in the case of Milton C (#40), active in white citizens' councils. But for the most part they were more pallid than that, less militant, claiming to be non-political and shunning the taking of a stand "except as it affects me personally." Whenever it did affect their private world, their customary "tolerance" dropped out and they promptly found "reasons" for shutting out blacks. Busing and open housing were the test issues that readily smoked out these blander racists. During these years, furthermore, the phenomenon of the Show Black became quite widespread, so that businesses which earlier refused to serve blacks came to hire one token black and put him in a conspicuous place. Fire insurance, some militants called it.

In some ways, the most confused or perplexed about racism were those parents who were derived from northern backgrounds. As "northerners" they perceived themselves as racially liberal. They often surprised themselves with the magnitude of their racism. The special problems of the northern white liberal living in the southeast have led many civil rights activists to observe that "Northern white liberals will do blacks in quicker than Southern."

A type of rigidity characterized the life style of these unsteady, ambivalent middle class people. These two terms—uncommitted and rigid—seem paradoxic and contradictory but they are not. Salzman (1968, p. 43) explained it in this way:

> The patient's rigidity is manifested in his posture and muscular tonus as well as in the persistent, ritualized, inflexible, and singleminded style of thinking and acting . . . .
>
> The rigidities of the obsessional are observable in every aspect of his living since the adherence to prescribed rules or established patterns of behavior provides an inner security.
>
> Such pervasive rigidity seems to be contradicted by the ambivalent attitudes which the obsessional displays. However, he is rigid about his instabilities and thus may resist inflexibly any effort to alter his more extreme ambivalent attitudes.

One ambivalence pervading the lives of these families was their preoccupation with dominance and subordination. They were highly aware of, and sensitive to, power in interpersonal dealings. At times, this familial preoccupation very directly harmed the child.

These children and their families certainly embodied the accelerating urbanization of the South. By 1969 only one-fourth of the U.S. population remained rural. I noticed, in the cases that I gathered, that those from the early 1970's were much more often urban than those gathered in the late 1950's. And the youngsters showed more "content" that applied to an urban setting, in dream reports as well as in casual remarks about their everyday living. Likewise, in the later years of my case-finding, mobility had become a more prominent feature of their lives. Families moved, often between states and at times across the entire continent. Their mobility remained considerably below the national norm, however, for their mobility was much less than that experienced by massive numbers of poor families. But, as time went on their state-to-state geographic mobility did heighten and move them increasingly toward the picture typical of the U.S. where ordinary households change location more than once every three years.

The societal picture formed by these families was of an ascendant, urban, middle class, white, racist group. Bathed in alienation and lacking in commitment, they believed only the more stringent truth of propositions, and attempted to speak the language of bland objectivity. Even blatant nonsense was made to sound rational and scientific. They talked their way around life, and they strove to be sensible. Militancy and excess turned them off. They exalted what worked for them and their more fortunate ancestors: orderliness, cleanliness, perseverance, deliberation, reflection, conformity, rectitude, verbalizing and keeping busy. In short, they revered the "virtues" of the Nordic, Protestant middle class. I have the feeling that they'll go on revering them when some of the virtues are totally antiquated and dysfunctional.

They only wanted "to do the best by their children." Alas, their fate was to see their children take up those very virtues which the parents idolized and use them to form symptoms. It could be that *the children have the symptoms but the parents have the disease, calling it a virtue.* Often, to make matters worse, the obsessive child used the parental virtue/filial symptom *against* the parents, going the parents one better, and battering his parents through a display of moral superiority. As the mother of Alfred Y (#12) said of her son, many other of these children "took a good thing and overdid it." An obsessive neurosis lacks the virtuousness of an obsessive character, and a neurosis is less adaptive and usable in everyday life.

Social Uses of Obsessional Character. If one wished to prepare a child for later Jesuit training and practice, or even for a career in a military bureaucracy (Michaels and Porter, 1949), the child would surely find it easier had he learned obedience, rectitude, orderliness, perseverance, and so on. A one-track mind helps one to concentrate and learn anatomy and biochemistry; but it aids most in memorization, not in creatively grasping principles and making cognitive bridges and syntheses. Cleanliness, for instance, may be a virtue "next to godliness," but it becomes an end in itself only for those who, as the Freudian metaphor has it, are embarked upon extreme reaction formation against their wishes to smear, eat, and smell feces. In corroboration we can cite many non-Western groups who do not show the reaction formation of disgust at the smell of feces or body odors which did characterize the group under study here. Similarly, orderliness may be helpful in planning a conference or running a library; but when it becomes a rigid defense against insecurity and is used magically to control the unforeseeable, it blends over into suffering. Honoring and obeying parents has been an important and essential *commandment* in many cultures throughout many ages; but in our era it can quickly become an inessential vestige of authoritarian dogma. It can lead to great inner conflict for those children who blindly obey out of fear not love. And, keeping busy at instrumental tasks helps us to accomplish our goals; but working for the sake of denying fear or expunging guilt is compulsive and dysfunctional. Even if Richard Nixon spurs us on to hold fast onto the "work ethic," it would be far better for us to play and recreate rather than to perform slave labor.

Gerda Willner (1968, p. 201) commented on that striving for busy-ness in our society that is closely related to obsessiveness. She enunciated that such characters do not want any leisure, and keep "on the go" in order to avoid self-understanding.

He therefore throws himself into his work. He takes on more jobs, makes more money and invents more time- and labor-saving devices. It is as if he were trying not only to build, use and depend on computers, but to become a computer himself. Out of necessity he focuses on knowing, planning and plotting, on making absolutely certain and eliminating any chance-taking. He has forgotten how to live with imperfection and insecurity. However, in his frantic search for perfection and security he makes his life more and more miserable. Our culture breeds compulsiveness . . .

Our culture breeds, or at least condones, a life style in which occurs partial (intellectual, for example) involvement, for brief time periods, in small sectors of a whole life. Our culture does not make room for the imperfection, shame, and insecurity (or anxiety) that are *there* whenever whole human beings meet. But our culture looks at the perfect parts, not the imperfect entirety of a human being. We produce human beings devoid of naturalness. We make "progress," dehumanization increases, alienation runs rampant, but our obsessive style has accomplished progress for us.

Certainly the obsessive character has social uses, *if only it would not progress into obsessive neurosis.* To stop that progression was what these parents whom we studied seemed unable to do. They might stop it for themselves, but not for their children. The children read their minds and became sick with the same good raw materials their parents had handed them.

Sigmund Freud gave testimony to the effect that anal and obsessive traits were socially useful. Freud (1930) opined that a life of repression—of alienation, renouncing one's longings, being out of touch with one's self—was the prerequisite, at the level of individuals, for the existence of civilization. I find the thought disquieting, but Freud believed that repression and guilt were by-products of the reality principle's necessary triumph over the pleasure principle. Freud was pleased, apparently, that he had "no illusions about alienation" when he believed that alienation was both universal and desirable for civilized life. Herbert Marcuse (1955) Géza Róheim (1943), Wilhelm Reich (1970) and Norman O. Brown (1959) picked up some parts of Freud's message and made of them a more trenchant and radical critique than Freud himself seemed to propound. They have been surveyed in a book by Paul A. Robinson (1969). Freud was busy fighting other battles, and he was inclined to be accepting of the politico-cultural status quo, even saying some favorable words on occasion for his Kaiser and for Benito Mussolini, among others. Hence, Freud acknowledged that there are some "benefits" attendant to anality. Even if they reluctantly conceded its "advantages," so did Ernest Jones (1950), Harry Stack Sullivan (1954), Karl Abraham (1949), and Otto Fenichel (1945). But the virtues of anality were thoroughly questioned and criticized by the radical Freudians. Particularly Róheim and Reich attacked anality because it interfered with the genitality that they equated with being whole men, mature, pure in heart. Róheim insisted that we, as well as our uncivilized brothers, whom Róheim, as a psychoanalytic ethnographer, also studied, were more repressed than we needed be. He latched onto the liberating, nonconformist possibilities of psychoanalysis. Róheim insisted as did Reich and many early Freudians upon the need for diminished sexual coercion, suppression and repression; he was no apologist for the *status quo.* Culture necessarily showed the workings of all our oedipus complexes, Róheim insisted, but culture need not be antagonistic to our genital lusts and need not enshrine the *anal* stage of our childhood. Wilhelm Reich, in the frame of mind of Róheim but more politically engaged and more socially relevant, also sought to "advance unsuppressed genitality" as a social program.

Norman O. Brown (1959), however, spoke out prophetically against even our "genital establishments." Neither anus nor genital should be enshrined, according to Brown, for a full life requires that polymorphous perversion of childhood be accepted, condoned, kept viable, and perpetuated actively in all stages of life—not just childhood. Brown came down effectively as an orthodox Freudian who perceived a revolutionary ethic within psychoanalysis. Brown's "Studies in Anality" in his book, *Life Against Death,* is an excellent speculative treatise constructed in the psychoanalytic mode. Jonathan Swift, Martin Luther, and the generic economic actions of spending, saving, lending at interest, and giving money are all subjected to Brown's psychoanalytic-social criticism. Brown's heroes are those who accepted and then transcended their anality, personally and socially.

Erich Fromm (1941, 1944, 1947) and Herbert Marcuse (1962)

went further, in my opinion, and—all the while paying homage to Freud—re-stated Freud's ideas in such a way that we have, after all of the modifications, a view that is truly post-Freudian, that does not vaunt anality or the political *status quo*. Marcuse and Fromm did not agree with one another's politics or philosophical *Weltanschauung* (as shown explicitly by Marcuse (1955) and Fromm (1955)), but both were students of Marx *and* Freud, and each attempted in his way to bring these two thinkers into a unified view. Marcuse warns against "surplus repression" and Fromm, meaning more or less the same thing, against "irrational authority." Marcuse was considerably the more bitter and negative of the two. Each, moreover, advanced a view of a unified Man that required a restructuring of social institutions along humanistic-socialist lines if a healthy humanity was to be ensured.

Certainly, in some social arrangements and institutions, and in some sub-groups, the obsessive character is rewarded, and is regarded as socially useful and beneficial. The psychiatrists Joseph J. Michaels and Robert T. Porter (1949) raised the possibility that

> Many of the compulsive tendencies represented by normal concern with cleanliness, orderliness, industriousness, responsibility, respect for law and discipline, etc., may hardly be considered pathologic in a civilized society, for they are practically prerequisites for the high standard of living and the continual striving for improvement which characterize the goals of present-day civilization.

Indeed, Michaels and Porter contended that, like higher IQ's, compulsion neurosis might represent a "useful" deviation from the mean. Certainly, they stated, obsession facilitated adjustment to military service, and the point of their wartime article was to consider why severe obsessives got into so little trouble in the army. They concluded, "the individual with a compulsive character finds himself (in military service) in a compulsive milieu in which his tendencies harmonize."

In their discussion, Michaels and Porter said some very interesting things about the desirability of obsessive behavior and about *the necessity* for certain "anal-obsessive" influences upon children by their parents. Their comments are not to be easily passed off, in my opinion, as being merely armchair philosophical anthropology. Their views, very moderately and judiciously put, have a lot to do with the everyday, practical child rearing of obsessive children. They advance, at least adumbrate, ten important postulates, it seems to me:

1) Restraint on some impulses is *necessary* for social living.
2) Not all impulses need to be restrained *severely*.
3) *No* impulses need to be restrained fully.
4) Moral restraint is *not* logical and rational, just as impulses themselves are irrational.
5) Impulse-restraint is the *sine qua non* of conscience development.
6) Conscience (superego, or moral judgments and attitudes) is "the essentially compulsive component of personality" (p. 130)—compulsion being making oneself do what he doesn't long to do, or *not* do what he craves to do!
7) Religion and "parents or parent substitues" induce compulsive character traits in children.
8) Children *must* have parental values "imposed authoritatively by those whose love and approval the infant needs." The parents must carry out "early training which instills some compulsive character traits in children by virtue of respect for authority." Parents need, in some small measure, to break a child's will. The big question remains, *how much* sexual repression and compulsive work are needed for social life.
9) The only ways out of irrational obedience to parentally imposed instinctual renunciation are to obtain psychoanalytic therapy for the individual or "to interpret the teachings of infancy during later childhood, introducing the logical reasons for behavior patterns whose enforcement in infancy was sought through authority instead." It all boils down to derepression whether done in the home or the consulting room. Precisely. To me, it seems that the parents of our obsessive children are parents

who are unable to "shift gears" away from that certain amount of will-breaking of the infant child which may be required in all cultures. They are rigid parents. They do not keep up, empathically, with the growth of their child.

10) When the parents lack flexibility to keep current in empathy with their children, and, for example, continue will-breaking beyond the child's age two or three years, in the words of Michaels and Porter (p. 130), "they may impose burdens of guilt, inferiority, frustration and neurosis."

Consequently, Michaels and Porter came closer to one fact than most writers have done—childhood is a developing, a shifting existence, a becoming; parenthood that does not shift appropriately with the child's changes will breed neurosis. If parents cannot "interpret" their earlier pontifications, or in some way release the growing child from their early brow beating, obsessive disorder may result. *Parenthood* is a developing, shifting existence also, and is most healthy when it is carried out with a developmental perspective. Parenthood itself must stay "phase appropriate." There was a great shortage of timeliness, and of a developmental outlook among the parents of our 49 obsessive children. They expected their children to persist in obeying the illusions with which they had been enshrouded in infancy. Parents can help their children, within limits, to break free of the chains of illusion that parents themselves helped to forge.

Were we to borrow the imagery of Marcuse, and to some extent of the radical Freudians generally, we might say that the parents of obsessive children bring them up to feign hyper-rationality. Control of all of one's behavior is their goal. They are preparing their children for a life of conformity to mass society. These parents and their children will not undergo "future shock" since they are already living an *ad hoc* existence, largely devoid of living, passionate organic ties ("libidinal bonding" is an apt term in this context, I think). Their current lives show a highly extended rationalization and repression.

Following Marcuse (1970, p. 56) we can at least envision a

utopical alternative to the mounting repression seen in the "administered reality principle" which now prevails. That other way is a socialist society, I believe, with an economic order that is collectivized and a political order that is democratized. This democratic socialist society would be characterized by an ever-advancing technology in combination with derepression and desublimation. Individual liberty would flourish, perhaps as never before, according to Oscar Wilde (n.d.) in his essay "The Soul of Man Under Socialism." Primitivism and savagery would not erupt; instead as Marcuse wrote:

> In other words, technical progress would be accompanied by a lasting *desublimation* which, far from reverting mankind to anarchic and primitive stages, would bring about a less repressive yet higher stage of civilization.

Naturally, no such progressive changes will come automatically. We are warned against being too sanguine, for we have seen the miscarriage of too many socialist efforts, when they have not been accompanied by programs of sexual derepression, democratic procedures, pacifist reverence for life, and guarantees of personal liberties. Even Marcuse showed some strong authoritarian inclinations: Socialism in and of itself is not enough, for the economic changes brought by socialism can become thoroughly corrupted if democracy is not guaranteed simultaneously.

False Consciousness. Anal characters, obsessive characters, have that sort of an inappropriate outlook that makes them examples of what a Marxist might call "false consciousness." Freud (1894) had referred to the obsessive's "false connections in consciousness" but it was not to the overall cognitive derangement (or impairment) that Freud pointed; only to the narrower symptom picture. The Marxist concept helps to broaden Freud's medical concepts. I think that if we look at the concept of *false consciousness* for a moment it can help us to clarify some features of the life of the obsessive family.

False consciousness refers to those distortions in thinking that have highest relevance to societal living. Originally, Marxist social scientists used the term to cover any distortions of *class conscious-ness*—any interference with an accurate, veridical perception of class position, class affiliation and role in class struggle. Later gen-erations have modified this, and have so generalized the concept that it now refers to any kind of bias or distortion in perception, thought and memory. All too often, also, unfortunately, "false consciousness" has come to mean "the part of your outlook with which I disagree." Too often, the term has come to be a kind of Marxian insult hurled at one's ideological opponents when one labels their perspective as "false consciousness." Modern life, of course, is filled with usage of this type of epithet designed to unmask, as exemplified by the Freudians who insult and label their opponents as *neurotic, showing unanalyzed resistances*, and so forth. Sullivanian invective too seems less brutal but sometimes only more sly. Harry Stack Sullivan, we must recall, made the parliamentary step required to "unchurch" Otto Rank from offi-cial psychoanalysis in the U.S.

False consciousness, by these standards, was very much a part of the lives of these obsessive children and their parents. Neurotic fog, predilections for water-muddying speech, indecision, inability to make changes and to take risks, worship of the concrete and literal or cut-and-dried, a compulsion to render the world into black and white—these were all part of their anal-obsessive false consciousness. They all had vague feelings of unreality and that things aren't as they seem. They seemed to sense that they did not know how to think straight. Their cognitive difficulties required some alleviation by psychotherapy. Psychotherapy, I believe, does not supplant political action; so to the need for psychotherapy we must add the need for social change. But ordinarily psychotherapy concentrates upon emotional and affective problems. Psycho-therapists stay non-cognitive. Yet, some voices are emerging to say otherwise. Harley Shands (1960) and Joseph Barnett (1966, 68, 69) have been among the most outspoken writers who regard the "cognitive repair" of what I have called false consciousness to be a major task of the psychotherapy with an obsessive patient. Shands described *psychotherapy as epistemology*, in fact. The formulations of Shands and Barnett are highly relevant to work with obsessive families. These people do not think straight, and the psychiatrist must help them to know a spade as a spade.

To the extent that an obsessive life style blinds us to our human condition, and leads us to misperceptions, it is not an effective and happy cognitive mode for human beings. If obsession does have social utility we nonetheless quickly reach the point of diminishing returns. Whether we call the institutionalized misperception by the term *false consciousness* is not so serious. It is very serious, however, that societally patterned misperception is a central part of these families' way of life. Obsessive children suffer from the unreal "reality" their parents perceive.

Neither obsessive children nor their parents will be in the vanguard of needed democratic social change, I predict. They are too close to the way things are and too dependent upon keeping them unchanged. With our very best psychiatric results, at present we can only give some amelioration to obsessive children and their parents. Undoubtedly, societal and institutional changes are required, added onto psychiatry, to bring a fuller liberation to obsessive children.

APPENDIX

NOTES TOWARD A PSYCHIATRIC CHRONOLOGY
OF OBSESSION

1522-23: Ignatius Loyola produced, despite horrific temptations to spiritual pride, the "Spiritual Exercises to Conquer Self and Regulate One's Life and to Avoid Coming to a Determination Through any Inordinate Affection," while at Manresa tending the sick, clad in a hair shirt and a girdle woven of a prickly plant, and undergoing severe austerities unwarmed and untouched by either Renaissance or Reformation. The Jesuit disciple of Loyola was to spend time forcing himself to think of sin's foulness and the attraction of righteousness while fasting, praying, practicing self-loathing, and imagining the tortures of hell.

1533: Paracelsus referred to "obsessio," meaning imperious cravings derived not from one's "spiritual nature" but from man's "animal nature." *Obsessio* in Catholic theology referred to demonic influences while one is awake in contrast with demonic "possession" while asleep. [Ellenberger, 1970]

1602: Felix Plater lumped obsessions with other manifestations of an overstimulated consciousness *(alienato)*.

1658: Richard Flecknoe, *Enigmaticall characters* . . . described the "irresolute Person"—an obsessive—who "when he begins to deliberate, never makes an end."

251

1660: Jeremy Taylor published *Doctor Dubitantium, or the Rule of Conscience* giving case materials to show how religious scruple merges into severe obsessional disorder and then on into mental breakdown. "They repent when they have not sinn'd. [Scruple] is a trouble where the trouble is over, a doubt when doubts are resolved." (See Hunter and Macalpine, 1963.)

1666: *Grace Abounding to the Chief of Sinners*, an obsessive spiritual autobiography by John Bunyan, was published during the author's 12-year imprisonment. Described were his temptations to blaspheme, his despair, his loneliness, isolation, agony, and his belief that he had betrayed Christ to Satan—other than that it was all joyous Puritanism, doing for Protestantism what Loyola did for Roman Catholicism.

1749: David Hartley, English philosopher and physician, described the obsessive's one-track inclinations as "he becomes narrow-minded, strongly persuaded of the Truth and Value of many Things in his particular Study, which others think doubtful or false, or of little Importance."

1759: Samuel Johnson, scrofulous lexicographer and famous English writer, himself obsessive, published his only novel *Rasselas* in which he wrote of obsessions and fixed ideas and false consciousness in this wise:

> . . .the mind, in weariness or leisure, recurs constantly to the favourite conception, and feasts on the luscious falsehood whenever she is offended with the bitterness of truth. By degrees the reign of fancy is confirmed; she grows first imperious, and in time despotick. Then fictions begin to operate as realities, false opinions fasten upon the mind, and life passes in dreams of rapture or of anguish. . .
> "No disease of the imagination . . . is so difficult of cure, as that which is complicated with the dread of guilt. (Cited by Hunter and Macalpine, 1963)

1774: Johann Joseph Gassner, an Austrian miracle healer, used the term *obsessio* to indicate an illness resulting from sorcery. A kind of empiricist, Gassner sent patients, if they did not respond well to "a trial of exorcism," on to a physician who healed disorders of "natural causation."

1798: John Haslam, head of the dispensary at Bethlehem Hospital in London, described obsession: ". . . certain notions are forced into their minds, of which they see the folly and incongruity, and complain that they cannot prevent their intrusion." (cited by Zelmanowits, 1953)

1838: Jean-Etienne-Dominique Esquirol observed obsessive doubting and called it "monomanie raisonnante," a catchy term suggesting something like "reasoning madness."

1850: Jean-Pierre Falret named obsession "la maladie du doute."

1861: Benedict A. Morel, French psychiatrist and medical historian, a friend of Claude Bernard, first used (probably) the term *obsession* in the modern sense of an unwelcome recurring thought.

1866: Benedict A. Morel, "Du Délire Emotif" in the *Archives Générales de Médicine*, contended that intellectuals and professionals had more obsessions. Psychiatrists had found this a most appealing viewpoint. In the 10th century an Arabian physician, Najab, had attributed ruminating and doubting bouts to "too much love for philosophy and law." (See Zilboorg and Henry, 1941)

1875: Legrand du Saulle, questioning adults, concluded that the obsessive malady began only at puberty or later. This idea persisted for many years, causing psychiatrists to assert in good faith that obsessions were exclusive property of adults.

1878: Carl Friedrich Westphal described the obsessive-compulsive syndrome:

> ideas . . .come to consciousness in spite of and contrary to the will of the patient and which he is unable to suppress although he recognizes them as abnormal and not characteristic of himself.

1879: Henry Maudsley, an eclectic materialist in Great Britain, viewed obsessions as intimately related to affective disorders such as manic-depressive psychosis, a view that was to be prevalent among the Meyerians, and, out of the ranks of the psychoanalysts, Karl Abraham most notably.

1894: Daniel Hack Tuke of the British Quakers published "On Imperative Ideas" in which he gave an empirical listing of 14 cases of "obsessive pathology in everyday life." Tuke concluded that obsessive doubting is "counter-productive"—"for in a man's questioning thus, his last state is worse than his first." As an eclectic Tuke posited a brain dysfunction underlying the imperative ideas.

1894: Sigmund Freud, in "The Neuro-Psychoses of Defense" explained *isolation of affect*, a defense in obsessional neurosis, as a "false connection in consciousness."

1894: J. Séglas in a conference at Salpetrière agreed that obsessions often begin at puberty, *but may begin even before*, he said.

1895: Sigmund Freud's paper, in English called "Obsessions and Phobias: Their Psychical Mechanisms and Their Aetiology," published in *Revue Neurologique*. Freud classified phobia with anxiety neurosis, separating it from "Zwangsneurose." He mentioned in passing an 11-year-old girl "who already showed obsessions."

1896: Freud's paper "Further Remarks on the Neuro-Psychoses of Defense" appeared. He classified obsessions as ideas, affects, and actions; contended that obsessive ideas are self-reproaches because of an enjoyed childhood sexual act. The latter idea was made totally explicit in his 1896 paper on "Heredity and the Aetiology of the Neuroses," in which he said the hysteric child had *not* enjoyed his childhood sexuality but the obsessive child *did* get pleasure. Freud stated openly in "Further Remarks on the Neuro-Psychoses of Defense" that the therapeutic task was to make conscious the link between the obsession and the "repressed memory" of the sexual "crime" in early childhood.

1897: Krafft-Ebing first used the term "obsessive idea" and set a rather popular precedent.

1902: Pitres and Régis studied 100 cases and found 46% had onset between ages five and 15 years. The famous dilemma started, of rarely treated child cases but of many adults recalling childhood illness.

1903: Pierre Janet published *Les Obsessions et La Psychasthenie.* Included under "psychasthenia" were obsessions, depersonalization, tics, phobias, neurasthenia, etc. Classified obsessive ideas in a way that makes interesting and relevant reading today. Janet insisted that tics are the earliest signs—*de la petite enfance*—of obsessional neurosis. Janet cited a case of a five-year-old obsessive child.

1904: L. Löwenfeld's book on Psychic Compulsions appeared in Wiesbaden with a chapter by Freud on "Freudian Psychoanalytic Method."

1907: Sigmund Freud, "Obsessive Acts and Religious Practices." Equated ceremonials and obsessive acts. He ventured the idea that while obsessional neurosis is "individual religiosity," religion is "a universal obsessional neurosis." Began to de-emphasize the basis of obsession as childhood sexuality and to emphasize the *repression* of instinctual drives, or impulses.

1908: Sigmund Freud, "Character and Anal Erotism." Freud still did not publish his in-private view that obsession had to do with anality.

1909: Sigmund Freud, "Notes on a Case of Obsessional Neurosis." The famous Rat Man case. (See Anita Bell, 1961) Freud chided himself for, in his 1896 discussion, being too systematic and taking "as its model the practice of obsessional neurotics themselves—"

1910: E. Sadger published "Analerotik und Analcharakter" *(Die Heilkunde)*, summarized the Freudian views on anality.

1910: Alfred Adler began to do his most voluminous writing on "compulsion neurosis" as a distorted struggle against feelings of inferiority, of insecurity, of being slighted—and an effort to "achieve a feeling of personal significance and value."

1911: Karl Abraham linked melancholia with obsessional neurosis.

1912: Theodor Ziehen published in *Charité Annalen* a study of the obsessive personality, emphasizing the pedantry and rigidity of this subtype of "psychopathic constitution."

1912-13: Freud's *Totem and Taboo* still retained the view that the obsessive as a child had committed a sexual crime.

1913: Sigmund Freud emphasized the *pregenital* libido organization of the obsessive in "Predisposition to Obsessional Neurosis." He assigned age six to eight years as the usual age of onset, an idea that has remained very influential, and often cited. Freud now made explicit his belief of a relation between anal erotism and obsession, although he had adumbrated it more than 16 years earlier in letters to Wilhelm Fliess.

1913: Ernest Jones, "Hate and Anal Erotism in the Obsessional Neurosis" appeared in German.

1917: Sigmund Freud's paper "On Transformations of Instinct as Exemplified in Anal Erotism." He described obsessional neurosis as "the result of a regressive debasement of the genital organization."

1918: Ernest Jones, "Anal-Erotic Character Traits" summarized the Freudian characterology of the obsessive.

1921: Emil Kraepelin wrote in 8th ed. of his *Textbook of Psychiatry* that obsessives are highly intelligent. That assertion has been a popular one for the others to quote often.

1921: Karl Abraham, "Contributions to the Theory of the Anal Character" appeared, giving a succinct literature review.

1922: Eugenia Sokolnicka, a psychoanalyst, first reported in detail (14 pages) the analysis (lasting six weeks) of a boy aged ten and one-half years. Her paper had a pleasantly non-doctrinaire "aura" and stressed the interpersonal relations or object relations of the obsessive boy studied by her.

1923: Phyllis Greenacre published a "pre-Freudian" paper, a "Study of the Mechanisms of Obsessive-Compulsive Conditions."

1923: Freud, in *The Ego and The Id*, conjectured that obsessives in their libidinal regression do so by a "defusion of instincts." Love, for example, is defused into aggression. He introduced doubt on this point, however, by saying it might be either *defusion* or *insufficient instinctual fusion* (either a regression or a developmental deficiency).

1924: J. B. Watson followed by Mary C. Jones in behavioristic view of phobias and obsessions.

1924: Freud explained he had thought in 1896 that obsessives as children had actually committed sexual "crimes" because he had not distinguished, *then*, between "patients' phantasies about their childhood years and their real recollections."

1925: Arnold Gesell described *normal ritualization* in the child aged two and three years. His work gave a tremendous boost to many aspects of the child development field and added authority to the view that obsessions might be mistaken for normal repetitive behavior in two- and three-year-old children.

1926: Sigmund Freud, *Inhibitions, Symptoms and Anxiety*. Freud considered ceremonialism in latency as a defense against masturbation; said no obsessional neurosis till the phallic stage was reached; tried to account for the harsh, tormenting superego as an effect of libidinal regression.

1926: Anna Freud's lectures discussed the obsessive child as in need of "liberation" from the moral strictures of an introjected parental value system.

1927: Melanie Klein's contribution to a "Symposium on Child Analysis" showed the incipiency of many of her ideas, to be filled out and spelled out later, regarding the obsessive child. The case of Erna, in particular, illustrated the Kleinian approach to obsessive symptoms in younger children.

1928: Wilhelm Reich introduced the concept of character analysis, in contrast to the analysis of symptomatic neurosis. Described obsessive character in orthodox Freudian terms emphasizing sexuality, adhering to libido theory and to the Freudian mechanistic metaphysics which he ultimately carried further than most Freudians cared to go.

1928-30: Harry Stack Sullivan advanced, to a small circle of associates, an inter-personal viewpoint on obsessions (of adults, especially).

1932: Melanie Klein advanced the view of obsessive symptoms' appearance in infancy as a defense against psychosis, and of early conscience development, in her book, *The Psycho-Analysis of Children*.

1934: Ivan P. Pavlov propounded the uncertain theory that obsession reflects a brain dysfunction—areas of "pathological inertness" and also areas of an "ultra-paradoxical phase."

1935: Muriel B. Hall, "Obsessive-Compulsive States in Childhood: Their Treatment," an optimistic view of the prognosis of obsessive-compulsive neurosis in children.

1935: Leo Kanner published first textbook of *Child Psychiatry*, and by 1957, 3rd edition, gave 11 pages to obsessions and compulsions of children.

1936: Aubrey Lewis produced an eclectic and already a classical review of the literature on obsessional illness. Lewis pointed to the youthfulness of onset, and reported that obsessions in adolescence may herald a schizophrenic illness.

1937: Anna Freud's *The Ego and the Mechanisms of Defence* delineated the concept that unevenness of drive and ego progression was responsible for obsessional neurosis. The ego became of more focal import to psychoanalysis forever after this book.

1938: Viktor E. von Gebsattel described the existential world of the obsessional neurotic and Erwin Straus likewise: devoid of calm, perpetually tense, living with dirt and death but also showing distortions of space and time.

1938: Paul Schilder enunciated his views on the organic background of obsessive-compulsive disorders, trying to integrate neurologic and psychoanalytic theories.

1939: Sullivan's memorial lectures concerning William Alanson White. These lectures later appeared as *Conceptions of Modern Psychiatry*.

1940: Lauretta Bender and Paul Schilder, "Impulsions . . ." ego syntonic, "circumscribed interest patterns"—see Robinson and Vitale (1954).

1941: Bingham Dai, trained in the Chicago Psychoanalytic Institute, but returned to China, began a series of publications dealing with obsessive-compulsive adolescents and adults in both China and United States. Horney's and Sullivan's influences were prominent in his work, as was his sociology training.

1942: Leo Berman published a study of six obsessional children, viewing them within a Freudian perspective.

1944: Erich Fromm published "Individual and Social Origins of Neurosis" in the *American Sociological Review*. Neo-Freudian in scope and perspective, this was to be a milestone in the sociopsychiatric view on neurosis generally, and obsessional neurosis in particular.

1947: Lydia Jackson and Kathleen Todd devoted seventeen pages of book on *Child Treatment and the Therapy of Play* to "Obsessional Patterns." Generally eclectic approach with even Jung considered.

1952: Selma Fraiberg published "A Critical Neurosis in a Two-and-a-Half-Year-Old Girl"—clinical study of a very young obsessive child by someone not a Kleinian.

1952: American Medical Association and American Psychiatric Association, as published in *Mental Disorders: Diagnostic and Statistical Manual* (DSMI), "officially" separated phobias from obsessions-compulsions and described also an "obsessive-compulsive personality."

1954: Berta Bornstein, "Fragment of an Analysis of an Obsessional Child: The First Six Months of Therapy"—Freudian but orthodoxy not total.

1962: David Shapiro's article "Aspects of Obsessive-Compulsive Style" appeared in *Psychiatry*. The author explored the interpersonal significance of varied "character" or "ego" styles of the obsessive—including his rigidity, compulsions, sense of should or ought and less of reality. A most admirable and too seldom acclaimed essay, a brilliant accomplishment. Appears in his book, *Neurotic Styles*.

1965: Humberto Nágera and associates at Hampstead Child Therapy Clinic, London, review the psychoanalytic literature on obsessional neurosis—an admirable and monumental work, unfortunately available only in mimeographed form.

1965: 24th Congress of the International Psychoanalytic Association held in Amsterdam dealt with theme of obsessional neurosis with much time and discussion devoted to obsessive illness, to the Rat Man and to "Frankie," a man who as a child was analyzed as a phobia by Berta Bornstein and as an adult came for psychoanalysis, to Samuel Ritvo, as an obsessive. Anna Freud's summary of the Congress was intended as an "occasional piece" but was to become a brilliant statement of her general views on obsessions, sick children and psychoanalysis.

1965: Anna Freud's *Normality and Pathology in Childhood* presented the view that obsessions at all childhood stages are
likely to be fluid and often indistinct from hysteria or from
antisocial reactions or phobias. Ideas of developmental assessment for libido, aggression, object relations, ego functions,
etc. systematically set forth. A "bible" for the analytic ego
psychology approach.

1965: Lewis L. Judd undertook a clinical, descriptive study of six
obsessive children seen in Los Angeles—a milestone in empirical research, in critique and as a review of the literature, on obsessive children.

1965: Leon Salzman published an article on therapy of (adult)
obsessive patients. It articulated, effectively and succinctly,
the viewpoint of "post-Freudian psychoanalysis." Later, a
book, *The Obsessive Personality*, carried this viewpoint further.

1966: Joseph Barnett published two papers describing obsessive
illness as a cognitive disturbance, in need of cognitive repair.
Barnett operated within the Sullivanian framework—
eschewing libido theory and looking at the deficit in cognition or intellection within the interpersonal setting.

1968: DSM-II, *Diagnostic and Statistical Manual of Mental Disorders* (Second Edition) appeared as an official publication of
the American Psychiatric Association. Code 301.4 was given
over to "Obsessive compulsive personality (Anankastic personality)" while 300.3 was "Obsessive compulsive neurosis."

BIBLIOGRAPHY

Abraham, Karl, "Contributions to the Theory of the Anal Character", (original 1921) in *Selected Papers of Karl Abraham* London: Hogarth Press, 1949: 371-393.

Ackerman, Nathan W., *The Psychodynamics of Family Life: diagnosis and treatment of family relationships.* New York: Basic Books, 1958.

Adams, Paul L., Schwab, John J., and Aponte, Joseph. "Authoritarian Parents and Disturbed Children", *American Journal of Psychiatry* 121 (1965): 1162-1167.

Adams, Paul L., "Empathic Parenting of the Elementary School Child", *Southern Medical Journal* 58 (1965): 642-647.

Adams, Paul L., *et al.*, *Children's Rights.* New York: Praeger Publishers, 1971.

Adams, Paul L., "Family Characteristics of Obsessive Children", *American Journal of Psychiatry* 128 (1972): 1414-1417.

Adler, Alfred, *The Individual Psychology of Alfred Adler*, Edited by Ansbacher, H.L. and Ansbacher, R.R. New York: Basic Books, 1956.

Adler, Alfred, *Superiority and Social Interest: a collection of later writings.* Edited by Heinz L. and Rowena R. Ansbacher. Evanston: Northwestern University Press, 1964.

Adorno, Theodor W., and Frenkel-Brunswik, Else *et al.*, *The Authoritarian Personality*. New York: Harper & Brothers, 1950.

American Psychiatric Association. *Diagnostic and Statistical Manual of Mental Disorders*. Washington, D.C.: American Psychiatric Association, 1952.

American Psychiatric Association, *Diagnostic and Statistical Manual of Mental Disorders*, (DSM-11) Washington, D.C.: 1968.

Anderson Camilla, *Saints, Sinners and Psychiatry*. Portland, Oregon: The Durham Press, 1950.

Aronfreed, Justin, *Conduct and Conscience: the Socialization of Internalized Control Over Behavior*. New York: Academic Press, 1968.

Bakwin, H., and Bakwin, R.M., *Behavior Disorders in Children*. Philadelphia, 1953.

Balslev-Olesen, Th. and Geert-Jørgensen, Einar, "The Prognosis of Obsessive-Compulsive Neurosis", *Acta Psychiatr. Scandinav.*, *Suppl.* 136 (1959): 232-241.

Barcia, Demetrio and Fuster, Pilar, "Relación entre Obsesiones y Psicosis Epilépticas en los Niños". *Revista Española de Otoneuro-oftalmologia y Neurocirugia* 28 (1969-70): 311-318.

Barnett, Joseph, "Cognition, Thought and Affect in the Organization of Experience" in Jules H. Masserman, ed., *Science and Psychoanalysis*, Volume XII. New York: Grune and Stratton, 1968.

Barnett, Joseph, "Cognitive Repair in the Treatment of the Obsessional Neurosis" in J. Lopez-Ibor, ed., *Proceedings of the Fourth World Congress of Psychiatry*, Excerpta Medica International Congress Series No. 150. Madrid, 1966: 752-757.

Barnett, Joseph, "On Aggression in the Obsessional Neurosis", *Contemporary Psychoanalysis* 6 (1969): 48-57.

Barnett, Joseph, "On Cognitive Disorders in the Obsessional", *Contemporary Psychoanalysis* 2 (1966): 122-134.

Bateson, Gregory, Jackson, Don D., Haley, Jay, Weakland, John H., "A Note on the Double Bind—1962", *Family Process* 2 (1963): 154-161.

Bell, Anita I., "Some Observations on the Role of the Scrotal Sac and Testicles", *J.Am.Psychoanal. Assn.* 9 (1961): 261-286.

Bell, Anita I., "The Significance of Scrotal Sac and Testicles for the Prepuberty Male", *Psychoanal. Quart.* 34 (1965): 182-206.

Bender, Lauretta, *A Dynamic Psychopathology of Childhood*. Springfield: Charles C Thomas, 1954.

Berman, Leo, "The Obsessive-Compulsive Neurosis in Children", *Journal of Mental and Nervous Disease* 95 (1942): 26-39.

Bernard, F. and Flavigny, H., "Le Rôle du Père dans les Obsessions de L'Enfant", *Revue de Neuropyschiatrie Infantile* 13 (1965): 730-739.

Bijou, Sidney W. and Baer, Donald M., "Operant Methods in Child Behavior and Development". In Honig, Werner, *Operant Behavior: Areas of Research and Application.* New York: Meredith Publishing Company, 1966.

Blos, Peter, *The Young Adolescent.* New York: Free Press, 1970.

Bollea, G. and Mazzei, G., "The Rorschach Picture in the Compulsive Syndrome of the Preverbal Period", *Acta Paedopsychiatrica* 30 (1963): 77-87.

Bonnard, Augusta, "The Mother as a Therapist in a Case of Obsessional Neurosis", *Psychoan. Study of the Child* 5 (1950): 391-408.

Bornstein, Berta, "Fragment of an Analysis of an Obsessional Child: The First Six Months of Therapy", *Psychoanalytic Study of the Child* 8 (1954): 313-332.

Boszormenyi-Nagy, Ivan, "The Concept of Change in Conjoint Family Therapy". Chapter 23 in Alfred S. Freedman *et al.*, *Psychotherapy for the Whole Family.* New York: Springer Publishing Company, 1965.

Boszormenyi-Nagy, Ivan, and Framo, James L., eds., *Intensive Family Therapy: theoretical and practical aspects.* New York: Harper & Row, 1965.

Braconi, L., "La Psiconevrosi Osessiva nei Gemelli", *Acta Genetica Me⅃. Gemellol.* 19 (1970): 318-322.

Braganza, T. and Dai, Bingham, "Culture as a Factor in Obsessive-Compulsive Neurosis", *North Carolina Medical Journal* 20 (1959): 142-145.

Brown, Felix W., "Heredity in the Psychoneuroses", *Proceedings the Royal Society of Medicine* 35 (1942): 785-790.

Brown, Norman O., *Life Against Death: the psychoanalytical meaning of history.* Middletown, Connecticut: Wesleyan University Press, 1959.

Buxbaum, Edith, *Troubled Children in a Troubled World.* New York: International Universities Press, 1970.

Camus, Albert, *The Rebel: an essay on man in revolt.* New York: Alfred A. Knopf, 1956.

Carrera, Frank and Adams, Paul L., "An Ethical Perspective on Operant Conditioning", *Journal of the American Academy of Child Psychiatry* 9 (1970): 607-623.

Chess, Stella and Thomas, Alexander, *et al.*, "Implications of a

Longitudinal Study of Child Development for Child Psychiatry", *American Journal of Psychiatry* 117 (1960): 434-441.

Chethik, Morton, "The Therapy of an Obsessive-Compulsive Boy: Some Treatment Considerations", *Journal of the American Academy of Child Psychiatry* 8 (1969): 465-484.

Clancy, John and Norris, Albert, "Differentiating Variables: Obsessive-Compulsive Neurosis and Anorexia Nervosa", *American Journal of Psychiatry* 118 (1961): 58-60.

Coddington, Robert Dean and Offord, David R., "Psychiatrists' Reliability in Judging Ego Function", *Archives of General Psychiatry* 16 (1967): 48-55.

Corbett, J. A., Mathews, A. M. *et al.*, "Tics and Gilles de la Tourette's Syndrome: a Follow-up Study and Critical Review", *British Journal of Psychiatry* 115 (1969): 1229-1241.

Corey, Lewis, *The Decline of American Capitalism* New York: Covici-Friede, 1934.

Dai, Bingham, "A Sociopsychiatric Approach to Personality Organization", *American Sociological Review* 17 (1952): 44-49.

Dai, Bingham, "Culture and Delusional Systems of Some Chinese Mental Patients", *International Journal of Social Psychiatry* 11 (1965): 59-69.

Dai, Bingham, "Obsessive-Compulsive Disorders in the Chinese Culture", *Social Problems* 4 (1957): 313-321.

Dai, Bingham "Divided Loyalty in War: a study of cooperation with the enemy", *Psychiatry* 7 (1944): 327-340.

Dai, Bingham, "Personality Problems in Chinese Culture", *American Sociological Review* 6 (1941): 688-696.

Dai, Bingham, Personal Communication, 1972.

Despert, J. Louise, "Differential Diagnosis Between Obsessive-Compulsive Neurosis and Schizophrenia in Children", *Psychopathology of Childhood*, edited by Paul Hoch and Joseph Zubin. New York: Grune and Stratton, Inc., 1955.

Dugas, M., "The Diagnosis of Obsessional Neurosis in the Child", *Méd. Infant.* 68 (1961): 5-11.

Dührssen, A., "The Problem of Compulsion Neurosis as Based on Cases of Children", *Praxis der Kinderpsychologie und Kinderpsychiatrie* 3 (1954): 15-5.

Ehrenwald, Jan, *Neurosis in the Family: a study in Psychiatric Epidemiology*, *Arch. General Psychiatry* 3 (1960): 232-242.

Ehrenwald, Jan, *Neurosis in the Family and Patterns of Psychosocial Defense: A Study of Psychiatric Epidemiology*. New York: Harper, 1963.

Elkisch, Paula, *Diagnostic and Therapeutic Value of Projective*

Techniques: A Case of a Child Tiqueur. Monograph Series of the American Journal of Psychotherapy, Number 2, 1948.

Ellenberger, Henri F., *The Discovery of the Unconscious: The History and Evolution of Dynamic Psychiatry.* New York: Basic Books, 1970.

Engels, Frederick, *The Origins of the Family, Private Property and the State in the Light of the Researches of Lewis H. Morgan.* (Original 1884) New York: International Publishers, 1942.

Epstein, Nathan B. and William A. Westley, "Patterns of Intra-Familial Communications", *Psychiatric Research Reports* 11 (1959): 1-12.

Erikson, Erik H., *Childhood and Society.* New York: W.W. Norton & Co., 1950.

Erikson, Erik H., "Growth and Crises of the Healthy Personality", *Psychological Issues* 1 (1959): 50-100.

Eysenck, Hans Jurgen, *The Scientific Study of Personality*, London: Routledge and Kegan Paul, 1952.

Fedor-Freiberg, P. and Dobrotka, G., "Obsessions in Children", *Acta Paedopsychiatrica* 31 (1964): 346-355.

Fenichel, Otto, *The Psychoanalytic Theory of Neurosis.* New York: W.W. Norton & Company, Inc., 1945.

Fernando, S. J., "Gilles de la Tourette's Syndrome: a Report on Four Cases and a Review of Published Case Reports", *British Journal of Psychia.* 113 (1967): 607-617.

Finney, Joseph C., "Maternal Influences on Anal or Compulsive Character in Children", *Journal of General Psychoanalysis* 103 (1963): 351-367.

Fisher, Seymour and David Mendell, "The Communications of Neurotic Patterns Over Two and Three Generations", *Psychiatry* 19 (1956): 41-46.

Foster, R.M., "Parental Communication as a Determinant of Child Behavior". *American Journal of Psychotherapy* (1900): 579-590.

Fraiberg, Selma, "A Critical Neurosis in a Two-and-a-Half-Year-Old Girl", *Psychoanalytic Study of the Child* 7 (1952): 173-215.

Freedman, Alfred S., *et al.*, *Psychotherapy for the Whole Family*, New York: Springer Publishing Company, Inc. 1965.

Freud, Anna, *Normality and Pathology in Childhood: Assessments of Development.* New York: International Universities Press, 1965.

Freud, Anna, "Obsessional Neurosis: A Summary of Psycho-Analytic Views as Presented at the Congress", *International Journal of Psycho-Analysis* 47 (1966): 116-122.

Freud, Anna, Fourth Lecture, In *Psychoanalytical Treatment of Children.* New York: Schocken, 1964.

Freud, Sigmund, (1894) "The Neuro—Psychoses of Defense". In volume I of *The Standard Edition of the Complete Psychological Works of Sigmund Freud.* Edited by James Strachey. London: Hogarth Press, 1953.

Freud, Sigmund, (1895) "Obsessions and Phobias: Their Psychical Mechanisms and Their Etiology", *Collected Papers* I, 128-137.

Freud, Sigmund, (1896) "Further Remarks on the Neuro-Psychoses of Defense", in *Standard Edition* III.

Freud, Sigmund, (1896) "Heredity and the Aetiology of the Neuroses", in *Standard Edition* III.

Freud Sigmund (1907) "Obsessive Actions and Religious Practices", in *Standard Edition* IX.

Freud, Sigmund (1908) "Character and Anal Erotisms, in *Standard Edition* IX.

Freud, Sigmund, (1909) "Notes Upon a Case of Obsessional Neurosis", in *Collected Papers* III.

Freud, Sigmund, (1912) "Totem and Taboo", in *Standard Edition* XII.

Freud, Sigmund, (1913) "The Predisposition to Obsessional Neurosis", in *Collected Papers* II.

Freud, Sigmund, (1917) "On Transformations of Instinct as Exemplified in Anal Erotism", in *Standard Edition* XVII.

Freud, Sigmund, (1923) "The Ego and the Id", in *Standard Edition* XIX.

Freud, Sigmund, (1924) "Neurosis and Psychosis", in *Standard Edition XIX.*

Freud, Sigmund, (1926) "Inhibitions, Symptoms and Anxiety", in *Standard Edition* XX.

Freud, Sigmund, (1930) "Civilization and Its Discontents", in *Standard Edition* XXI.

Fromm, Erich, *The Art of Loving.* New York: Harper Brothers, 1956.

Fromm, Erich, *Beyond the Chains of Illusion: my encounter with Marx and Freud.* New York: Pocket Books, 1962.

Fromm, Erich, *Escape from Freedom.* New York: Rinehart & Company, 1941.

Fromm, Erich, "The Human Implications of Instinctual Radicalism", *Dissent* II, No. 4, (Autumn, 1955): 342-349.

Fromm, Erich, "Individual and Social Origins of Neurosis", *American Sociological Review* 9 (1944): 380-384.

Fromm, Erich, *Man for Himself*. New York: Rinehart & Company, 1947.

Fromm, Erich, *Sigmund Freud's Mission: an analysis of his personality and influence*. New York: Harper & Brothers, 1959.

Gans, Herbert J., *The Urban Villagers: group and class in the life of Italian-Americans*. New York: Free Press of Glencoe, 1962.

Gebsattel, V.E. "Die Welt des Zwangskranken", *Monatschrift fur Psychiatrie und Neurologie* 99 (1938): 10-74.

Gebsattel, V.E., "Zeitbezogenes Zwangsdenken In der Melancholie", *Nervenartz* 1 (1928): 275-287.

Gero, George, "Defenses in Symptom Formation", *Journal of American Psychoanalytic Association* 1 (1953): 87-103.

Gero, George and Rubinfine, L. "On Obsessive Thoughts", *Journal of American Psychoanalytic Association* 3 (1955): 222-243.

Gesell, Arnold, and Ilg, Frances L., *Infant and Child in the Culture of Today*. New York: Harper & Row, 1943.

Golovan, L.I., "On the Prognostic Significance of Obsessive Phenomena During the Course of Schizophrenia", *Zhurnal Neuropatologii i Psikhiatrii imeh S. S. Korsakova* 65 (1965): 1218-1224.

Goodwin, Donald, Guze, S.B., and Robins, E., "Follow-up Studies in Obsessional Neurosis", *Arch. Gen. Psychiat.* 20 (1969): 182-187.

Green, Lawrence W., "Manual for Scoring Socioeconomic Status for Research on Health Behavior", *Public Health Reports* 85 (1970): 815-827.

Greenacre, Phyllis, "A Study of the Mechanism of Obsessive-Compulsive Conditions", *American Journal of Psychiatry* 79 (1922-23): 527-538.

Greenberg, Harvey A., "Transaction of a Hair-Pulling Symbiosis", *Psychiatric Quarterly* 43 (1969): 662-647.

Grimshaw, Linton, "The Outcome of Obsessional Disorder: a follow-up study of 100 cases", *British Journal of Psychiatry* 111 (1965): 1051-1056.

Grimshaw, Linton, "Obsessional Disorder and Neurological Illness", *Journal of Neurology, Neurosurgey and Psychiatry* 27 (1964), 229-231.

Haley, Jay, "Marriage Therapy". *Archives of General Psychiatry* 8 (1963): 213-234

Haley, Jay, *Strategies of Psychotherapy*. New York: Grune & Stratton, 1963.

Hall, Muriel B., "Obsessive-Compulsive States in Childhood and

Their Treatment", *Archives of Disease in Childhood* 10 (1935)" 49-59.

Hartmann, Heinz, *Essays of Ego Psychology: selected problems in psychoanalytic theory.* New York: International Universities Press, 1964.

Henderson, Sir David and Gillespie, R.D., *A Textbook of Psychiatry for Students and Practitioners.* London: Oxford University Press, 1956: 212-221.

Henrikson, Lars V., "Risk-Taking and the Behavior Disorders", *Corrective Psychiatry and Journal of Social Therapy* 8 (1962): 133-144.

Henry, Jules, "Family Structure and the Transmission of Neurotic Behavior", *American Journal of Orthopsychiatry* 21 (1951): 800-818.

Henry, Jules and Warson, Samuel, "Family Structure and Psychic Development", *American Journal of Orthopsychiatry* 21 (1951): 59-73.

Heuyer, G., Moses, R., Lelord, G., Laroche, J., "Syndrome Obsessionnel chez un Enfant de Dix Ans: Problèmes Cliniques et Pronostiques", *Rev. Neuropsychiat. Infant.* 6 (1958): 343-348.

Hill, Reuben and Hansen, Donald A., "The Identification of Conceptual Frameworks Utilized in Family Study", *Marriage & Family Living* 22 (1960): 299-311.

Højer-Peterson, W., "The Compulsive Personality Type", *Acta Psychiatrica Scandinavica* 44 (1966): 156-171.

Horkheimer, Max, ed., *Autorität und Familie.* Paris: Alcan, 1934.

Horney, Karen, *The Neurotic Personality of Our Time.* New York: W.W. Norton & Company, 1937.

Hunter, Richard and Macalpine, Ida, *Three Hundred Years of Psychiatry, 1535-1860.* London: Oxford University Press, 1963.

Ignatius de Loyola, *Spiritual Exercises of Saint Ignatius,* New York: Doubleday. No date given.

Ingram, I.M., "Obsessional Illness in Mental Hospital Patients", *Journal of Mental Science* 107 (1961): 382-402.

Ingram, I.M. and McAdams, W.A., "The Electroencephalogram, Obsessional Illness, and Obsessional Personality", *Journal of Mental Science* 106 (1960): 686-691.

Inouye, Eiji, "Similar and Dissimilar Manifestations of Obsessive Compulsive Neurosis in Monozygotic Twins", *American Journal of Psychiatry* 121 (1965): 1171-1175

Jackson, Don D., *Etiology of Schizophrenia*. N.Y.: Basic Books, 1960.

Jackson, Lydia and Todd, Kathleen, *Child Treatment and the Therapy of Play*, London: Methuen, 1947.

Jaeger, Werner, *Paideia: The Ideals of Greek Culture*. 3 Volumes. Translated from the Second German Edition by Gilbert Highet. New York: Oxford University Press, 1943.

Janet, Pierre, *Les Obsessions et La Psychasthenie*. Volume I. Paris: Felix Alcan, 1903.

Jessner, Lucie, "The Genesis of a Compulsive Neurosis", *Journal of Hillside Hospital* 12 (1963): 81-95.

Jones, Ernest, "Anal-Erotic Character Traits". Chapter XXIV of *Papers on Psycho-Analysis*. Fifth Edition. London: Bailliere, Tindall and Cox, 1950.

Jones, Ernest, "Hass und Analerotik in der Zwangsneurose", *Internationale Zeitschrift fur Aerztliche Psychoanalyse* 1 (1913): 425-430.

Joseph, Betty, "Persecutory Anxiety in a Four Year Old Boy", *International Journal of Psychoanalysis* 47 (1966): 184-188.

Judd, Lewis, L., "Obsessive Compulsive Neurosis in Children", *Archives of General Psychiatry* 12 (1965): 136-143.

Kalmanson, Denise, "Psychoanalysis of an Obsessional Neurosis in an Eleven Year Old Child", *Revue Francaise de Psychanalyse* 21 (1957).

Kanner, Leo, *Child Psychiatry*, Third Edition. Springfield, Illinois: Charles C. Thomas, 1957.

Kanner, Leo, Discussion of Robinson and Vitale (1954)

Kardiner, Abram, "The Concept of Basic Personality Structure as an Operational Tool in the Social Sciences", in Linton, Ralph, ed., *The Science of Man in the World Crisis*. New York: Columbia University Press, 1945.

Kardiner, Abram, *The Individual and His Society*, New York: Columbia Univ. Press, 1939.

Kardiner, Abram, *et al.*, *The Psychological Frontiers of Society*. New York: Columbia University Press, 1945.

Kasanin, J.S., "The Psychological Structure of the Obsessive Neurosis", *Journal of Nervous and Mental Disease* 99 (1944): 672-692.

Kayton, L. and Borge, G.F., "Birth Order and the Obsessive-Compulsive Character", *Archives of General Psychiatry* 17 (1967): 751-754.

Khan, M. Masud R., "Infantile Neurosis as a False Self Organization", *Psychoanalytic Quarterly* 40 (1971): 245-263.

Klein, Melanie, "Symposium on Child Analysis". (Original 1927)

In *Contributions to Psycho-Analysis: 1921-1945.* New York: McGraw-Hill, 1964: 152-184.

Klein, Melanie, *The Psycho-Analysis of Children.* London: Hogarth Press, 1932. (Appeared as Number 22 of the International Psycho-Analytical Library).

Kluckhohn, Clyde, Murray, Henry, and Schnieder, David, *Personality in Nature, Society and Culture.* Second Edition. New York: Alfred A. Knopf, 1954.

Kringlen, Einar, "Natural History of Obsessional Neurosis", *Seminars in Psychiatry* 2 (1970): 403-419.

Kringlen, Einar, "Obsessional Neurotics", *British Journal of Psychiatry* 111 (1965): 709-722.

LaBarre, Weston, "Family and Symbol", in George B. Wilbur and Warner Muensterberger, eds., *Psychoanalysis and Culture: Essays in Honor of Géza Róheim.* New York: John Wiley and Sons, 1967 (Original Edition, 1951).

LaBarre, Weston, "Some Observations on Character Structure in the Orient: The Japanese". *Psychiatry* 8 (1945): 319-342,

Laughlin, Henry P., *The Neuroses.* Washington: Butterworths, 1967

Lebovici, Serge and Diatkine, R., "Les Obsessions chez L'Enfant", *Rev. Fran. Psychan.* 21 (1957): 647-681.

Legrand Du Saulle, Cited by Léon Michaux (1957).

Leonhard, K., "Individual Therapy of Severe Obsession Neurosis", *Psychiatrie, Neurologie and Medizinische Psychologie* 19 (1967): 2-10.

Lewis, A., "Problems of Obsessional Illness", *Proceedings of the Royal Society of Medicine* 29 (1936): 325-335.

Llorens, L.A. and Bernstein, S.P., "Fingerpainting with an Obsessive-Compulsive Organically-Damaged Child", *American Journal of Occupational Therapy* 17 (1963): 120-121.

Lo, W.H., "A Follow-Up Study of Obsessional Neurotics in Hong Kong Chinese", *British Journal of Psychiatry* 113 (1967): 823-832

Lucas, Alexander R., Morris, P.E. and Morris, E.M., "Gilles de la Tourette's Disease: a Clinical Study of Fifteen Cases", *Journal of the Amer. Academy of Child Psychiatry* 6 (1967): 700-722.

Luxenburger, H., "Heredität und Familientypus der Zwangsneurotiker", *V. Kongressber. f. Psychotherapie in Baden-Baden,* 1930. (Cited in Rüdin, 1953).

Lynd, Helen M., *On Shame and the Search for Identity.* New York: Science Editions, 1961.

Lynd,Robert S., *Knowledge for What?* Princeton: Princeton University Press, 1939.

Mahler, Margaret S., "A Psychoanalytic Evaluation of Tic in Psychopathology of Children", *Psychoanalytic Study of the Child 3/4* (1949): 279-310.

Mailloux, N., "Delinquency and Compulsive Repetition", *Archives di Psicologia, Neurologia, e Psichiatria* 25 (1964): 7-17.

Marcuse, Herbert, *Eros and Civilization*. New York: Vintage Books, 1962.

Marcuse, Herbert, *Five Lectures: Psychoanalysis, Politics and Utopia*. Translations by Jeremy J. Shapiro and Shierry M. Weber. Boston: Beacon Press, 1970.

Marcuse, Herbert, "The Social Implications of Freudian 'Revisionism' ", *Dissent* II (Summer 1955): 221-240. (Also appeared in "Epilogue" to *Eros and Civilization*.)

Marks, I.M., Crowe, M., Drewe, Young, J., and Dewhurst, W.G. "Obsessive Compulsive Neurosis in Identical Twins", *British Journal of Psychiatry* 115 (1969): 991-998.

Marks, I.M., *Patterns of Meaning in Psychiatric Patients*, Maudsley Monograph #13. London: Oxford University Press, 1965.

Matousek, M. and Nesnidalova, R., "Obsession in Children as a Manifestation of Cerebral Immaturity", *Ceskoslavenska Psychiatrie* 60 (1964): 164-172.

Mendell, David and Fisher, Seymour, "An Approach to Neurotic Behavior in Terms of a Three Generation Family Model", *Journal of Nervous and Mental Disease* 123 (1956): 171-180.

Merton, Robert K., *Social Theory and Social Structure*. Revised and Enlarged Edition. The Free Press of Glencoe, 1957.

Michaels, Joseph J. and Porter, Robert T., "Psychiatric and Social Implications of Contrasts Between Psychopathic Personality and Obsessive Compulsive Neurosis", *Journal of Nervous and Mental Disease* 109 (1949): 122-132.

Michaux, Léon, "Etude Clinique de la Nevrose Obséssionnelle de L'Enfant", *Rev. Neuropsychiat. Infant. Hygiene Ment. Enfance* 5 (1957): 467-493.

Milner, A.D., Beech, H.R. and Walker, V.J., "Decision Processes and Obsessional Behavior", *British Journal of Social Clinical Psychology* 10 (1971) 88-89.

Morel, M., "Du Délire Emotif: Nevrose du Systeme Nerveux Ganglionnaire Visceral", *Archives Générales de Médecine* 7 (1866): 385-402, 530-551, 700-707.

Muramatsu, Tsuneo, "Japan" in George W. Kisker, Ed., *World Tension: The psychopathology of international relations*. New York: Prentice Hall, 1951.

Nágera, Humberto, *Early Childhood Disturbances, the Infantile Neurosis, and the Adulthood Disturbances: Problems of a Developmental Psychoanalytic Psychology*. New York: International Universities Press, 1966. (The Psychoanalytic Study of the Child Monograph No. 2)

Nágera, Humberto, (In collaboration with Burgner, M.) "On Obsessional Neurosis". London: Hampstead Child Therapy Clinic, 1965.

Nunberg, Herman, *Principles of Psychoanalysis*. New York: International Universities Press, 1955.

Ollendorff, Robert H.V., *The Juvenile Homosexual Experience*. New York: The Julian Press, Inc., 1966.

Ollendorff, Robert H.V., "The Rights of Adolescents", in Paul Adams *et al.*, *Children's Rights*. New York: Praeger Publishers, 1971.

Pacella, Bernard *et al.*, "Clinical and EEG Studies in Obsessive-Compulsive States", *American Journal of Psychiatry* 100 (1944): 830-838.

Parker, Neville, "Close Identification in Twins Discordant for Obsessional Neurosis", *British Journal of Psychiatry* 110 (1964): 496-504.

Parsons, Talcott, "Family Structure and the Socialization of the Child". In T. Parsons and R.F. Bales, eds., *Family Socialization and Interaction Process*. Glencoe, Illinois: Free Press, 1955.

Pavlov, Ivan P., "An Attempt at a Physiological Interpretation of Obsessional Neurosis and Paranoia", *Journal of Mental Science* 80 (1934): 187-197.

Piaget, Jean, *Play, Dreams and Imitation in Childhood*. New York: Norton, 1962. (First English translation by C. Gattegno and F.M. Hodgson, 1951).

Pitres, A. and Regis, E., *Les Obsessions et les Impulsions*, Paris: Doin, 1902.

Pollitt, John D., "Natural History of Obsessional States: A study of 150 cases", *British Medical Journal* 1 (1957): 194-198.

Pollitt, John D., "Natural History Studies in Mental Illness", *Journal of Mental Science* 106 (1960): 93-113.

Rado, Sandor, *Adaptational Psychodynamics*. New York: Science House, 1969.

Rado, Sandor, "Obsessive Behavior: So-called Obsessive-Compulsive Neurosis", in Arieti, Silvano, ed., *American Handbook of Psychiatry*, Volume I. New York: Basic Books, 1959: 324-344.

Ramzy, I., "Factors and Traits of the Compulsive Neurosis in

Childhood", *Revue Francaise de Psychanalyse* 31 (1967): 611-628.

Ramzy, I., "Factors and Features of Early Compulsive Formations", *International Journal of Psycho-Analysis* 47 (1966): 169-176.

Rank, Otto, *Modern Education: A Critique of Its Fundamental Ideas*. New York: Alfred A. Knopf, 1932.

Rank, Otto, *Will Therapy*. Translated by Julia Taft. New York: Alfred A. Knopf, 1945.

Reich, Wilhelm, *Character Analysis* (Original 1933). New York: Farrar, Straus and Giroux, 1971.

Reich, Wilhelm, *The Mass Psychology of Fascism*. (Original 1933). New York: Farrar, Straus and Giroux, 1970.

Reiss, A., Duncan, O., Hatt, P., and North, C., *Occupations and Social Status*. New York: Free Press of Glencoe, 1961.

Ritvo, S., "Correlation of a Childhood and Adult Neurosis: Based on the Adult Analysis of a Reported Childhood Case". *International Journal of Psycho-Analysis* 47 (1966): 130-131.

Robinson, J. Franklin, and Vitale, Louis J., "Children with Circumscribed Interest Patterns", *American Journal of Orthopsychiatry* 24 (1954): 755-766.

Robinson, Paul A., *The Freudian Left: Wilhelm Reich, Géza Róheim, Herbert Marcuse*. New York: Harper Colophon Books, 1969.

Rockwell, Fred V. and Simons, Donald J., "The Electroencephalogram and Personality Organization in the Obsessive-Compulsive Reactions", *Archives of Neurology and Psychiatry, Chicago*, 57 (1947): 71-77.

Róheim, Géza, The Origin and Function of Culture. New York: *Nervous and Mental Disease Monographs* 69, 1943.

Rosen, Ismond, "The Clinical Significance of Obsessions in Schizophrenia", *Journal of Mental Science* 103 (1957): 773-785.

Rosenberg, C.M., "Obsessional Neurosis", *Australian and New Zealand Journal of Psychiatry* 2 (1968): 33-38.

Rosenberg, C.M., "Familial Aspects of Obsessional Neurosis", *British Journal of Psychiatry* 113 (1967): 405-413.

Rosenberg, C.M., "Complications of Obsessional Neurosis", *British Journal of Psychiatry* 114 (1968): 477-478.

Rüdin, Edith, "Ein Beitrag zur Frage der Zwangskrankheit Insbesondere Ihrer Hereditären Beziehungen", *Archiv fur Psychiatrie und Zeitschrift Neurologie* 191 (1953): 14-54.

Ruesch, Jurgen and Bateson, Gregory, "Communication and Mental Illness", *Communication: The Social Matrix of Psychiatry*, New York: W.W. Norton & Company, Inc., 1951.

Ruesch, Jurgen, "Disturbing Modes of Inner Experience", *Therapeutic Communication*, New York: W.W. Norton & Company, Inc., 1961.

Ruesch, Jurgen, *Disturbed Communication*, New York: W.W. Norton & Company, 1957.

Salzman, Leon, *The Obsessive Personality*, New York: Science House, 1968.

Salzman, Leon, "Therapy of Obsessional States", *American Journal of Psychiatry* 122 (1966): 1139-1146.

Sandler, J. and Joffe, W.G., "Notes on Obsessional Manifestations in Children", *The Psychoanalytic Study of the Child* 20 (1965).

Satir, Virginia, *Conjoint Family Therapy*. Palo Alto: Science & Behavior Books, 1967.

Schilder, Paul, "The Analysis of Ideologies as a Psychotherapeutic Method, Especially in Group Treatment", *American J. Psychiatry* 93 (1936): 601-615.

Schilder, Paul, "The Organic Background of Obsessions and Compulsions", *Amer. Jour. Psychiat.* 94 (1938): 1397-1416.

Schilder, Paul, "The Structure of Obsessions and Compulsions", *Psychiatry* 3 (1940): 549-560.

Scott, M.E., "Treatment of Obsessive Behavior in a Child", *Southern Medical Journal* 59 (1966): 1087-1089.

Seeley, John, *The Americanization of the Unconscious*. New York: International Science Press, 1967.

Shands, Harley C., *Thinking and Psychotherapy: An Inquiry into the Process of Communication*. Cambridge, Mass.: Harvard University Press (Published for the Commonwealth Fund), 1960.

Shapiro, A.K. and Shapiro, E., "Treatment of Gilles de la Tourette's Syndrome with Haloperidol", *British Journal of Psychiatry* 114 (1968): 345-350.

Shapiro, David, "Aspects of Obsessive-Compulsive Style", *Psychiatry: Journal for the Study of Interpersonal Processes* 25 (1962): 46-59.

Shapiro, David, *Neurotic Styles*. New York: Basic Books, Inc., 1965.

Sikkema, Mildred, "Observations on Japanese Early Training". *Psychiatry: Journal of the Biology and the Pathology of Interpersonal Relations* 10 (1947): 423-432.

Skoog, Gunnar, "Onset of Anancastic Conditions: a Clinical Study", *Acta Psychiatrica Scandinavica*, Suppl. 184, 41 (1965): 1-81.

Slater, Eliot, "Genetical Factors in Neurosis", *British Jour. Psychol.* 55 (1964): 265-269.

Slater, Eliot, and Cowie, Valerie. *The Genetics of Mental Disorders (Oxford Monographs on Medical Genetics.)* London: Oxford University Press, 1971.

Sokolnicka, E., "Analysis of an Obsessional Neurosis in a Child", *Interna. J. Psychoanal.* 4 (1922): 306-319.

Solomon, Joseph C., "The fixed idea as an internalized transitional object", *Amer. Jour. of Psychotherapy* 16 (1962): 632-644.

Stengel, E., "A Study on Some Clinical Aspects of the Relationship Between Obsessional Neurosis and Psychotic Reaction Types", *Jour. Ment. Sci.* 91 (1945): 166-187.

Stengel, E., "Some Clinical Observations on the Psychodynamical Relationship Between Depression and Obsessive-Compulsive Symptoms", *Journ. Ment. Sci.* 94 (1948): 650-653.

Stolorow, R.D., "Mythic consonance and dissonance in the vicissitudes of transference", *Amer. Jour. Psychoanal.* 30 (1970): 178-179.

Straus, Erwin W., "An Existential Approach to Time", *Annals of the N.Y. Academy of Sciences* 138 (1966-67): 759-766.

Straus, Erwin W., *On Obsession: A Clinical and Methodological Study*. New York: Nervous and Mental Disease Monographs (#73), 1948.

Straus, Erwin W., *Phenomenological Psychology*. New York: Basic Books, 1966.

Sullivan, Harry Stack, "Obsessionalism", *Clinical Studies in Psychiatry*, Edited by Helen S. Perry, *et al.*, New York: W.W. Norton Company, 1956: 229-283.

Sullivan, Harry Stack, *The Psychiatric Interview*. Edited by Helen S. Perry and Mary L. Gawel, with an Introduction by Otto Allen Will. New York: Norton, 1954.

Szasz, Thomas, *The Myth of Mental Illness: Foundations of a Theory of Personal Conduct*. New York: Dell, 1967.

Taylor, James G., "A Behavioural Interpretation of Obsessive-Compulsive Neurosis", *Behav. Res. Ther.* 1 (1963): 237-234.

Theophrastus, *Characters*. Cambridge: Harvard University Press, 1946.

Tuke, Daniel Hack, "Imperative Ideas," *Brain* 17 (1894): 179-197.

Weiner, Irving B., "Behavior Therapy in Obsessive-compulsive Neurosis: Treatment of an Adolescent Boy", *Psychotherapy: Theory, Research, and Practice* IV (1967): 27-29.

Weisner, W.M. and Riffel, A., "Scrupulosity: Religion and Obsessive-Compulsive Behavior in Children", *American Journal of Psychiatry* 117 (1960): 314-318.

Weissman, P., "Characteristic Superego Identification of Obsessional Neurosis", *Psychoanalytic Quarterly* 28 (1959): 21-28.

Westley, William A. and Epstein, Nathan B., *Silent Majority: Families of Emotionally Healthy College Students*. San Francisco: Jossey-Bass, 1969.

White, Mary J., "Sullivan and Treatment" in Patrick Mullahy, ed., *The Contributions of Harry Stack Sullivan*. New York: Hermitage House, 1952.

Whitehead, Alfred North, *Science and the Modern World*. New York: MacMillan, 1925.

Wilde, Oscar, "The Soul of Man Under Socialism", in *Collected Works of Oscar Wilde*. New York: Greystone Press, no date, 474-497.

Willner, Gerda, "The Role of Anxiety in Obsessive Compulsive Disorders", *American Journal of Psychoanalysis* 28 (1968): 201-211.

Winnicott, D.W., "Comment on Obsessional Neurosis and 'Frankie'", *International Journal of Psychoanalysis* 47 (1966): 143-144.

Wisdom, J.O., "What is the Explanatory Theory of Obsessional Neurosis?" *British Journal of Medical Psychology* 39 (1966): 335-348.

Woodruff, Robert and Pitts, Ferris, N., Jr. "Monozygotic Twins with Obsessional Illness", *Amer. Jour. Psychiat.* 120 (1964): 1075-1080.

Woolley, L.F., "Exploration of the Psychoneurotic Borderland", *Psychiatric Quarterly* 11(1937): 74-93.

Woolley, L.F., "Psychasthenia, Definition, and Delimitation", *Psychiatric Quarterly* 11 (1937) 465-480.

Woolley, L.F., "Etiology, Dynamics and Genesis of Psychasthenia", *Psychiatric Quarterly* 11 (1937): 654-676.

Woolley, Lawrence F., "Studies in Obsessive Ruminative Tension States: III. The Effects of Erratic Discipline in Childhood on Emotional Tensions", *Psychiatric Quarterly* 11 (1937): 237-252.

Yorukoglu, Atalay. "The Psychodynamics and the Psychotherapy of an Obsessive-Compulsive Reaction in an Adolescent", *Turkish Journal of Pediatrics* 9 (1967): 165-173.

Zelmanowits, Joseph, "A Historical Note on the Simple Dementing Form of Schizophrenia", *Proceedings of the Royal Society of Medicine* 46 (1953): 931-933.

Zetzel, E.R. "1965: Additional Notes Upon a Case of Obsessional Neurosis: Freud 1909", *International Journal of Psychoanalysis* 47 (1966): 123-129.

Ziehen, Theodor, "Zur Lehre von den psychopathischen Konstitutionen", *Charite Annalen* 36 (1912): 130-148

Ziehen, Theodor, *Die Geisteskrankheiten. Einschliesslich des Schwachsinns und die Psychopathischen Konstitutionen im Kindesalter.* Berlin: Reuther and Reichard, 1926: 372-390.

Zilboorg, Gregory, and Henry, George W., *A History of Medical Psychology*, New York: W.W. Norton & Co., 1941.

INDEX OF NAMES

277

SUBJECT INDEX

Adoption, frequency among children
  studied, 107
Affects *(see also* Defense mechanisms), 92–98
  basic anxiety in obsessive child,
    92–93
  ceremonialism, 95
  changes in, with treatment, 226–
    227
  clarification of, in therapy,
    215–216
  and defenses, 92–98
  displacement, 96
  foremost in obsessive child, 93, 98
  intellectualization, 84
  isolation, 85, 93–95
  rage and rectitude, 203–204
  repression, 85, 93–95
  undoing, 96–97
Age
  of children studied, 106
  of onset, 106
  at time seen, 106
Anality, 10, 15, 62, 81, 200, 201
  importance in child development,
    35

and money, 64
obsessions, 79
sadism, anal, as cause of obsession
  (Freud), 198
vs. genitality, 244
Ananke (Anancasm)
  definition, 5
  elimination of in treatment, 226
Antisocial reactions
  abundant, 18–19
  prognosis if obsessive also, 98
Anxiety neurosis, coexistent with
  obsession, 13
Authoritarianism *(see also* Empathy,
  Family, Fascism), 23–28, 194
Authority, rational vs. irrational
  (Fromm), 36

Behavior modification
  approach to family, 52–53
  bandwagon, 43
  "training" and overenculturation,
    233–235
Biology, of obsession, 43–52
Biosocial approach to obsession, 30